Chattanooga

—A DEATH GRIP
ON THE CONFEDERACY

Chattanooga

—A DEATH GRIP
ON THE CONFEDERACY

James Lee McDonough

The University of Tennessee Press
KNOXVILLE

Library of Congress Cataloging in Publication Data

McDonough, James L., 1934–
    Chattanooga—a death grip on the Confederacy.
    Bibliography: p.
    Includes index.
    1. Chattanooga, Battle of, 1863. I. Title.
E475.97.M45 1984   973.7′359   83–23582
ISBN 0–87049–425–2 (cloth: alk. paper)
ISBN 0–87049–630–1 (pbk. alk. paper)

If we can hold Chattanooga . . . I think the rebellion must dwindle and die.

—Abraham Lincoln to
General William S. Rosecrans at Chattanooga,
October 4, 1863

You . . . now have (the enemy) by the throat, and he must break your hold or perish.

—Abraham Lincoln to
General William S. Rosecrans at Chattanooga,
October 12, 1863

For Nancy

Contents

Illustrations

Preface

This book is about the struggle for Chattanooga during the American Civil War. Beginning with the climax of the engagement at Chickamauga, September 19 and 20, 1863, the story focuses upon the siege of Chattanooga and the battles that finally determined which side would control that strategic railroad town.

Some readers may wonder: Why Chattanooga but not Chickamauga? The answer to that question is easy. There was no reason to treat Chickamauga extensively because the late Glenn Tucker's book, *Chickamauga: Bloody Battle in the West*, is a solid work. The ensuing fight for Chattanooga, however, is another matter. A comprehensive, historical treatment has long been needed. Even Fairfax Downey's *Storming of the Gateway: Chattanooga, 1863*, is devoted primarily to Chickamauga, with only a very limited coverage of the events that followed that struggle. Several biographies, together with some general war narratives and a few campaign histories, have touched upon the siege and battles for Chattanooga, but these obviously were never intended to be full historical treatments of the subject. There is one in-depth, excellent study of the Confederate army, particularly the high command, during the siege: Thomas L. Connelly's *Autumn of Glory: The Army of Tennessee, 1862–1865*. Connelly's and Archer Jones's *The Politics of Command: Factions and Ideas in Confederate Strategy* is also helpful. And Grady McWhiney's *Braxton Bragg and Confederate Defeat*, although the biography ends before the Chattanooga campaign, is "must" reading for anyone seeking to understand the Confederate commanding general.

But, to my knowledge, no one has previously published a full, documented history, covering Yankees and Rebels in more or less equal balance, and presenting in detail and analysis both the siege and the fascinating battles for Chattanooga—above all, that intriguing struggle for Missionary Ridge, climaxed by the collapse of the center of the Confederate line. Even Shelby Foote's highly readable narrative, which devotes many pages to events during the siege, disposes of the perplexing fight for Missionary Ridge in brief fashion.

My introductory chapter, covering the Confederate breakthrough of the Union line at Chickamauga, depends heavily on secondary sources, although primary sources were consulted. Afterward, the accounts of the fighting at Brown's Ferry, Wauhatchie, Orchard Knob, Lookout Mountain, and Missionary Ridge are based upon extensive research in the *War of the Rebellion: A Compilation of the Official Records of the Union and Confederate Armies*. And, for Missionary Ridge, where the decisive struggle occurred, several Confederate After Action Reports, which never appeared in the *Official Records*, were of material assistance. These are found in the P.K. Yonge Library of Florida History at the University of Florida, Gainesville, and the Western Reserve Historical Society, Cleveland, Ohio. Also particularly helpful were the memoirs of Confederate General Arthur M. Manigault, and the account of the Tunnel Hill fighting by Captain Irving Buck of Patrick Cleburne's staff, in the Southern Historical Society Papers, Richmond. While many secondary works have been consulted, and numerous letters, diaries, journals and memoirs used, the narrative and analysis of the Chattanooga fighting is founded upon the After Action Reports.

Naturally I have wondered why the battles for Chattanooga, abundant with lessons and implications for the study of military tactics and strategy today, have received so little attention. Perhaps the answer might involve, to a degree, the long overemphasis on the Eastern theater of the war. Maybe it has to do with the complications of the Chattanooga campaign; a campaign which seemed relatively simple to me until I began to examine it in some depth, after which its complexities loomed fully the equal of any Civil War campaign that I have studied extensively. Yet again, perhaps Chattanooga has been relatively ignored because the casualty lists were not horrendously long. Thomas L. Livermore, in his *Numbers and Losses in the Civil War in America, 1861–65*, pages 106–8, computed Confederate casualties at 6,667 and Union at 5,824. Chickamauga, for instance,

was far more bloody than Chattanooga—and has received more attention. Sometimes it seems that the popular acclaim given to a battle is
almost in direct ratio to the number slain. Maybe, in a sense, it is an
attempt to compensate; to justify the loss of life. Thus the dead are
honored by hallowing the names of the places where they fell in great
numbers, like Chickamauga, while neglecting a more decisive struggle, like Chattanooga, in which the loss of life was relatively small.

One of the fascinating themes in developing such a book as this is
the tension between accident and intentionality—between what people thought they were doing and what actually happened. Consequently, a number of "what if?" questions are posed, usually by
implication, but sometimes specifically. The overall effect, providing
part of the major structure of the work, constitutes something of a
lesson in the complexities of history. Historical judgments are very
tricky, and I will be pleased if this book, to a degree, serves as a
warning against over-simplified interpretations of the war which
relegate human factors, chance occurrences and campaign results to
the background while presenting the outcome of the struggle as a
mere matter of materials, organization, communication and logis-
tics.

Nashville, Tennessee   JAMES LEE MCDONOUGH
August 1983

Acknowledgments

Many people assisted me in the preparation of this book; and, although I cannot name every person, I am grateful to all. A few deserve special recognition. Among those, again, is Phil J. Hohlweck, Milwaukee, Wisconsin. Just as when I was writing *Stones River—Bloody Winter in Tennessee,* Phil allowed me to research in his extensive collection of regimental histories, while his wife Clara fortified us with assorted delicacies of the table. Particularly I recall the delicious pancakes one morning in early August. The Hohlwecks were also hosts to my wife, Nancy, and two of our children upon that occasion in 1981.

The National Park Service, as represented by Ed Tenney, Woody Harrell and Robert Housch, at the Chickamauga-Chattanooga National Military Park, was generous and helpful when I studied the terrain and did research in the Park library. The staff of the Crisman Memorial Library at David Lipscomb College deserves recognition for assisting in the location of sources which are scattered throughout the nation. Dr. Thomas Connelly of the University of South Carolina generously allowed me to use source materials he has collected through the years. Jim Moon, Nashville, Tennessee, is to be acknowledged for his work in preparing the maps which the reader will undoubtedly find welcome. Jo Ann Harwell and Julia Shipp, who typed large portions of the manuscript, were always accommodating, even when I wanted a chapter finished quickly.

And finally, again, I am grateful to everyone associated with the University of Tennessee Press for their work in producing an attrac-

tive book on quality paper. Working with the U.T. Press has continued to be a pleasant experience.

Nashville, Tennessee   JAMES LEE MCDONOUGH
August 1983

Chattanooga
—A DEATH GRIP
ON THE CONFEDERACY

1

The Dead Lie So Thickly

The time neared eleven o'clock in the morning, Sunday, September 20, 1863. The sun was high and the day was hot. Only moments separated the Union Army from disaster. Screened from the eyes of Federal pickets by the deep woods west of Chickamauga Creek in north Georgia, Confederate Lieutenant General James Longstreet had massed an assault column 11,000 strong, under the immediate command of Major General John B. Hood, supported by a division on each side and one in reserve, the total force numbering 23,000.[1]

Longstreet's command, the bulk of which had come with him from Virginia to reinforce the Army of Tennessee, was superior in weight and depth and was assembled on a more compact front than his attacking force on the last day at Gettysburg. The soldiers were also relatively fresh, many not having seen action since the circuitous train ride from the Virginia theater, whereas, at Gettysburg, four of the nine attacking brigades had been badly shot up in the earlier action. To the inherent strength of the general's compact formation and numbers would be added the element of surprise, the dense woods providing concealment during most of their approach. Longstreet was supremely confident. Corps commander General Hood said he manifested "that confidence which has so often contributed to his extraordinary success," stating that Longstreet had assured him that "we would *of course* whip and drive [the Yankees] from the

3

field."[2] Very possibly Longstreet's assault would have been irresistible under any circumstances on that Sabbath morn.

But across the way in the Union lines, only a few hundred yards from the Rebel jump-off point, Brigadier General Thomas J. Wood, an old army regular from Kentucky, was unwittingly completing a tragic Union blunder, instigated at Major General William S. Rosecrans's army headquarters, which would make absolutely certain the success of the Rebel attack. Wood commanded a division located a little to the right of center on the Federal line. Skirmishing along his front was active, but nothing very threatening seemed to be developing. He did not know of the Rebel troops massing in the heavy woods to his front.

And then, from Rosecrans's headquarters, Wood received a fateful order, which would be the determining factor in one of the most desperately fought battles of the war. The dispatch was brief: "Headquarters Department of the Cumberland, September 20—10:45 A.M. Brigadier General Wood, Commanding Division: The General Commanding directs you to close up on [Brigadier General John F.] Reynolds as fast as possible, and support him. Respectfully, etc. Frank S. Bond, Major and Aide-de-camp."[3]

Back at army headquarters, it was thought that a gap existed in the line, no one realizing that Brigadier General John M. Brannan's division rested in position between Wood and Reynolds. All morning, responding to continuing Confederate pressure, Rosecrans had been reinforcing the left wing of his army, drawing troops from the right and center. Chief of Staff James A. Garfield had been marking the shifting positions of the Union divisions on his improvised map. "Even Garfield," observed Glenn Tucker, historian of the Chickamauga battle, "must have been confused, for no human being could possibly follow the devious course of the deadly brigade clashes occurring all along the line in the dense, vine-matted woods and jungle-like thickets." But Garfield, even if he could have identified the position of Brannan's division, was not on hand at the critical moment when General Rosecrans received the alarming news that "a chasm" existed on the right center of his line. Two staff officers of Major General George H. Thomas, apparently independent eyewitnesses, reported the dire situation. Evidently, to one passing in the rear of Reynolds and Wood, Brannan's troops were not visible in the woods to the south.[4]

When the battle opened, Brannan had been on the far left of the line. Later, he was shifted to the center; then, at Rosecrans's council

1. General John Bell Hood. Dahlgren Collection. *Tennessee State Library and Archives.*

2. General Jefferson C. Davis. G.M.L. Johnson Papers. *Tennessee State Library and Archives.*

of war the previous evening, it was decided that Brannan's division would be returned to Thomas if required again on the left. Rosecrans did not know Brannan's location, but he probably assumed that his division had gone to reinforce Thomas. Not taking time to check on the accuracy of the staff officers' reports, Rosecrans moved to close the supposed "gap" as quickly as possible before the enemy discovered it.

As Rosecrans understood the situation, he merely was ordering Wood to shift over to his left, linking up with the nearest division's right flank. When Wood, however, got orders "to close up on Reynolds," it seemed to him, knowing as he did that Brannan lay immediately on his left flank, that headquarters was instructing him to pull his men out of the fighting line, march to the rear, pass behind Brannan's division, and move up to assist Reynolds, whose division was located about a third of a mile farther north. If Wood had any question about the movement, he probably was highly disinclined to voice it. Only an hour or so before, Rosecrans had spoken harshly to him in the presence of his subordinates, deploring Wood's "damnable negligence," and criticizing him with a string of expletives for being slow in obeying a previous order. This time Wood was not slow. He did what any general is supposed to do on the battlefield. He obeyed orders—as he understood them.

Thus, through a misunderstanding of the situation, an entire division vacated its place in the Federal line and, moving to fill a gap that did not exist, actually created one. By a strange coincidence, for certainly gaps have occurred in the lines on other battlefields and not been critical, Longstreet hit the precise point left open by the Union mistake. Through this hole the attackers poured, divisions of Brigadier General Bushrod R. Johnson, Brigadier General Joseph B. Kershaw, and Brigadier General E. McIver Law, supported on the right by Major General Alexander P. Stewart and on the left by Major General Thomas C. Hindman, with Brigadier General William P. Preston's division in reserve. Bushrod Johnson's attack was one of the most dramatic and successful of the war. Leading the Rebel onslaught, he sliced through the right center of Rosecrans's army, advancing for a mile and cutting off the Federal commander—who had moved his headquarters only a few moments earlier to a ridge that turned out to be in the very path of the breakthrough—from the main body of his army to the north.[5]

Fragments of Rosecrans's broken line were scattered to the left

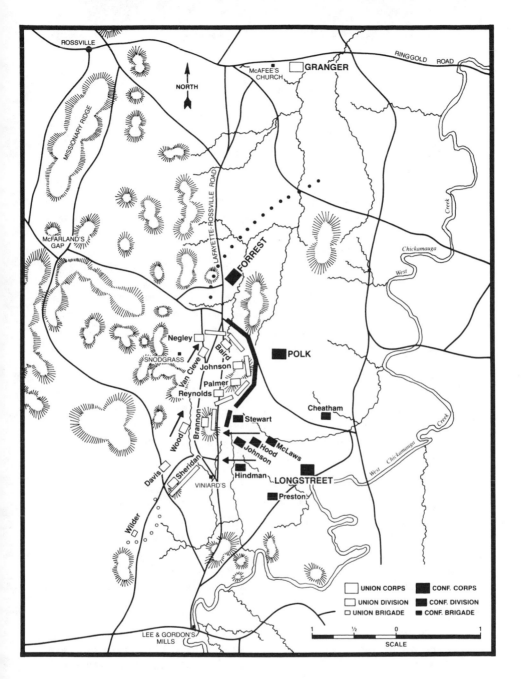

Map 1. Chickamauga: About 11:30 A.M., September 20, 1863. *Map by J.L. Moon, Jr.*

and right, and the divisions of Brigadier General Jefferson C. Davis and even Major General Philip H. Sheridan, who had fought so stubbornly at Stones River nine months before, collapsed and fled from the field. They were soon followed by large segments of the divisions of Brigadier General H.P. Van Cleve and Major General James S. Negley. The whole right wing of the Federal army disintegrated. Besides Rosecrans, corps commanders Major General Alexander McD. McCook and Major General Thomas L. Crittenden were also cut off. Unable to rally the troops around them, and apparently thinking the entire army was being destroyed, Rosecrans, McCook, and Crittenden all fled northwest through McFarland's Gap to Rossville and Chattanooga.

General Hood was elated by the triumph. Riding alongside Bushrod Johnson, he yelled an order to "Go ahead, and keep ahead of everything!" Only a few minutes later, a minié ball hit Hood in his upper right leg and knocked the general from his horse. With one arm already useless at his side from a wound at Gettysburg, Hood was carried back to the division field hospital, where surgeons amputated his leg. Despite the loss of their corps commander, the Confederates surged ahead.[6]

A Confederate officer described the Rebel charge: "On they rushed, shouting, yelling, running over batteries, capturing trains, taking prisoners, seizing the headquarters of the Federal commander, . . . until they found themselves facing the new Federal line on Snodgrass Hill."[7]

One of the Federals who watched the disaster was Assistant Secretary of War Charles A. Dana, "a sort of glorified snooper and trouble-shooter for [Secretary of War Edwin M.] Stanton," according to historian Stanley Horn. Dana had lain down on the ground, explaining that he had not slept much for two nights, when he was startled by "the most infernal noise I ever heard." Sitting up in the grass, Dana claimed that "the first thing I saw was General Rosecrans crossing himself—he was a very devout Catholic. 'Hello,' I said to myself, 'if the general is crossing himself, we are in a desperate situation.' " Dana recounted how he was on his horse "in a moment . . . I saw our lines break and melt away like leaves before the wind. Then the headquarters around me disappeared. The gray-backs came through with a rush. . . . The whole right of the army had apparently been routed. My orderly stuck to me like a veteran, and we drew back for greater safety into the woods a little way. There I came upon

General Porter—Captain Porter he was then—and Captain Drouil-
lard, an aide-de-camp infantry officer attached to General Rosecrans'
staff, halting fugitives. They would halt a few, get them into some
sort of line, and . . . then there would come a few round of cannon shot
through the treetops over their heads and the men would break and
run. . . . I attempted to make my way from this point in the woods to
Sheridan's division, but when I reached the place where I knew it had
been a little before, I found it had been swept from the field. . . . I
turned my horse and . . . rode to Chattanooga. . . . The whole road was
filled with flying soldiers. . . . Everything was in the greatest disorder.
When I reached Chattanooga, a little before four o'clock, I found
Rosecrans there."[8]

The Confederates had enjoyed a "run of luck" that, in retrospect,
seems almost uncanny. Longstreet himself could easily have been
killed or captured the previous evening. While trying to find the
headquarters of the Army of Tennessee, he lost his way in the woods
and, together with two members of his staff, blundered into the
Union lines. Fortunately, when the Yankees who challenged him
identified their unit with a numerical designation (Rebels normally
used commanders' names), Longstreet recognized what had happened before the Federal soldiers did. Quickly and quietly he disappeared in the dark.[9] Then came the Federal confusion about a
reported gap in the line while Garfield, who might have straightened
out the mess, was momentarily absent from headquarters. Also, by
pure chance, the Rebel attack struck the hole left by Wood's departure—and Wood, despite the less than precise wording of Rosecrans's
order, the meaning of which was subject to interpretation, had moved
out instantly upon receiving it. And finally, also good fortune for the
Confederates, Rosecrans had just moved his headquarters into the
very line of the Rebel attack.

In a matter of minutes, the whole battle had been changed by
Longstreet's breakthrough. Longstreet recognized this fact immediately and, contrary to his orders, which had been to bear to his left,
turned right to attack the remainder of the Union army. Longstreet's
change of direction brought almost a total rout of the Yankee forces.
Major General Thomas, soon to be known by the well-earned nick-
name *The Rock of Chickamauga,* remained on the field, turning the
divisions of Brannan and Wood, and marshalling remnants of the
shattered right wing, to slow Longstreet's advance. Hastily he formed
a new line on a ridge south of the house owned by a sixty-year-old

native of Virginia named George Washington Snodgrass.[10]

"This new Federal line," wrote historian Bruce Catton, "was not, strictly speaking, a military formation at all. It consisted of fragments of men from a number of commands, a squad here and a platoon there, formal organization completely lost, nobody in particular in general command of anything—except that Thomas was always there, moving back and forth, unhurried, holding this mixed-up line in place by sheer force of his own personality."[11] When James Garfield rode up, bringing Thomas reliable information that the right and part of the center of the army were driven from the field, and no ammunition, to his knowledge, was closer than Chattanooga, he said of the general: "I shall never forget my amazement and admiration when I beheld Thomas holding his own with utter defeat on each side and wild confusion in the rear."[12]

Now the Rebels prepared for what they hoped would be the final attack. Sensing a complete victory, Longstreet's men surged forward, assaulting the Yankee line again and again. Regardless of how imperturbable Thomas may have seemed outwardly, he had to be worried; and if some help had not been received, even he would have been defeated. But Thomas got reinforcements just as the Confederates were about to succeed in enveloping Brannan's right flank, which would have enabled them to cut off the remainder of the Federals from Chattanooga.

Through the morning, Major General Gordan Granger, a heavily bearded, profane-talking, West Point career man, had been near McAfee's church, in the army's left and rear, about four miles from where Thomas now desperately fought. In charge of Rosecrans's so-called "reserve corps," actually only a three-brigade division, Granger was frustrated as he heard the battle raging to the south and could not get involved. Shortly before noon, he and his chief of staff climbed a haystack in an attempt to gain a better view. All they could see was dust and smoke, but Granger had made his decision. Without orders and following the sound of battle, in what Mark Boatner called a "splendid example of battlefield initiative," Granger hastened to the aid of Thomas, despite his staff officer's warning that "if you go, it may bring disaster to the army and you to a court martial." But Granger was convinced that Bragg was "piling his whole army on Thomas"; and when Granger did arrive, Thomas indeed sorely needed help.[13]

As Granger's infantry moved rapidly toward the sounds of battle, Thomas and his staff could see, perhaps a mile or more off to the north, dense billows of dust rising from the treetops. Of course, General Thomas did not know who was coming. The dreaded Confederate cavalry commander, Major General Nathan Bedford Forrest, allegedly had been in that vicinity. Maybe the enemy, in force, was about to fall upon the right and rear of his position. If so, total disaster lay only moments away. The rising dust moved nearer and the tension mounted. Still, the colors of the approaching troops could not be identified. Finally, Thomas sent an aide riding to resolve the uncertainty. Returning at a gallop within a few moments, the officer relieved the suspense with the great news that Brigadier General James B. Steedman's lead division of Granger's reserve was coming up on the double.

They were barely in time. General Granger at once saw the threat to the Union flank. Telling Thomas something to the effect that his troops were "just the fellows for that work," that "they don't know any better than to charge up there," Granger ordered Steedman to go in and drive back the Confederates. Steedman, according to one account, told a staff officer to see that his name was spelled correctly in the obituary column, then turned and led the charge on horseback. Grabbing the regimental colors of an Illinois regiment, he roared encouragement to his men, only to have his horse shot from under him. Still holding tightly to the flag, he rose from the nasty fall, struggling forward and yelling "Follow me!" to his men.[14]

A terrible fight took place as the division drove the Rebels eighty or one hundred yards from the ridge, then received and threw back a counter-attack. Steedman himself survived, but his losses were appalling. In less than thirty minutes, between one-third and one-half of his force became casualties. But here the Confederate momentum was finally arrested. With Granger's second brigade soon at hand, lengthening and reinforcing Brannan's overlapped right flank, the Federals were fighting with stubbornness and gallantry. Thomas B. Van Horn, in his *History of the Army of the Cumberland*, candidly and succinctly stated the significance of Granger's reinforcements: "the opportune aid of these two brigades saved the army from defeat and rout."[15]

Yet, Longstreet would not stop trying. There was still time, in midafternoon, for the Confederates to strengthen their left wing, where they had been winning, and make one final grand effort. Longstreet asked Bragg for reinforcements, only to be told that none were available and that the army's right wing "had been beaten back so badly that they could be of no service."[16] Longstreet still had available one fresh division, commanded by Brigadier General Preston, formerly assistant adjutant general (chief of staff) to Albert Sidney Johnston, Preston's brother-in-law who died in his arms at Shiloh. Having failed to break the Union flank, Longstreet called for Preston, whom he met for the first time as he ordered the brigadier to assault Thomas's center (Brannan's division).[17]

The forty-six-year-old Kentuckian, a graduate of Harvard, got his soldiers in position, two brigades advancing in echelon with one held in reserve, and moved forward against the Union line. It was about four o'clock, and by now the Yankees had thrown up breastworks from stones and fallen trees. When Preston's division emerged from the woods at the foot of the slope, they were met by a heavy, well-aimed fire from the crest ahead. The attackers got to within one hundred yards or so of the defenders before their advance stopped. Then began an exchange of volleys, with many of the Confederates badly exposed to the enemy's fire, which lasted, some said, for the better part of an hour.

One of Preston's brigades was led by New York-born, thirty-year-old Brigadier General Archibald Gracie. A graduate of Heidelberg and West Point, Gracie was a merchant in Mobile before the war; his son would later research and write an excellent volume about the battle of Chickamauga and, incidentally, also survive the *Titanic* disaster. Colonel John H. Kelly—like Gracie an inspiring leader, who had fought at Shiloh, Perryville, and Stones River—commanded Preston's other brigade. While it is a tribute to Preston's division, and the example of their commanders, that the men fought so well in a difficult position—and lost over a third of their strength—they nevertheless could not break the Union line.

Now, however, Longstreet renewed his efforts on the flank (in later years, he claimed to have made twenty-five assaults altogether on Snodgrass Hill), and, at last, Lieutenant General Leonidas Polk, commanding the Rebel right wing, began to apply pressure once more on the Union left. Fighting was desperate and sometimes hand-to-hand, as men used their bayonets, shot their opponents at point-blank range, or smashed them out of action with the blows of musket butts. Valiant as his defense had been, Thomas was forced from his position by the combined assaults of Longstreet and Polk. He did not—despite later overly laudatory accounts that he did—hold his ground "until dark."[18]

Thomas's stand on Snodgrass Hill saved the Union army from

destruction, but his withdrawal to Chattanooga, through McFarland's Gap, really began around four-thirty, or soon after, a long time before dark. Most of his left wing was off the field by five-thirty. Perhaps the retreat may have been "in good order," as some reports said, but General John Beatty's vivid description of the march poignantly portrays the scene: "The march . . . was a melancholy one. All along the road for miles, wounded men were lying. They had crawled or hobbled slowly away from the fury of the battle, become exhausted, and lain down by the roadside to die." Describing the scene at Rossville, "between ten and eleven" that night, the general said, "at this hour . . . the army is simply a mob. There appears to be neither organization nor discipline. The various commands are mixed up in what appears to be inextricable confusion. Were a division of the enemy to pounce down upon us between this and morning, I fear the Army of the Cumberland would be blotted out."[19]

Already, Assistant Secretary Dana had telegraphed a dispatch to Stanton, beginning with the statement: "My report today is of deplorable importance. Chickamauga is as fatal a name in our history as Bull Run."[20] Dana did not exaggerate. Actually, in terms of casualties, it was far worse than Bull Run.

Chickamauga, the Indian name for the stream lazily winding northward across Georgia toward its confluence with the Tennessee River above Chattanooga, was said by some to mean "river of death"—presumably from some dark and hellish event forever lost in the far-distant, aboriginal past. Now, again, the name seemed fitting; and as never before. No battle of the war, relative to time and numbers, was more bloody than Chickamauga. In absolute terms, of course, the three-day engagement at Gettysburg witnessed the greatest number of casualties, approximately 51,000. But Chickamauga, totalling nearly 35,000 in only two days, saw slaughter at the same rate as Gettysburg—and this when total Union strength numbered some 25,000 less than in the Pennsylvania battle, and Rebel forces were nearly 10,000 less. The struggle along the west bank did indeed turn the creek into a "river of death."[21]

When Lieutenant General Daniel Harvey Hill later walked over the field, he said that he had "never seen the Federal dead lie so thickly on the ground, save in front of the sunken wall at Fredericksburg."[22] In fact, the Confederate dead lay even more thickly than the Union. Thomas L. Livermore's *Numbers and Losses in the Civil War in America, 1861–65*, calculated that the Confederate

3. General George H. Thomas. *Chickamauga-Chattanooga National Military Park.*

dead at Chickamauga numbered about 650 more than the Federal. In breaking down the figures by army, Livermore estimated the total effective Union strength going into the battle at 58,222, of which 16,170 became casualties. Confederate forces were estimated at 66,326, of which 18,454 were casualties. Glenn Tucker, in his extensive book on Chickamauga, noted that "there are blanks in the reports and discrepancies in the estimates" making it difficult to calculate totals accurately, but he concluded that Confederate casualties were considerably higher than Livermore's figures. Tucker totalled Rebel casualties at 20,950, of which he listed 2,673 killed, 361 more than Livermore's calculation. Whatever the precise figures, and Tucker came up with a total for both armies of 37,129, the Confederates, as the assailants, suffered more severely in gaining their victory than did the Yankees.[23]

When the triumphant yelling and roaring of the Confederates— cheers "such as I had never heard before, and shall not hear again," remembered Harvey Hill; while a Yankee, Ambrose Bierce, thought the sounds "the ugliest any mortal ever heard"[24]—had at last played out, the battlefield undoubtedly, on the testimony of seemingly endless witnesses, became a macabre panorama of cold, agony, and death. Sam Watkins of Company "Aytch," First Tennessee, told of a group of women looking over the battlefield with lanterns. They had turned over several bodies and then he heard a woman scream, "O, there he is! Poor fellow! Dead, dead, dead." She placed the dead man's head in her lap and began kissing it, all the while saying, "O, O, they have killed my darling, my darling, my darling." Watkins said he could stand no more of watching and hearing, and that his companion, William A. Hughes, was weeping.[25]

The scene of carnage presented strange and unexpected sights. "In a dense thicket," recorded John A. Wyeth, "I came upon a soldier in blue sitting upright against the trunk of a tree, one hand on his gun, which rested across his thigh, and the other tightly gripping the brim of his hat, which was drawn down on one side of his face, as if shielding his eyes from the sun. I had no idea," said Wyeth, "that a dead man would be sitting upright, but such was the case. He was stiff and stark. From under the knee of one leg a pool of clotted blood told the story. A minié ball had cut his . . . artery or vein, and I reasoned that he grew faint and sought the tree, leaned back against it, held on faithfully to his gun with one hand, with the other pulled down the brim of his hat to shade his eyes, then fainted from loss of blood and died." Continuing his graphic account, Wyeth described how he came to one of the field hospitals where the surgeons were busy with the wounded, who were stretched out on their blankets under the trees. He wrote, "One fellow was walking up and down holding the freshly amputated stump of his forearm with the remaining hand. His jaws were firmly set, and his face wore the hard fixed expression of pain, yet he made no complaint. In fact, I do not think I heard a groan or cry in all that experience. . . . Fragments of arms and legs completed the gruesome picture."[26]

Tragic were the stories of soldiers whose wounds might not have been so serious if medical attention had been received earlier. Such a case was that of W.W. Gifford, Thirty-sixth Illinois infantry, wounded in the fighting on September 20, and told by a doctor that his leg could be saved only if he were transported to a hospital quickly. But Gifford lay on the battlefield until September 26! When at last he reached a hospital the leg was amputated. On the last day of the month Gifford was loaded into a wagon and sent into the Union lines at Chattanooga. Passing the Chickamauga battlefield, he noted that all the dead were still not buried, even though a week and a half had passed.[27]

Civilian residents of the battlefield area had established a temporary camp near the D.C. Reed house. Realizing that the fight had gone in favor of the Southerners, many broke out rejoicing; some of the women, so it was reported, sang with joy. But those who tried to return home were to find their houses crowded with wounded soldiers. The Snodgrass house, for example, had become a gory shambles, the furniture broken and bloodstained, the bullet-riddled structure filled with the wounded and the dead, as also were the outhouses. Many of the residents of the area continued sleeping in the open, without sufficient blankets or food, enduring the chilly nights for a week or more. In the early mornings the heads of the little children sometimes glistened white with a heavy coat of frost. Soon the Snodgrass family moved to Ellis Springs near Ringgold and did not return home until after the war.[28]

Possibly, Chickamauga illustrated that the nature of the war had changed. Across the almost thirty months since Fort Sumter, tens of thousands of men had died; some instantly and cleanly, others in untold agony; some bravely, others lonely and afraid. The killing and maiming had gone on and on; and still it would continue.

Yet, there may have been a difference at Chickamauga—if some

Federal accounts are to be believed. And it was more than that men had been hardened and made cold by killing; more than that the old, Medieval concepts of chivalric conduct were being destroyed by so much struggle, suffering, and loss; more even than that, for the numbers engaged, Chickamauga had been the bloodiest battle of the war. It was that the deepest, primeval emotions had been released, manifested in the mutilations and atrocities to which some Union wounded and dead were said to have been subjected.

S.S. Canfield, Twenty-first Ohio Infantry, reported that one of the surgeons who went out after the battle to care for the Union wounded informed him that on a part of the field there was a head of a Federal soldier on every stump. W.W. Lyle, Eleventh Ohio Infantry, in his book entitled *Lights and Shadows of Army Life,* devoted a chapter to "Rebel Barbarities," in which he claimed that the Chickamauga battlefield, when he went over it weeks later, "was then seen as a terrible record of worse than savage brutality. No full description of the revolting scenes which our soldiers then beheld has ever been given, and probably never will." Lyle stated that "in several places we found bodies, or rather remains, lying between logs, part of which— an arm or leg, for instance—was calcined, as if subjected to intense heat, while other parts of the body were crisp and dry. It is firmly believed by all who saw those revolting scenes, that many of our wounded were burned alive, horrible as it may seem, for bodies were found partly consumed, where the contraction of the muscles, and the clenched fingers, seemed to indicate an attempt to grasp something, while the general appearance gave evidence of a violent struggle of some kind. In one place, the body of a Union soldier was found, with both ears cut off, and in another, several bodies from which the heads had been removed. These had been set up on stakes and rails of the fences, or fastened on limbs of trees." Lyle concluded the specific examples with the laconic sentence: "The details are sickening."[29]

Whatever the facts behind such atrocity charges may have been, the Rebels had won a very bloody and hard-fought engagement. General Bragg, as so often was true of both sides whenever a victory was experienced, dispatched a telegram to Richmond praising the Lord for the triumph. "It has pleased Almighty God," he said on September 22, "to reward the valor and endurance of our troops by giving our arms a complete victory over the enemy's superior numbers. Thanks are due and are rendered unto Him who giveth not the battle to the strong."[30]

From the triumph, many throughout the Confederacy expected that much would be achieved. The "Rebel war clerk" in Richmond, John B. Jones, probably voiced the thoughts of thousands when he recorded in his now-famous diary, on the same date as Bragg's above dispatch: "The effects of this great victory will be electrical. The whole South will be filled again with patriotic fervor, and in the North there will be a corresponding depression. Rosecrans' position is now one of great peril; for his army . . . may be utterly destroyed, and then Tennessee and Southern Kentucky may fall into our hands again. . . . Surely the Government of the United States must now see the impossibility of subjugating the Southern people, spread over such a vast extent of territory; and the European governments ought now to interpose to put an end to this cruel waste of blood and treasure."[31]

But, in actual fact, the possibility of foreign intervention seemed very slim by the fall of 1863. The British had survived the worst of the "cotton famine," and other British industries were booming as a profitable market developed in America for war supplies for the Union armies. Too, traditional British policy never knowingly recognized a lost cause—even one with which the British sympathized. And London certainly doubted the South's chances to win.

The closest France ever came to taking an active role in the American question had been in June 1863. Napoleon III needed Southern cotton and American allies for his dream of a New World Empire based in Mexico. Clearly, a warm reception could not be expected from the United States; the Confederacy, on the other hand, in desperation, made overtures of friendship to France and the Austrian Archduke Maximilian, whom Napoleon had installed as Emperor of Mexico. But Napoleon hoped for concert with the British, who remained cool, unconvinced that the French venture could be in their best interest. Napoleon finally decided not to act alone. After Gettysburg and Vicksburg, both England and France withheld ships for which the Confederates had contracted. By the fall of 1863 the diplomatic tide had turned in favor of the North, and for that tide to be reversed—for there to be any chance of even arresting it—the Confederates probably would have needed not only to regain Tennessee and Southern Kentucky, but to march to the Ohio River as well.[32]

Aside from diplomatic considerations, *if* such a Confederate advance had been possible, it would indeed have undone much that the Union had accomplished, because the Civil War was not being won or

lost on the Virginia front. There great battles were waged and dramatic chapters, which now loom larger than life, were writ in history and
legend; but no major army was ever captured or destroyed by the
other side and neither capital fell until a week before Lee's surrender.
Rather, beyond the northern Virginia theater, west of the Allegheny
Mountains, where the border between Union and Confederacy
stretched for a thousand miles, the outcome of the war was ultimately decided. In that vast, sprawling region the Confederacy was losing
the war, as the Union, by the fall of 1863, had won West Virginia,
most of Missouri, and much of Kentucky and Tennessee, along with
parts of Louisiana and Arkansas. The Union had also occupied key
islands around the 3,500 miles of coastal perimeter, penetrated the
major rivers, captured the largest city, and clamped an ever-
tightening blockade on the Confederacy.[33]

Although the Rebels certainly failed to exploit the opportunities
presented by the Chickamauga victory, any dream of driving the
Yankees all the way back to the Ohio while recovering vast territory
appears to have been unrealistic. Two of the three ways in which the
Confederacy might have succeeded were already locked away in the
irretrievable past: military victory and foreign intervention. The
third, attrition of the Northern will to fight, in essence a weariness of
war, was now the only real hope for the South. If the triumph at
Chickamauga had been effectively followed by forcing the Federals
back into Middle Tennessee—a realistic possibility that would have
denied them the staging base of Chattanooga for a later drive into the
heart of the deep South—the war might have been significantly prolonged. TIME, in the overall canvas and in historical retrospect,
constituted what the fight for Chattanooga was actually all about.

2

War Between the Generals

A Confederate cavalry column pounded northward on the La Fayette road on the morning of Monday, September 21, rapidly approaching Rossville, Georgia. Personally leading the advance guard of the Rebel pursuit was Major General Nathan Bedford Forrest. Just out of Rossville, Forrest and his advance came up on a segment of the Union rear guard under Colonel Robert H.G. Minty. Typically, like a god of war, rising in his stirrups and roaring "Charge!," Forrest led some 400 of his troopers headlong toward the enemy. The Federals fired a volley, perhaps aimed at the general himself, and one of the shots severed a large artery in his horse's neck. Seeing the blood spurting from the wound, Forrest leaned over, poked a finger into the artery, and thus scotched the bleeding and continued to plunge forward in pursuit. The Yankees were driven toward Chattanooga. When the action was over Forrest dismounted, removed his finger from the artery, and the horse fell dead.[1]

A few moments more and the aggressive cavalry commander stood high on a spur of Missionary Ridge. Climbing an oak tree, the general swept the country with a pair of field glasses taken from a Union prisoner, surveying Lookout Mountain, the Tennessee River, and Chattanooga. When he came down from his vantage point in the tree, Forrest dictated a message to Lieutenant General Leonidas Polk, to be forwarded to General Bragg.

We are in a mile of Rossville. have been on the point of Missionary Ridge. Can see Chattanooga and everything around. The Enemy's trains are leaving, going around the point of Lookout Mountain.

The prisoners captured report two pontoons thrown across [the Tennessee River] for the purpose of retreating. I think they are evacuating as hard as they can go. They are cutting timber down to obstruct our passage. I think we ought to press forward as rapidly as possible.[2]

In later years General Longstreet declared that this brief message "fixed the fate of the Confederacy. . . ." General Bragg, according to Longstreet, had decided to march around Rosecrans, leaving him in Chattanooga, but when Forrest's dispatch was received, causing Bragg to think that the town would be abandoned, he decided to march through Chattanooga rather than around it. Then, when the Yankees did not evacuate the town, Bragg became unsure of his next move, precious time was wasted, the potential fruits of the Chickamauga victory were lost, and momentum gradually shifted to the Federals. A chance to regain Middle Tennessee and even control central Kentucky to the Ohio, thought Longstreet, had been frittered away.[3]

Probably the significance of Gettysburg and Vicksburg in deciding the war's outcome has been overemphasized, as Longstreet's interpretation of the opportunities at Chickamauga-Chattanooga would imply. Clearly the costly Confederate victory at Chickamauga, the greatest the Army of Tennessee ever had, was not followed up effectively. Even so, Chickamauga both prevented an early fall of Atlanta, with all the dire repercussions that would have ensued, and lifted Southern hopes, which had been despairing after Gettysburg and Vicksburg. The Confederacy would fight on for another year and a half. Still to be endured by the North were the horrendous Federal casualties of Grant's campaign against Lee in the spring of 1864. Still to come was the nadir of Northern war weariness (now potentially the Confederacy's greatest asset if she could only prolong the conflict), which would not be reached until the following summer. Indeed, it is likely that it was neither on the rich, picturesque farm land of Pennsylvania nor along the bluffs and swamps of the Mississippi that the war finally assumed an irreversible course against the South. Rather, perhaps that moment came after the confused, smoke-enveloped, hellish fighting swirling among the charred timbers at the Battle of the Wilderness in early May 1864, when Grant simply accepted the awful casualty rate of two Federals lost for every Confederate and unprecedentedly kept driving, continued attacking, maintaining the pressure on an enemy with far fewer manpower resources; whereas, in the past, the Union army had always retreated in the face of such losses.

Or maybe the decisive struggle came still later, when Sherman's legions fought to break into the besieged city of Atlanta in the late summer of 1864. Atlanta was the key to survival of the Confederacy. It symbolized the gritty determination of the deep South to resist subjugation. But Atlanta was far more than a symbol. The city's workshops and factories throbbed with armament production. Atlanta, said Sherman, "has done more and contributed probably more to carry on and sustain the war than any other city. . . ." If Atlanta had stood, Lincoln's administration well might have fallen in the November election, and a war-weary North likely would have been ready to make peace.

Or yet again, perhaps it was the combination of Grant and Sherman in 1864—the tremendous offensive pressure applied simultaneously on two fronts—that at last turned the war irretrievably against the Confederacy. If the importance of Gettysburg and Vicksburg in determining the war's outcome has been exaggerated, and at the expense of the significance of Grant's and Sherman's 1864 campaigns, then Longstreet's claim that Forrest's dispatch sealed the fate of the Confederacy appears grossly overstated. Even in the immediate context, the aftermath of Chickamauga, Longstreet's claim is misleading.

Forrest's message was only one of several such reports Bragg received during the two days following the battle. Longstreet himself, complying with Bragg's directive on the night of September 21, sent Lafayette McLaws's division to push toward Chattanooga on a reconnaissance mission. Like Forrest, McLaws was convinced the Federals were retreating and said, in fact, that the enemy was already crossing the river on pontoon bridges. Bragg also told Polk to send a division to the top of Missionary Ridge, from which the Yankees in Chattanooga might be observed. Brigadier General George Maney of B. Franklin Cheatham's division reported on September 22 that all evidence— heavy dust clouds moving from the city toward East Tennessee, as well as around Lookout Point toward Middle Tennessee, while wagons appeared to be crossing the Tennessee River on pontoons— indicated that the Union army must be retreating from Chattanooga.

And another message came in from Forrest ("almost beside himself at the delay," according to one of his troopers) again indicating an enemy retreat and stating that every hour lost would be worth 10,000 men. W.W. Mackall, Bragg's chief of staff, even telegraphed Lieutenant General Joseph E. Johnston that Rosecrans was burning Chattanooga as he retreated. Obviously, responsible people besides Forrest had thought the Federals were abandoning the town.[4]

There was also testimony, for what it was worth, and Bragg did not think it was worth much, from a man in the ranks. A well-worn, but interesting and later favorite story among the old veterans concerned a Confederate soldier who had been captured and carried into Chattanooga, only to escape amid the confusion there of the Federal army. Making his way back to his unit with an account of Yankee demoralization and intentions to retreat, the soldier was taken to General Bragg, for whom he repeated his story. Doubtful of the man's judgment on the subject, the haggard, austere Bragg dourly asked him, "Do you know what a retreat looks like?" Irritated by his stern commander's skepticism, the private allegedly replied: "I ought to know, General; I've been with you during your whole campaign."[5]

At last, on September 22, Bragg gave orders for Forrest and Wheeler to cross the Tennessee River and move to cut off Rosecrans's line of retreat. However, when General Bragg reached the summit of Missionary Ridge about noon the next day and viewed Chattanooga, he saw no evidences of a Federal withdrawal. On the contrary, his scouts were now bringing in reports that the enemy was busily strengthening the fortifications that the Confederates themselves had thrown up around the city earlier. And Bragg's question for the private—"Do you know what a retreat looks like?"—must have seemed like a very pertinent query.

Actually, it is not at all surprising that some Confederates mistakenly supposed that Union forces were withdrawing from Chattanooga. Federal losses at Chickamauga were severe. Evidences of trauma and devastation—dead and wounded men, dead horses, abandoned equipment—were everywhere for anyone to see. Many Federals had fled to Chattanooga in panic and, initially, some of them fully expected to continue the withdrawal beyond the city. "What was very nearly a stampede . . . began on the twenty-third," according to one Federal soldier, who wrote that crowds of wounded, many critically wounded, "streamed over the pontoon bridge and up the slopes of Walden's Ridge." The jolting of the ambulances and wagons was excruciatingly painful to the badly wounded, but regardless of the cries of agony the procession moved on. "A dozen or more died that night," he said, "and were buried in rude graves, without coffins or ceremony, on the summit of the ridge."[6] Doubtless there were Rebels who found it easy to see what they wanted to see—a badly beaten Union army, which had fallen back from Chickamauga in confusion and near riot, proceeding to hasten away from Chattanooga.

But once they were concentrated and positioned behind defensive works, which were being strengthened hour by hour, the Federals' resolve soon stiffened and thoughts of retreat began to fade. Letters from many soldiers attest to such determination. Although private Benjamin Mabry described Chickamauga as "the hardest fight that ever was," he also noted that the Federal army was fortifying and would "hold this place or die on the ground. . . ." A few days later, a Federal by the name of John Lewis wrote his fiancée that the army had "fortified behind strong works"; it was "not whipped and I don't think we will be either." A few days later, an Indianian, Henry W. Howard, became even more emphatic in a letter to his brother. "Now we are well fortified," he wrote, "and I believe the hole [sic] Confederacy couldn't whip us out of Chattanooga." And sometimes, even Yankees, such as private Abraham Kipp of Pennsylvania, whose letters admitted that the army was "in a pretty critical position," would nevertheless convey a positive, determined tone, saying, for example: "I don't think the Rebels can drive us out of this place unless they starve us out."[7]

While the Union soldiers, or at least many of them, regained their composure and confidence, the Confederates occupied Missionary Ridge and Lookout Mountain, established a line of posts across the valley of Chattanooga Creek, which lay between these heights, and opened a long-range artillery fire upon the Federal works. Meanwhile, Bragg pondered his next move.

Several possibilities were open to the general. Obviously, he might attack the Federals straight on. Or he might attempt to turn them out of their position by crossing the Tennessee, gaining their rear, and breaking their supply line from Louisville and Nashville. Also, by establishing a siege line, he might attempt to starve them into either surrendering or attacking against long odds. Or, still another move would be for Bragg to divide his army, keeping part of his troops in an investment posture at Chattanooga, while sending a superior force against the small Union army of 15,000 at Knoxville, compelling Major General Ambrose E. Burnside to evacuate that city or fight at a disadvantage.

Although Bragg was slow both to realize he had won a victory at Chickamauga and to pursue the beaten Federals, there was nothing wrong with his initial strategic thinking once he had arrived at Chattanooga. To attack at Chattanooga made no sense. Bragg knew his own losses were severe. A week after Chickamauga he learned just how heavy they had been, reports showing his effective strength to be less than 36,000 men. The Yankees had a strong defensive line, built upon the former Confederate works. And history provides more than one instance of seemingly beaten soldiers stubbornly rising to fight and win when placed behind good entrenchments. While Bragg credited Rosecrans with many more troops than he in fact commanded, the Union general did have ample numbers for a defensive engagement.

If an assault on the Federal position seemed highly risky, a flanking movement appeared impossible—at least for a while. Food was short, pontoons for bridging the river were not at hand, and Longstreet's corps was totally without transportation. Faced with these problems, and still puzzled about Rosecrans's intentions (some Confederates yet thought the Union commander would retreat, his strengthening of fortifications being merely a ruse to cover plans for crossing the Tennessee), Bragg's strategy, which crystallized by the end of September, was to gather the necessary supplies for a flanking movement against Rosecrans's rear, while laying siege to the city. Evidently, Bragg believed the flanking movement would be unnecessary, expecting that his investment of Chattanooga would prove decisive.

The strategy seemed sound enough, but Bragg had a major problem—a problem that was becoming obsessive and destructive of whatever chance he might have had to successfully implement his siege campaign. The problem was the "war" within his own army, a war he waged against several of his generals.

There was nothing new, of course, about dissension and bitterness within the Army of Tennessee. Even before Bragg became the army's commander in the aftermath of the Battle of Shiloh, some officers had lost confidence in a general who had ordered charge after costly charge against the Federal stronghold in the Hornets' Nest, when it appeared to many subordinates that other tactics were essential.

4. General Braxton Bragg. *Library of Congress.*

Once appointed to lead the Army of Tennessee, Bragg proved that his reputation for stern, even stubborn, and sometimes unreasonable discipline was well deserved; worse, he failed in the Kentucky campaign, leaving his soldiers convinced that their commander had thoroughly muddled a promising invasion. Several officers had been highly critical, Major General Edmund Kirby Smith requesting a transfer, preferably to Mobile, but anywhere, he said, if staying in his present position would require further cooperation with Bragg. The complaints had been disturbing to the point that Jefferson Davis had summoned General Bragg to Richmond for a conference. And several weeks later, the Confederacy's president had visited the army at Murfreesboro, Tennessee. Although Davis had chosen to sustain Bragg in his command after the dismal Kentucky campaign, the dissension within the army was not abated and mounted again after the Battle of Stones River.

Once more, as in Kentucky, a great opportunity seemed to have been frittered away in the bloody struggle along the banks of Stones River near Murfreesboro. Recriminations and placing of blame enveloped the high command. Probably not thinking the matter through before he spoke, Bragg had told a gathering of officers that he would resign his command if it were true that he no longer enjoyed the army's confidence. Yet, when he did not receive the support for which he had hoped, Bragg did not resign. Instead, he lashed out at several brigadiers, blaming the army's failings on John P. McCown, B. Franklin Cheatham (who reportedly said after Stones River that he would never serve under Bragg again), and John C. Breckinridge, with whom Bragg carried on the longest and most bitter struggle. The situation had been so bad that corps commanders William J. Hardee and Leonidas Polk had requested Jefferson Davis to place Joseph E. Johnston in command. Clearly, the Rebel high command, in the aftermath of Stones River, had been racked with dissension.[8]

But now, following Chickamauga, the situation was even worse. The Army of Tennessee faced a near mutinous internal crisis—the worst of the war. Again, and this time even though the enemy had been driven from the field, many corps and division leaders thought the Army of Tennessee had failed to achieve its potential. A terrible sacrifice of manpower had been the price of a glorious victory—a victory that promised much, but from which little tangible had actually been garnered. As usual, Bragg attempted to shift the fault to someone else. In fact, he seemed determined to purge the army of those who opposed him, just as, at the same time, several of his generals were determining to be rid of their commander. "The tone of the army among its higher officers toward the commander was the worst conceivable," wrote G. Moxley Sorrel, Longstreet's chief of staff. "Bragg was the subject of hatred and contempt, and it was almost openly so expressed. His great officers gave him no confidence as a general-in-chief."[9]

The clash might be said to have begun two days after Chickamauga, when General Polk received a blunt note from Bragg demanding to know why his attack on the morning of September 20 had been delayed. Bragg had also decided to move against Thomas C. Hindman, for his conduct earlier in the month at McLemore's Cove, despite the fact that Hindman handled his troops well at Chickamauga. General Polk took the better part of a week before responding with a long explanation that placed much of the blame for the delay on another general, D. Harvey Hill. Bragg replied that the explanation was unsatisfactory and, on September 29, suspended Polk and Hindman from command, charging both with disobedience and directing them to Atlanta where they were to await further instructions. Apparently Bragg's mind had been set against Polk even before he read that general's explanation, for already he had sent two letters to Jefferson Davis, discussing the problems and indicating that Polk probably would be replaced as a corps commander. Soon Bragg moved against Hill also, recommending to Richmond that he be suspended from duty like Hindman and Polk. His qualifications for high command were inadequate, said Bragg, charging that Hill had "greatly demoralized the troops. . . . , and sacrificed thousands at Chickamauga."[10]

In the meantime, none of these three generals had been standing by idly; they, along with several others, were busily plotting against General Bragg. At a secret meeting on September 26, Generals Polk, Hill, Simon Buckner, and James Longstreet conferred with one another, planning to work for the removal of Bragg from command. Bragg's "palpable weakness and mismanagement manifested in the conduct of the military operations of this army" could not be tolerated any longer, they thought.[11] Polk and Longstreet, who possessed the most influence in Richmond, would launch a letter-writing campaign. Longstreet began the effort the very same day, writing Secretary of War James A. Seddon. "Our chief has done but one thing that he ought to have done since I joined his army," alleged Longstreet.

"That was to order the attack upon the 20th. All other things that he has done he ought not to have done. I am convinced that nothing but the hand of God can save us or help us as long as we have our present commander." Longstreet urged Seddon to replace Bragg with Robert E. Lee. The Army of Northern Virginia, theorized Longstreet, could operate on the defensive during Lee's absence, while the Army of Tennessee, guided by Lee, could assume offensive operations with a good prospect of recovering the state of Tennessee. Longstreet wrote to Lee as well, explaining the Chattanooga situation as he interpreted it and raising the possibility of Lee's taking command in Tennessee.[12]

Polk also wrote Lee and urged that he consider moving south to replace Bragg. Too, Polk wrote his long-time friend President Davis, blaming Bragg for not pursuing Rosecrans into Chattanooga. "The troops at the close of the fight were in the very highest spirits, ready for any service. . . . General Bragg did not know what had happened. He let us down as usual," declared the lieutenant general, "and allowed the fruits of the great but sanguinary victory to pass from him by the most criminal negligence, or rather incapacity. . . . By that victory, and its heavy expenditure of the life-blood of the Confederacy, we bought and paid for the whole of the state of Tennessee to the Mississippi River at the very least. . . ." In a letter to his wife, Polk stated, "The truth is General Bragg has made a failure, notwithstanding the success of the battle, and he wants a scapegoat." Bitterly Polk remarked that Bragg's actions against him were "a part of that long-cherished purpose to avenge himself on me for the relief and support I have given him in the past. . . ."[13]

Polk suggested to Davis that Lee or Beauregard should take Bragg's command. After being sent to Atlanta, Polk again asked Davis to replace Bragg and, in a letter to his daughter, he complained about Bragg: "I feel a lofty comtempt for his puny effort to inflict injury upon a man who dry-nursed him for the whole period of his connection with him, and has kept him from ruining the cause of the country by the sacrifice of its armies."[14]

With Polk gone, the leadership of the anti-Bragg faction fell squarely upon Longstreet. Lee had written to Longstreet, and Polk as well, disclaiming any special genius for leading the western army, but this in no way lessened the efforts of Longstreet and the others to remove Bragg from command. In fact, as Thomas L. Connelly suggested in *Autumn of Glory*, Longstreet's request that Lee replace Bragg may have been no more than a token gesture.[15] Clearly Longstreet wanted the western command for himself. He knew that Lee had turned down the command when Davis sent a corps to reinforce Bragg before Chickamauga; also, when rumors circulated among Longstreet's staff and through the army that he would take Bragg's place, the general did not discourage their spread. On the contrary, he openly criticized Bragg and suggested how he would have conducted the campaign if he had commanded the Army of Tennessee.

And then, on October 4, Longstreet had a secret meeting with the corps commanders and several other high-ranking dissidents. The result was a petition to Jefferson Davis, recounting the army's recent triumph but focusing upon the trauma of lost opportunity and calling for the removal of Bragg on the ground that "the condition of his health unfits him for the command of an army in the field." The petition read, in part: "Two weeks ago this army, elated by a great victory which promised to prove the most fruitful of the war, was in readiness to pursue its defeated enemy. That enemy, driven in confusion from the field, was fleeing in disorder and panic-stricken across the Tennessee River. Today, after having been twelve days in line of battle in that enemy's front, within cannon range of his position, the Army of Tennessee has seen a new Sebastopol rise steadily before its view. . . . Whatever may have been accomplished heretofore, it is certain that the fruits of the victory of the Chickamauga have now escaped our grasp." The Confederate army was now, the petitioners continued, "stricken with a complete paralysis" and would soon be "thrown strictly on the defensive, and may deem itself fortunate if it escapes from its present position without disaster."[16]

Possibly this remarkable document struck President Davis as alarmist in tone; actually, as would soon be proved, it was amazingly prophetic. The authorship of the petition has remained something of a puzzle, Longstreet denying that he wrote the document and claiming that Hill was responsible, while Hill maintained that Buckner wrote it. Very possibly the author was Buckner. General Polk's son William, writing a biography of his father, reached that conclusion also after questioning and interviewing various people. Also, Bragg's staff evidently thought Buckner instigated it. And Bragg later maintained he had confirmation that it was decided at the meeting that Buckner would be a good successor to Bragg, thus, supposedly, giving Buckner something more than ordinary motivation.

Whoever actually penned the document, it clearly expressed the sentiment of Longstreet, Hill, Buckner, and a number of others who

5. General Leonidas Polk. *Chickamauga-Chattanooga National Military Park.*

wanted to be rid of Bragg. In all, twelve general officers signed the document, including such people as Patrick Cleburne, William Preston, and Randall Gibson. And one would suppose that Polk, Hindman, and Cheatham would have affixed their signatures if they had been present, although such known Bragg critics as John C. Breckinridge and St. John Liddell did not sign.

The journal Liddell kept is interesting in this regard. "The fruits of victory [after Chickamauga] were before us, if our general would only reach forth and grab them," wrote Liddell. Instead, he continued, there was "the unpardonable delay of two days," while "no council [of war] was held," and Bragg was "wrapt up in his own self-opinion— and at present was unapproachable; . . . at least until his pride and elation had subsided." Liddell said further that Bragg was lacking in "strategic ability" and "determination of purpose, so necessary to a commanding general. . . ." Nevertheless, in spite of such obvious conviction that Bragg was incompetent, General Liddell refused to sign the "round-robin" petition, on the ground that "indifferent as Bragg was, I did not know any better general to take his place." In fact, Liddell feared that John C. Pemberton might be the choice if Bragg were removed, thinking that Davis, for personal reasons, would never appoint Joseph Johnston or P.G.T. Beauregard, and Lee was not likely to be sent away from Virginia. With all Bragg's faults, Liddell preferred him to anyone whom he thought likely to receive the appointment if Bragg were removed.[17]

Probably Liddell represented a minority point of view. Many of the high-ranking officers obviously desired Bragg's departure, and at least one general, Forrest, apparently threatened to kill the commander if he interfered with him further. Bragg had a low opinion of Forrest's capabilities. General Liddell made a pertinent, summary entry in his journal, recording that one morning soon after the Confederates had taken possession of Missionary Ridge, Bragg was pacing his room "in ill-humor" and saying: "I have not a single general officer of cavalry fit for command—look at Forrest; . . . the man . . . has allowed himself to be drawn off toward Knoxville in a general rampage, capturing villages and towns, that are of no use whatever to me. . . . The man is ignorant, and does not know anything of cooperation. He is nothing more than a good raider." Such a judgment perhaps reflects more upon Bragg than Forrest; it also helps explain Bragg's decision to order Forrest to turn over all of his corps to Joseph Wheeler, retaining only one regiment and one artillery battery.[18]

6. General Nathan Bedford Forrest. *Tennessee State Library and Archives.*

Forrest was enraged. Bragg had done something similar in the Kentucky campaign, giving a command to Wheeler that Forrest had raised. Bragg had also issued Forrest some curt messages during the campaigning about Nashville before the battle at Stones River. And Forrest's relationship with Wheeler, which was anything but cordial, further complicated the problem. After the Fort Donelson failure back in the winter of 1863, the two cavalrymen well might have come to blows if Wheeler had been as volatile as Forrest, the latter vowing never to serve again under Wheeler's command. Now, Forrest immediately protested Bragg's order, only to receive a coldly worded reissue for the transfer of his troops to Wheeler.

As Robert Selph Henry observed in his biography of Forrest, the "accounts of what happened and the exact sequence of events vary and cannot be entirely reconciled,"[19] but clearly the cavalry commander was incensed beyond the point of writing letters or signing petitions. An enraged Forrest, convinced that Bragg was both incompetent and pursuing a personal vendetta against him, stormed into Bragg's quarters, passing the sentry without acknowledging his salute. Then, according to Forrest's kinsman and chief surgeon, Dr. J.B. Cowan, who claimed to have been present and gave the story to both Dr. John A. Wyeth and Captain Harvey Mathes, whose biographies of Forrest were written near the turn of the twentieth century, Forrest refused to shake the hand Bragg offered and, punctuating his points with a stabbing motion of his finger, bitterly and rapidly addressed the commanding general, saying: ". . . You robbed me of my command in Kentucky. . . , men whom I armed and equipped. . . . You drove me into West Tennessee in the winter of 1862, with a second brigade I had organized, with improper arms and without sufficient ammunition. . . . In spite of all this I returned well equipped by captures . . . and now this second brigade, organized and equipped without thanks to you or the government . . . you have taken from me. I have stood your meanness as long as I intend to." Forrest then proceeded, Cowan related, to call Bragg "a damned scoundrel," saying that if Bragg "were any part of a man," he would slap his jaws and force him to resent it. "You may as well not issue any orders to me," concluded Forrest, "for I will not obey them, and . . . if you ever again try to interfere with me or cross my path it will be at the peril of your life." At that point, recorded Cowan, Forrest turned and stalked out of the commanding general's quarters with the doctor following him.[20]

Considering Forrest's personality, such a story is not difficult to believe. There is another story, not recorded by Dr. Cowan, that a few days later Forrest sent his resignation to Bragg to be forwarded to Richmond, and it was only through the intervention of President Davis that Forrest was not lost to the service of the Confederacy. Whatever precisely occurred, Forrest was transferred from Bragg's command in late October, taking up new responsibilities in Mississippi and West Tennessee. The dissension within the Army of Tennessee was at this time so widespread that Davis, in early October, decided to inspect the army himself. Too, the president was disturbed about information recently received that the army's effective strength was only about 36,000.[21]

Aboard a special train Davis headed south from Richmond on October 6. The long, roundabout route wound through the Carolinas to Columbia, then westward to Atlanta, and finally north to Chickamauga Station. In Atlanta the president conferred with his old friend Polk, agreeing that Bragg's charges were unfounded and attempting, unsuccessfully, to persuade Polk to return to the army. Polk adamantly said that he would resign rather than serve again under Bragg's command. The president, of course, was in an embarrassing position, now realizing just how deep was the breach between the two generals, both of whom had been his long-time friends. Polk even seemed disappointed that Davis planned to dismiss the charges against him, desiring to have a court of inquiry convened so that he could officially make his case against Bragg in a public manner. Finally, before Davis started the train ride through northwest Georgia, Polk did offer one concession, telling the president that he would accept a transfer to another department.

Bragg was equally determined not to have Polk under his command again and, when Davis conferred with him at Missionary Ridge, also poured forth denunciations of various subordinates, refused the services of Lieutenant General John C. Pemberton, the "hero" of Vicksburg for whom Davis sought an assignment, and concluded by submitting his resignation as commander of the Army of Tennessee. Davis refused to accept the resignation, apparently having already determined to sustain Bragg in command before he held his famous council of war with Bragg and his corps commanders, Longstreet, Hill, Buckner, and Cheatham, the last having temporarily replaced Polk. At least, within twenty-four hours of the president's arrival, Bragg told P.G.T. Beauregard's brother, Armand, that Davis was retaining him as the army's commander. Because of conflicting accounts, it is impossible to know the exact sequence of events and the exact role Davis played in guiding the subjects of discussion at the council of war.

Later Davis would write that he had "read with surprise" a statement by General Cheatham alleging that Cheatham and the other generals had been requested to express, in the presence of General Bragg, their views about the propriety of retaining Bragg as commander of the army. "In the conference I held with General Bragg and his four highest generals," said Davis, "I desired them to give their views on their military condition and future operations." It was only after "a discussion of various programmes," Davis continued, that "I inquired whether there were any other suggestions. . . . General Longstreet then, unexpectedly to me, said in substance that he thought a change of commander desirable, and he was sustained in this by the others, to what extent by General Cheatham I do not recollect. . . ."[22]

Nevertheless, from all the accounts available, those of Longstreet, Buckner, Cheatham, and Hill, it seems probable that Davis himself brought up the subject of Bragg's fitness to command. In his memoirs, *From Manassas to Appomattox*, Longstreet claimed that Davis "made known the object" of calling the meeting "and asked the generals, in turn, their opinion of their commanding officer, beginning with myself." Longstreet declared that he attempted to evade the issue, presumably because of the presence of Bragg, but the president "would not be satisfied, and got back to the question." Doubtless the situation was embarrassing. For Bragg, who had to sit and listen to the criticisms of his leadership, and for the generals who were compelled to give their low estimates of their commander in his presence, that conference on the night of October 9 must have been excruciating. Davis emerges from the episode as lacking in tact, even more, as cold and imperceptive.[23]

The Confederacy's president had conducted a "council of war" as merely a showpiece, his decision on retaining Bragg already being made. The truth is that Davis, for personal reasons, never seriously considered replacing Bragg with either Joseph E. Johnston or P.G.T. Beuregard. He was not convinced of Longstreet's competence, nor was he about to order Lee away from Virginia. It was not that Davis regarded Bragg so highly, but rather that, at least in Davis's mind, no one else possessed sufficient stature to replace him.

The president did devise a plan for resolving the Bragg-Polk controversy. Polk would be exchanged for Lieutenant General William J.

Hardee, who was acceptable to Bragg. But the president had done nothing to relieve the dissension within the army's high command. If anything, he had contributed to making it worse by the manner in which he proceeded, first, sustaining Bragg after compelling his critics to voice their objections in their commander's presence; second, three nights later, giving a speech publicly praising Bragg as "worthy of all confidence"; and third, when leaving Bragg's headquarters, issuing a proclamation highly laudatory of the army's commander. All this had to be frustrating and embarrassing to the generals, not to mention how disappointed they must have felt about Davis's judgment and ability to evaluate and resolve the problems of the army.

Predictably, the victorious and vengeful Bragg was now aroused to do much more than merely savor his triumph over the generals. To General St. John Liddell he said that Davis had "fully authorized him" to relieve "any and every officer who did not cheerfully and zealously sustain him." Liddell wrote that he at once tried to advise Bragg of "the propriety of making friends and quieting this dissatisfaction amongst his general officers—but to my distress, *his* mettle was also up and beyond the control of dispassionate reason." According to Liddell's record, and he seemed to have more rapport with Bragg than most officers, Bragg said with emphasis: "I want to get rid of all such Generals. I have better men now in subordinate stations to fill their places. Let them send in their resignations. I shall accept every one without hesitation." Liddell wrote that he then despaired of successfully appealing to Bragg to change his course. "I ceased to listen or talk upon the subject, letting the thing take its course. I truly regret that Longstreet, Buckner, D.H. Hill, Cleburne, Cheatham, and many subordinate officers had joined either directly or indirectly in this thing, at such a critical period too."[24]

Thus the war between Bragg and his generals, especially Hill, Longstreet, and Buckner, continued to rage. Now Bragg turned on Hill in earnest. He had been critical of the general soon after Chickamauga, in letters both to his wife and to Davis. In fact, two of Bragg's letters to the president contained criticisms of Hill, particularly complaining that Hill was slow in attacking on the last day at Chickamauga. Polk, of course, as previously noted, had blamed Hill for delaying the Confederate attack on the morning of September 20. Apparently this was Polk's explanation to his friend the president when the two conferred in Atlanta. Polk even claimed that Hill had admitted that he was at fault for the failure to attack when Bragg had expected.[25]

Indeed, everything appeared to go against Hill. President Davis, seeking to shift the blame from his friend Polk, seemed to be suggesting to Bragg, in a letter as early as October 3, that Hill was the one upon whom the commanding general should focus his attention. Polk's shortcomings at Chickamauga ought not to be regarded, said Davis, as greater than the "disobedience of orders by another officer of the same grade; especially when to the latter is added the other offences you specify."[26] Bragg did not need much encouragement, particularly since Hill was hardly one of the more popular generals serving with the army and thus would have few friends to support him. Perhaps, by the time Davis visited the army, Bragg also realized that he must moderate his criticisms of Polk, simply because of Davis's fondness for the general. Yet, having made such an issue of the delay at Chickamauga, he had to find someone to bear the blame.

On October 11, Bragg took Davis's suggestion, placing the responsibility for the Chickamauga mistake on Hill, asking the president to relieve him, and charging that the lieutenant general had undermined "the morale and military tone" of his soldiers, as well as failing to obey orders. Two days later Davis approved, writing Bragg and expressing his regret that the expectations which had led to Hill's assignment had not been realized and authorizing Bragg "to relieve Lieutenant General D.H. Hill from further duty with your command."[27]

This Bragg did on October 15, simply relieving Hill from duty and ordering the general to report to the Secretary of War in Richmond. Although Hill demanded to know why he had been removed, Bragg would give him no reason. All Hill could ever draw out of Bragg was that no charges would be filed and that he had been relieved in order to contribute to the army's efficiency. Hill was sure that he knew what such vague language meant: he was being removed from command because he had expressed a lack of confidence in Bragg. Once in Richmond, Hill continued to demand the specific reasons for his removal, only to encounter more of the same type of evasion he had received from Bragg. Asking for a court of inquiry to investigate his conduct, he found the president's attitude just as frustrating as Bragg's had been. No court could be held because no charges had been preferred, Davis reminded him. A tense, tempestuous interview with Davis was as fruitless as his earlier contacts with General Bragg. Hill remained convinced that he had been removed only because he had been critical of Bragg. Very probably he was right.[28]

Bragg also moved against Buckner. Buckner had done more than join in the anti-Bragg movement; he had even attributed the Chickamauga victory to the genius of Longstreet; and Bragg had learned that Buckner had been mentioned as a possible successor to him. "Troubles are brewing in the command," wrote Colonel J. Stoddard Johnson, one of Bragg's staff officers, in his journal on October 20. Certainly they were. This was the day that General Bragg asked Davis to disband the East Tennessee Department, which Buckner had commanded. The president so ordered, and Buckner lost his status not only as a department commander but also as a corps commander, his position being reduced to that of a division commander.

Surprised and enraged, Buckner lashed out at Bragg in a severe letter, "complaining," as Stoddard Johnson expressed it, "in bold terms of the injustice which had been done him." The letter was certainly a harsh document, one that angered Bragg. In fact, he sent it back to Buckner with an inscription, dated October 23, 1863, which reads: "Returned to writer as a paper improper and unfit to go in the records of this office." But Buckner continued to write. Stoddard Johnson's October 29 journal entry reads: "Buckner files another paper, appealing to the war department for a redress of wrongs. He complains of tyranny, discourtesy, and usurpation of power on the part of General Bragg." Again, on November 1, Johnson recorded: "Another long document today from Buckner, . . . written in sharp and bitter terms, repeating his former charges against General Bragg and stating that he, General Bragg, is influenced by selfish ambition and . . . revenge." Buckner was also complaining to the president, of course. Still again, on November 8, he wrote Bragg, reiterating all his former complaints—and in the same tone.[29]

All of Buckner's efforts never changed anything. Bragg had succeeded in his war against yet another general, a general who participated in "a mutinous assemblage," as Bragg phrased it in his letter to Richmond on November 8, summarizing the whole episode and indicating his belief that Buckner had hoped to succeed him once he, Bragg, was removed from command.[30]

Finally, the feuding between Bragg and Longstreet, perhaps the most destructive of all the command problems in its ultimate effect on the fortunes of the Rebel army besieging Chattanooga, continued building to its taxing and fatal climax as October wore on. But, while the Confederate generals bickered, intrigued, and vacillated, a major change was occurring in the Federal army. The Confederates were allowing their enemy too much time to recover and regroup after the defeat at Chickamauga. And now the Union forces were acting energetically to take full advantage of their unexpected reprieve.

3

Stunned, Like a Duck Hit on the Head

Until about noon of September 20 at Chickamauga, forty-four-year-old Major General William Starke Rosecrans had possessed perhaps the most enviable reputation of any Union general in either the eastern or the western theater of the American Civil War. After successes against Robert E. Lee in western Virginia during the first year of the conflict and later at Corinth, Mississippi, where his troops made a determined stand, turning back generals Earl Van Dorn and Sterling Price, Rosecrans had entered 1863 with a hard-fought victory at Stones River, recovering from the near disaster of a surprise attack in that major engagement and holding his ground until the Confederates retreated. A somewhat impulsive, excitable personality, "Old Rosy," as the men called him, had inspired hope and confidence throughout the army.

Although there had been some criticism when the colorful general did not resume offensive operations for a long time after the battle at Stones River, the fault was more that of the war department than that of the commanding general. Rosecrans demanded the mules, horses, and equipment necessary for an advance, but the department seemed indifferent to his western army. The independent, outspoken commander had an unfortunate tendency to irritate his superiors. Secretary of War Edwin M. Stanton strongly disliked the devoted Catholic general, who carried a crucifix on his watch chain and a rosary in his pocket while freely employing profanity, and this was a factor in the lack of cooperation between the war department and Rosecrans's army. Major General George H. Thomas, as well as Rosecrans's other corps commanders, agreed with the commanding general that the army could not move offensively without adequate transportation.[1]

When at length the general had felt prepared and gone forward, he had conducted a series of brilliant strategical flanking movements, taking the Army of the Cumberland over three mountain ranges in three weeks. By these movements, "perhaps unequalled and certainly unsurpassed for boldness and effectiveness in the Northern armies during the four years of war," according to the assessment of Chickamauga historian Glen Tucker, Rosecrans thoroughly baffled and ousted Bragg from Tullahoma, and then from Chattanooga, Tennessee, the town long recognized as the gateway to the deep South, whose seizure Abraham Lincoln had said was "fully as important as the taking and holding of Richmond." Chattanooga itself had been occupied without losing a man, and only six had died during the whole campaign, four of these accidentally. It had been a magnificent triumph, startling the entire South and causing rejoicing in the North such as had followed Gettysburg and Vicksburg.[2]

If Rosecrans had then won at Chickamauga, as clearly was possible before the freakish mid-day blunder on that fateful September Sunday, he undoubtedly would have been the outstanding Northern general of the war in the fall and winter of 1863, with a series of impressive triumphs and no defeats to mar his record. He might have pushed on deep into Georgia, threatening to sever the eastern half of the Confederacy, and would have preempted both Ulysses S. Grant's opportunity to gain stature and promotion to the rank of lieutenant general at Chattanooga as well as William T. Sherman's later campaign through Georgia and the Carolinas. But the fact was that Chickamauga so unnerved Rosecrans that he seemed unable to recover his confidence and presence of command. Appropriate certainly was the title selected for William S. Lamers's biography of General Rosecrans, *The Edge of Glory.*

On the evening of September 20 the Union commander wired Henry W. Halleck: "We have met with a serious disaster; extent not yet ascertained. The enemy overwhelmed us, drove our right, pierced our center, and scattered the troops there." Discouraged as was President Lincoln ("Well, Rosecrans has been whipped, as I feared," he

7. General William S. Rosecrans. *Dahlgren Collection. Tennessee State Library and Archives.*

remarked), he tried to encourage his general with a late-night telegram, saying, "We have unabated confidence in you and in your
soldiers and officers. . . . We shall do our utmost to assist you." The
next morning, however, another message arrived from Rosecrans,
this one even more discouraging, stating, "after two days of the
severest fighting I ever witnessed, our left and center were beaten.
The left held its position until sunset. . . . Our loss is heavy and our
troops worn down. . . ." Then came the most alarming part of the
wire, as Rosecrans said, "We have no certainty of holding our position
here." Of course few things in war are certain, but the tone of this
message greatly alarmed Lincoln, for he thought that it sounded
defeatist in nature. Also, soon Stanton was interjecting his barbs at
Rosecrans, observing that corps commanders McCook and Crittenden had "made pretty good time away from the fight, but Rosecrans
beat them both."[3]

The important point strategically, as Lincoln saw it, was not that
Rosecrans had been beaten at Chickamauga, but that he still held
Chattanooga. As long as he did so, he could keep the Rebels out of
Tennessee while also denying them the use of one of their most
important railroads. A Federal force of 15,000 under Major General
Ambrose E. Burnside, aided immensely by the campaign Rosecrans
had been conducting, was at long last in the Knoxville area, having
effectively cut the direct railroad link between Chattanooga and
Virginia. The Rebels were now forced to use a roundabout route from
Virginia south through the eastern Carolinas, then to Atlanta and
back up to North Georgia and Bragg's army. The president sensed,
with a sure instinct, that regardless of the defeat at Chickamauga the
Union still held a death grip on the Confederacy. "If we can hold
Chattanooga and East Tennessee," the president wrote to General
Rosecrans on October 4, "I think the rebellion must dwindle and
die." The president told Halleck that if Rosecrans "can only maintain
this position, . . . the rebellion can only eke out a short and feeble
existence, as an animal sometimes may with a thorn in its vitals."
But, telegraphing Rosecrans to "Please relieve my anxiety as to the
position and condition of your army up to the latest moment," Lincoln learned that his general again seemed to have lost confidence in
any measures he might undertake. General Rosecrans replied: "We
are about 30,000 brave and determined men; but our fate is in the
hands of God, in whom I hope."[4]

Besides such messages from the army's commander, which were

far from the determined resolution Lincoln wanted to hear, Stanton's spy in the Federal camp, Charles A. Dana, was sending back reports that became progressively less favorable to Rosecrans. From saying that the soldiers had lost their attachment for "Old Rosy" since "he failed them in the battle, and that they do not now cheer him unless they are ordered to do so," Dana proceeded to castigate Rosecrans for lack of administrative powers, practical incapacity, no strength of will, and no concentration of purpose. "I consider this army to be very unsafe in his hands," Dana declared. "If the army is finally obliged to retreat, the probability is that it will fall back like a rabble," he complained, seemingly reaching the zenith of his criticisms when he wrote of Rosecrans that "it often seems difficult to believe him of sound mind."[5] Obviously such reports could not have improved the president's estimate of the army's commander; yet the general's own wires to the president were probably by themselves, in their cumulative effect, sufficient to destroy whatever confidence Lincoln might otherwise have still had in General Rosecrans.

When, on October 12, Lincoln telegraphed Rosecrans, still trying to implant his own grasp of strategy within the commander's thinking, saying, "You and Burnside now have the enemy by the throat, and he must break your hold or perish," the general's reply was a complaint that the corn was ripe on the Confederate side of the Tennessee River, but "our side is barren"; after which he still proceeded to avow his faith: "We must put our trust in God," he said, "who never fails those who truly trust." If Rosecrans had a stranglehold on the Confederacy, he clearly seemed unaware of the fact. Exasperated with the man who had been so successful for a while but now seemed to have lost his confidence and self-reliance, Lincoln remarked that, ever since Chickamauga, Rosecrans had been acting "confused and stunned, like a duck hit on the head."[6]

Undeniably, Rosecrans had experienced major problems at Chattanooga, the worst of which, and its intensity mounted daily, was keeping his army supplied—food, of course, being the most critical factor. Downstream from Chattanooga, about thirty miles away, lay the town of Bridgeport, Alabama, through which ran the Memphis and Charleston Railroad, a line connecting with the Nashville and Chattanooga Railroad a short distance to the southwest at Stevenson, Alabama. Thus, the Yankees could easily bring huge quantities of supplies from Louisville and Nashville to Bridgeport. But the route from there into Chattanooga, whether by rail, river, or road, was

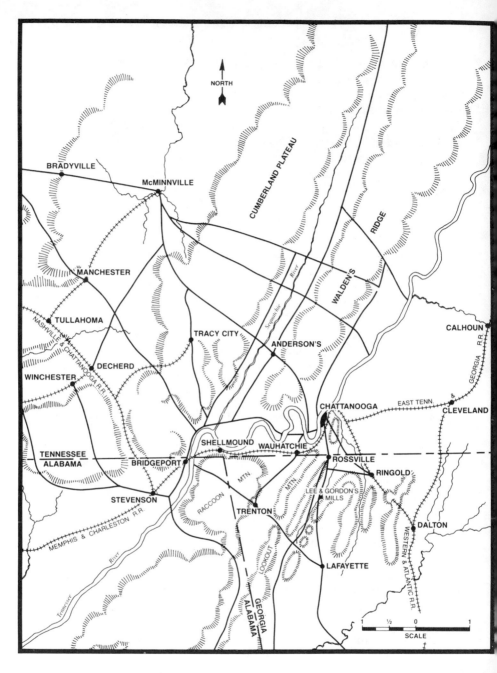

Map 2. Area Map of the Chattanooga Region. *Map by J.L. Moon, Jr.*

blocked by Confederate artillerists, sharpshooters, and pickets. These Rebels occupied Lookout Mountain, patrolled Lookout Valley, and were strategically strung across Raccoon Mountain, which paralleled Lookout Mountain farther to the west. The only route from Bridgeport to Chattanooga that the Rebels did not control (and parts of it were subject to enemy cavalry raids) was a wagon road, north of the Tennessee River, by which a supply train must first journey northward through the Sequatchie Valley and then toil eastward up and over a barren wasteland of almost impassable mountain country, before arriving at Chattanooga immediately north of the city. The Sequatchie Valley, which runs northeast-southwest, is bordered by the Cumberland Plateau on the west and the rugged terrain of Walden's Ridge to the east. Nearly forty miles up the valley, the road from Bridgeport intersected the Anderson Road (built in the 1840s by a farmer named Josiah Anderson in order to get produce to market at Chattanooga), which ran east over Walden's Ridge and on to the besieged city along the banks of the Tennessee River. It was, altogether, a tortuous, sixty-mile trek, the only route by which a mere trickle of supplies—food, warm clothing, medicine, and ammunition—came in to the besieged army.

The most treacherous part of this precarious route was the eastern descent of Walden's Ridge. In describing this road, Federal Colonel B.F. Scribner, of the Thirty-eighth Indiana Regiment, wrote that the "Ridge is steep and crooked; the road much of the way is composed of logs, one end of which rests on the side of the mountain, the other end supported in a horizontal position by props, thus forming a sort of corduroy road. At one point near the summit, a stream of water ran down the mountain's side through the interstices of the logs. It was a rickety, insecure, makeshift of a road and was so narrow that only in places could two teams pass each other."[7]

Thus the Federals tried to open a second road up the eastern slope of Walden's Ridge, in order that the loaded wagons, bound for Chattanooga, could use one, and the empty wagons, going to Bridgeport, might use the other. Because Confederate sharpshooters, stationed along the south shore of the Tennessee River on Raccoon Mountain, effectively prevented the use of the old Haley Trail, which ran directly across the river from them, the so-called Federal or Military Road was begun as an alternative.[8] This route, in the words of Cartter Patten, whose book *Signal Mountain and Walden's Ridge* is very helpful in understanding the problems of the Union army, went "up

Shoal Creek Gorge along somewhat the route of the present Signal Mountain Road. On reaching the top of the mountain, it ran west of the present Taft Highway and joined the Anderson Pike near the Shackleford place. It, too, was a steep, crude and makeshift affair but the empty wagon trains returning to Bridgeport had to use it."[9]

By mid-October, the Sequatchie Valley–Anderson Road route was horribly marred by the bodies of dead draft animals and the wreckage of broken wagons. With forage exhausted in the valley and the rugged terrain taking its toll, large numbers of mules died from starvation and overwork. John K. Duke, Fifty-third Ohio Infantry, wrote that "the poor, abused mule suffered the most. For instance, one of them got off the road and was hanging over a precipice, endangering the other mules of the team. This one was cut loose, and dropped 200 or 300 feet below." Duke also reported that because the mules were desperate for forage, "it was no unusual sight to see trees as high as animals could reach, barked and eaten as food."[10]

Conditions in Chattanooga were growing worse. The men were put on half rations of hard bread, which often served as their entire meal. The supply wagons were no longer transporting anything other than foodstuffs. As winter drew near, the men suffered increasingly from the lack of adequate shoes and clothing. Even fuel was becoming scarce, since all available trees had been cut down and even the stumps had been burned. Because mules were no longer available for hauling timber over any distance, soldiers sometimes managed to fell trees near the river, lashing them into rafts and floating them back to camp. The situation of the Federal army steadily deteriorated. If something were not done to alleviate the suffering, Chattanooga promised to become for the Federals what Vicksburg had been for the Confederacy. That something was the removal of General Rosecrans.

The relief of Rosecrans from command came exactly one month after the opening day of the battle of Chickamauga. His removal resulted, immediately and directly, from a Dana message, telegraphed to Stanton at Louisville, saying that Rosecrans was on the verge of retreating from Chattanooga and advising that he be ordered not to do so. Actually, Rosecrans had no such intention. To the contrary, he had been working for several days on plans for opening an adequate supply line, after which, despite his less than assuring communiqués to the president, he intended to resume offensive operations.

Although Dana was clearly unjust to Rosecrans, probably "Old

Rosy's" days in command would have been few even if Dana's telegram had never been sent. Already Major General Ulysses S. Grant had met with the Secretary of War in Louisville, where Stanton gave orders that, as Grant phrased it, "created the 'Military Division of the Mississippi.' (giving me the command)." Grant's Army of the Tennessee, Rosecrans's Army of the Cumberland, and Burnside's Army of the Ohio were now to compose a unified western command, with Grant authorized either to retain Rosecrans or place George H. Thomas in command of the Army of the Cumberland. Because Grant and Rosecrans disliked each other, and considering the shadow of defeat under which Rosecrans now labored, in contrast to the heroic stature of "the Rock of Chickamauga," it is difficult to conceive of Grant's retaining Rosecrans for very long under any circumstances—other than a swift and near miraculous triumph.

Regardless of what might have been, Dana's dispatch of Sunday, October 18, brought an abrupt end to Rosecrans's tenure as commander of the Army of the Cumberland. That evening Grant and his wife, Julia, were visiting some of her relatives in the Louisville area when a messenger from Stanton summoned Grant back to the Galt House for an urgent meeting with the secretary. Stanton was in a dressing gown, nervously pacing the floor, when Grant arrived at his room. Excitedly, he shoved Dana's message into Grant's hand. The general read it, bluntly stated that a retreat from Chattanooga would be "a terrible disaster," and immediately dispatched an order replacing Rosecrans with Thomas as commander of the Union forces and instructing Thomas to hold Chattanooga at any cost. On Monday, October 19, Rosecrans received the order, and Thomas sent back his famous response: "We will hold the town until we starve." On Tuesday morning Grant boarded a train for Chattanooga.

Spending the night in Nashville, where Andrew Johnson, Federal military governor of Tennessee, welcomed him with a long, tiring speech, Grant then passed through Murfreesboro the following day, his train going directly across the bloody Stones River battleground where Rosecrans and Bragg had first fought, nearly ten months earlier. The train next proceeded to Stevenson, Alabama, for Grant to have an early-evening conference with Rosecrans, who had left Chattanooga the day before. Thinking about the well-being of the Federal cause, and not wishing to encourage any demonstration of dissatisfaction at his departure (for, despite what Dana had written, many of the soldiers still esteemed him highly), Rosecrans had left Chattanooga soon after receiving Grant's wire. Now, although he had no fondness for Grant, Rosecrans generously shared his plans for lifting the siege with the incoming commander. "He came into my car," Grant later wrote, "and we held a brief interview, in which he described very clearly the situation at Chattanooga." Grant acknowledged that Rosecrans made some excellent suggestions about what should be done, but cuttingly, although pertinently, Grant added: "My only wonder was that he had not carried them out."[11]

These two men, conversing in a railroad car, were a study in contrasts. Forty-one-year-old Major General Ulysses S. Grant had a penchant for heavy drinking and enjoyed chomping on the butt of a cigar, but there any resemblance to General Rosecrans seemed to end. Grant was a short person and of slight build, while Rosecrans stood nearly six feet and possessed a wider frame.[12] Articulate and talkative, Rosecrans delighted in theoretical discussions of war; Grant said very little to anybody and went about, much of the time, wearing an old slouch hat and a plain, faded blue coat. Rosecrans was colorful, abounding with energy, a man who would readily "stand out" as attractive and interesting. Grant, on the other hand, was indeed, as wrote William S. McFeely, the general's biographer, "strikingly unnoticeable."[13] Nothing about his appearance would have caused the average man to remember him, unless possibly it was the worn, almost sad expression around his eyes. On the very day that Grant met with Rosecrans, a Union soldier observed him standing on the train platform and entered a description of the general in his diary: "He wore an army slouch hat with bronze cord around it, quite a long military coat, unbuttoned, no sword or belt, and there was nothing to indicate his rank. . . . When the boys called for a speech he bowed and said nothing."[14]

His later failures as president, nondescript looks, and sparse use of words were some of the factors contributing to the twentieth-century, popular image of Grant as a simple, shallow fellow who only succeeded in war because of either incredible luck or vastly superior manpower and material resources—or both. One of McFeely's contributions in *Grant: A Biography* is to convincingly dispel this simplistic view of the little man from Galena, Illinois.

McFeely's *Grant* unveils a character who, though certainly not brilliant, possessed some depth, keenness, and breadth of vision; also, ironically, a man who was anything but a "born soldier," in the West Point sense of a Douglas McArthur or a George Patton. Grant even detested Napoleon Bonaparte, then the idol of so many cadets as well as instructors at the Point. Of his years at the Academy, Grant wrote, "A military life had no charms for me," and once he referred to the day he left West Point as one of the two occasions that "possibly" were "the happiest of my life." Graduating twenty-first in a class of thirty-nine, the slight young cadet found drawing and painting, arts for which he demonstrated some talent, more intriguing than most of his subjects. And he spent considerable time reading fiction, although for some reason, about which one can only speculate, he was never willing to discuss literary matters at any stage of his adulthood—even though he recognized that people sometimes thought him ignorant of subjects that he really understood.

Perhaps the reading helped Grant learn to write briefly and clearly. The General's two-volume *Memoirs*, penned shortly before his death, are a classic of that type of literature. His accounts of the Mexican War, for example, both in the memoirs and in his letters home, reveal a sharp observer and even a rather sensitive man. With remarkable self-confidence, yet without arrogance or insubordination, he would sometimes analyze and criticize the military decisions of his superiors. Usually he was right. Grant could write about the American invasion of Mexico (of which he disapproved) with critical detachment, about the Mexican country and people with detail and sympathy, and about the fighting with vitality.

And precisely there—in the *fighting* of the Mexican War—"the real Grant" began to emerge. Grant possessed an almost scholarly detachment from most of life's concerns, but war proved to be one of the few things that could arouse him. Grant was not stimulated by West Point, by peacetime army posts, by talking about war, or by "army life." It was war itself—participating in it—that aroused Grant as nothing else ever had or would. Everything after the Civil War, even the presidency, which so stimulated Theodore Roosevelt that he called it "bully fun," was for Grant a drab, anticlimax to his days as a warrior.[15]

If then Grant had more substance than met the eye; if he was indeed, as McFeely has stated, "a man of limited though by no means inconsequential talents to apply to whatever truly engaged his attention,"[16] the general's success in war, the one thing that deeply aroused him, is easily understood. His triumph was not merely the result of chance, or of men and materials; Grant's ability accounted, at least in part, for his success. And his later failure in the presidency,

8. General Ulysses S. Grant. *Library of Congress.*

which neither stimulated nor satisfied him, is thus also more con-vincingly explained than by such condescending and unknowable assertions of some critics that he possessed the least intelligence of any man who ever occupied the White House. Both the "butcher" image of Grant, the warrior, and the bumbling figure of Grant, the politician, seem to be shallow over-simplifications of the small, quiet general who sat across the car from the more impressive appearing Rosecrans on that late October evening in 1863.

After the conference, Rosecrans continued his journey northward, and Grant proceeded to Bridgeport, Alabama, on the Tennessee bor-der. He was accompanied on this leg of the journey by Oliver O. Howard, a veteran of Chancellorsville and Gettysburg, whose com-mand had been hit hard in both engagements. Recently, in record time, he had been sent west, along with Joseph Hooker, leading reinforcements to help raise the siege of Chattanooga. Meeting his new commander for the first time, Howard was surprised by Grant's small size. He described the general as "rather thin in flesh and very pale in complexion, and noticeably self-contained and retiring." He also observed, as Grant met with Hooker—the latter a general who could be abrasive and overbearing—that Grant took the very first opportunity to assert himself and gain "a proper ascendency over subordinate generals. . . ."[17]

Perhaps Grant looked abnormally pale to Howard because he suffered considerable pain from a bruised and swollen leg sustained in a fall from a horse several days earlier. Although Grant was an excel-lent horseman, he liked to ride powerful and spirited animals. There are at least three versions of what happened. Certain only is that the general had been in New Orleans celebrating the Vicksburg triumph when he somehow took a very nasty spill from his mount. And now, particularly considering his bad leg, came the worst part of the trek into Chattanooga.

At Bridgeport the railroad line ended. The Rebels had destroyed the bridge to the south side of the Tennessee River, an area the Confederates held, of course, excepting only the town of Chattanooga itself. The only way into the Union encampment at the city was, as previously noted, via the north side of the river—a sixty-mile horse-back journey up the Sequatchie Valley and over Walden's Ridge on the rough, circuitous road the army trains had been laboriously traversing just to keep up a trickle of supplies for the Federal soldiers in the besieged town. At daybreak of October 22, with his crutches strapped to his saddle while James Rawlins lifted him into it, "as if he had been a child," Grant and his small party set off, in spite of a heavy storm that had blown in during the night.

If Grant ever had any doubt about what should be the first order of business after entering Chattanooga, this last miserable stretch of his journey would likely have eliminated the question. Carcasses of mules and horses, killed by the enemy or dead of starvation, were strewn along the roadway by the hundreds. (Possibly ten thousand mules and horses died during the siege of Chattanooga, and for a man who loved animals as Grant did, the overall scene would have been depressing indeed.) Sections of the road itself had been devastated by heavy rains. Washouts plagued hillside portions of the route, while low-lying areas might be knee-deep in mud. Grant, because of his bad leg, had to be carried over the worst of these. Surely, the establishment of a better line of food supply for the half-starved troops in Chattanooga—"opening up the cracker line," as Grant called it—was the top priority.

Late on October 23—the same day that an angry Bragg was returning one of General Buckner's letters "as a paper improper and unfit to go in the records of this office"—Grant finally arrived at the headquarters of General Thomas. Wet and filthy, but well other than for his leg, he declined an offer of dry clothes, slumped down in a chair in front of a fire, and lit a cigar. Without rising, Grant first shook hands with each of Thomas's staff officers and then immediately proceeded to have them, one by one, assess the army's military position. Perhaps Grant thought there was not time to be wasted. Probably he was making a statement, by example, both about his commanding position and about the seriousness with which he viewed the tactical situation.

Learning that hardly enough ammunition existed for even one day of battle, the need for opening up a new supply line took on an added dimension in Grant's thinking. Not only, according to the old cliché, does an army march on its stomach; it must also have something with which to fight. "It looked, indeed," the general later said, "as if but two courses were open; one to starve, the other to surrender or be captured." If some of the officers in the room thought Grant strangely inattentive—for example, Horace Porter found him "immovable as a rock and as silent as a sphinx"—the general was actually quite alert, watching for any signs from those who might have favored a retreat, or any solid ideas about the communications problem. And Porter noticed a change in Grant's demeanor when General William F.

Smith, the engineer whom Grant had known at West Point, began to speak. Smith had responsibility for bridges and roads. Porter wrote that Grant straightened up in his chair as he listened to Smith, while "his features assumed an air of animation, and. . .[he] began to fire whole volleys of questions. . . ."[18]

"Baldy" Smith, as some Academy classmates had called him because of prematurely thinning hair, had the answers—most of them anyway.[19] The thirty-nine-year-old West Pointer also had a reputation for being rather contentious, which seems to have been why the U.S. Congress had never confirmed his promotion to major general. But Grant had no problems with Smith's nature. He appeared genuinely pleased to see "Baldy," with whom he had not crossed paths since their West Point days. Above all, he liked Smith's plans about how to open a new and better supply line. "He explained the situation of the two armies and the topography of the country so plainly that I could see it without an inspection," Grant later wrote.[20] Considering the confusing complex of mountains, ridges, knobs, and valleys through and around which the Tennessee River winds like a monstrous serpent, Grant's tribute to Smith's description was no small compliment. To understand the plan one must grasp the geography of the region.

The Tennessee River follows a lazy, meandering course, flowing generally westward, but making two large loops in the vicinity of Chattanooga. After coursing due west past the city on the north, the river turns immediately south for a couple of miles, before bending abruptly back to the north from the base of Lookout Mountain. This famous loop of the river is known as Moccasin Bend. Continuing northward for several miles, the broad stream then gradually bears northwest, passing between Signal Mountain on the right bank and Raccoon Mountain on the left, afterward looping around the northern extremity of Raccoon to surge once more south and then west toward Bridgeport.

General Smith's plan for a new supply line involved crossing the Tennessee three times. The first crossing, of course, would be via the pontoon bridge already in use north of Chattanooga. The second was to be at Brown's Ferry, only a little more than a mile directly west across Moccasin Point; finally, after following a road through Cummings Gap in Raccoon Mountain, came Kelly's Ferry, the third crossing, from which a road ran along the north bank of the Tennessee to Bridgeport. Actually, such a route could hardly be more direct. Much

9. General U.S. Grant (seated, center) at the Headquarters of General George H. Thomas (second from right).*Chickamauga-Chattanooga National Military Park.*

easier to travel than the old one, it was also about half as long. The one big problem was that the Confederates held Raccoon Mountain, with pickets protecting Cummings Gap and advanced to the river at Brown's Ferry. Obviously, these Rebels would have to be eliminated, and Smith had devised a plan of attack.

From three directions Federal forces would converge on Brown's Ferry, establishing a beachhead on the west bank of the river. During the night, one column of infantry would march overland, west across the narrow neck of the peninsula formed by Moccasin Bend, while a second group would float downriver in pontoon boats. The latter would make the assault, hoping to surprise the Confederate outpost at Brown's Ferry, and holding on while the pontoons were assembled to provide a bridge across which the reinforcing column marching from Chattanooga could be brought up quickly. The third column, a force from Hooker's command, had the greatest distance to travel. Crossing to the south bank of the Tennessee at Bridgeport, and following the railroad eastward, these men would tramp around the south side of Raccoon Mountain, then move north under cover of darkness, still following the railroad through the valley of Lookout Creek, and close upon Brown's Ferry from the rear.[21]

Combining their forces, the Yankees would then be strong enough to drive the Rebels out of Cummings Gap (for General Bragg had not put enough Confederates there to withstand a real attack) and secure control of the road leading west to Kelly's Ferry. The plan was bold. It required timing and daring. Grant liked it and approved it—although not before, on the day after his arrival, riding with Smith and Thomas, along with some other officers, for an inspection tour of the base of Moccasin Point and the Brown's Ferry site. As he dismounted and walked along the bank of the Tennessee, Grant was in clear view of Confederate pickets on the other side, who saluted rather than opening fire.[22] Lieutenant Colonel John Atkinson described Grant's appearance about this time: "He wore his uniform more like a civilian than a graduate of West Point. His military coat was never buttoned up to the neck. He sat on his horse carelessly, although securely. He walked with his head down and without the slightest suggestion of a military step. Neither his face nor his figure was imposing."[23]

While on this inspection ride, Smith showed Grant both a sawmill, powered by a steam engine taken from a local factory, which he had set up to provide the lumber necessary for the pontoon bridge, and a steamboat being constructed for hauling supplies. Once the river had been opened up to traffic below (north of) Brown's Ferry, this boat could bring large quantities of bacon and hardtack upstream from Bridgeport to within easy reach at the ferry. Grant was so pleased that when he got back to Chattanooga that evening he issued orders for the plan to begin—and within two days.

Certainly there was no time to be wasted. From half rations the U.S. Army in Chattanooga had come down to quarter rations. Horses and mules were allowed three ears of corn each day, and hungry soldiers would steal the animals' food. When the livestock were fed, it became necessary to have armed guards to keep desperate soldiers from robbing them. C.C. Briant, Sixth Indiana Infantry, described the men in his company as "starved into walking skeletons—pale, thin-faced, sickly looking men, so weak that they would stagger as they walked. . . ." Briant said that he would go into the town and "buy anything I could find for sale in the way of food, regardless of price, and distribute among those most needy." Such resources were naturally soon exhausted. Finally, men were searching for items they had earlier thrown away, like meat skins, "hard as raw-hide leather," that had been trimmed off bacon. These gleanings, Brian reported, the soldiers would "wash and chew . . . as a sweet morsel."[24]

When a commissary wagon rattled by, soldiers would follow, hoping that something edible might fall out that they could pick up and devour. "We would draw our quarter rations," wrote Thomas J. Ford of the Twenty-fourth Wisconsin, "and eat them up right away, not having drawn for four days before, and take chances on foraging or gobbling or in any way that we could pick up anything to eat."[25] Edible articles obtained on foraging expeditions were always treasured and sometimes eaten of very sparingly. For instance, toward the last days of October, according to S.S. Canfield of the Twenty-first Ohio, a member of Company K secured a goose while foraging several miles from camp. "He took of it so sparingly," alleged Canfield, "that before the last of it was eaten, it went into decay, or what has since become the fashion to call, 'innocuous desuetude.' Finally, attracted to a hole in one of the bomb-proofs by a smell of something perishable, the remains of the goose were discovered, and although the owner protested that it was all right, for he had been partaking of it daily, it was buried from the sight and smell of men."[26]

Foraging expeditions might journey forty to sixty miles across the mountains to the north and east of Chattanooga. "Our animals were fast becoming unserviceable, and the foraging teams were so weak they were scarcely able to haul empty wagons as they started," wrote Canfield, "and soldiers had to help loaded wagons back to camp. Exhausted animals were often killed and wagons abandoned. In such cases returning soldiers brought in whatever they could carry on their backs." Canfield also said that when corn could be obtained (sometimes by foraging, or by robbing the animals of their ration, or even by finding stray pieces in the mud), it was parched and eaten or roasted and made into coffee, "and the grounds afterward eaten."[27] Another soldier's account in his journal is more detailed: "With a nail we punch our tin plates full of holes," he wrote, "and use the rough side for a grater; after a good deal of patience and hard work, the corn is grated into coarse meal, then mixed with water and salt, is baked over hot coals in other tin plates. This we relish with a diminutive piece of bacon and parched corn coffee. . . ."[28]

When occasionally a few cattle could be captured and slaughtered at the division slaughter yard, again quoting Canfield, "soldiers quarreled with each other for the offal of the animals; tails, hoofs, and even intestines. . . .The tails made the delicious ox-tail soup; from inwards, by a short process, was made a sort of tripe, while from hoofs and shanks we obtained an article not unlike common glue, which, while not the greatest delicacy in the world, was so much better than nothing, that he who secured a 'dose' of it deemed himself very fortunate."[29] An attempt was made to drive cattle overland from Nashville, but nothing could be found for the cattle to feed on anywhere near Chattanooga, and they arrived in a condition the soldiers referred to as "beef dried on the hoof."[30]

The stomach-turning ingenuity of some near-starving soldiers seemed to be unlimited. One desperate soldier claimed he hunted up an old discarded tin can, earlier filled with grease and rags to provide a wick for light after candles had been exhausted, and finding that it still had "considerable grease in it, mixed with some flies and the old rag wick, I ate them all and relished them very much at the time. . . ."[31] Compared to such gross fare, the braving of enemy picket fire by some Yankees to collect acorns in the area between Lookout Mountain and Missionary Ridge seems understandable, even preferable. It is hardly surprising that a Kansas infantryman related how one of the regiments in his division "caught, killed and ate a dog that wandered into camp."[32]

The soldiers' letters, diaries, and later regimental histories, almost without exception, abound with references to the sufferings endured throughout the siege of Chattanooga.[33] But the army was also being hardened by its trials. Determined to endure and prevail, Alfred L. Hough, wrote to his wife on October 18, 1863, in a letter representative of the thoughts of many. After speaking of the plight of the soldiers, Hough continued, "the poor horses, how they suffer, many die daily. If I had been suddenly thrown from the comforts of home, and the scenes of prosperity around me into such a place as this I should have thought it horrible, very horrible, but we have become used to it, we are as cheerful and as happy as you are; only when we think of home, then oh then how our hearts sicken."[34]

4

Rebels All Around

The view from atop Missionary Ridge is imposing at night, when lights are on all over Chattanooga, around Moccasin Bend of the Tennessee River, and also dot the distant heights, miles across the valley, on Signal Mountain (the southern extremity of Walden's Ridge), Raccoon Mountain, and Lookout Mountain. The murky outline of the slope and northern point of Lookout looms particularly massive and majestic on the horizon. At night, the serene panorama suggests a tastefully composed work of art. The irritating sounds from the city below wane under the cover of darkness—unless the vantage point is too close to the interstate highway that today crosses the ridge, bringing the all-pervading dronings of the big trucks on their cross-country journeys, replete with the screeching tires, wailing sirens, revving motors, and other all-too-familiar noise pollutions endemic to the monotonous expressways.

In the daytime, the aggravating sounds of machines and industry are more pronounced, and the evidences of contamination, poverty, and ugliness, drably characteristic of most cities, dominate and obscure the natural beauty of Chattanooga's setting. How lush and virgin the valley must have been for countless millennia and still was in the days when the American Indians roamed and hunted in the region and called Lookout Point "the Eagles' Nest." One senses that something irretrievably precious was destroyed in the onward march of American civilization. Understandable (beyond mere status seeking) is the desire of many who can afford better homes and landscaped lawns to live on the ridge rather than in the valley.

Already, in the fall of 1863, just as now, the town and the valley did not look very attractive in the clear light of day. Much of the timber on the ridge and in the valley had been cut away, used for fuel, buildings, and breastworks. In many places the land looked as if it had been scalped. Artillery shelling had torn up various structures. Smoke from chimneys and trains had darkened and dirtied the appearance of the small town. Occupied first by one army and then by the other, Chattanooga had suffered in the manner that any place does when tens of thousands of soldiers are tramping about for weeks at a time. Then, as now, the view from Missionary Ridge was much more pleasing at night than during the day.

General Bragg wrote to his wife about the unusual scene from Missionary Ridge: "Just underneath my headquarters are the lines of the two armies, and beyond with their outposts and signal stations are Lookout, Raccoon, and Walden Mountains. At night all are brilliantly lit up in the most gorgeous manner by the miriads of camp fires. No scene in the most splendid theater ever approached it."[1]

Among the Confederates stationed atop the ridge was Brigadier General Arthur Middleton Manigault of South Carolina. Intelligent, well-educated, and sensitive, the general's memoirs, written soon after the war ended, when his memory of events was fresh, are among the most valuable and interesting penned by any officer on either side. Describing the scene from Missionary Ridge, Manigault recalled that "at night just after dark, when all the camp fires were lighted, the effect was very grand and imposing, and such a one as had seldom, I take it, been witnessed." Continuing, the general said that "over and over again I have spent an hour or more in the quiet of the evening on a large, prominent rock that jutted out from the face of the ridge, at one of its highest points (the place is as familiar to me now as though it were but yesterday) admiring this grand illumination, thinking of home, family and friends, or speculating as to the future."[2]

Manigault was not alone in his contemplations. All around on the uplands, whether strung out along Missionary Ridge, positioned across the way on Lookout Mountain, or patrolling Raccoon Mountain, many Confederates were speculating about the future. Some, in fact, were deeply disillusioned and disheartened. After the elation of the Chickamauga victory came days of drudgery, interspersed with scenes of horror. Dr. W.J. Worsham of the Nineteenth Tennessee Infantry wrote, "our men were busy burying the dead, caring for the wounded that remained on the field and gathering up the guns, blankets, swords, broken caissons and broken ambulances." Mortally wounded men were sometimes in a crazed condition. Worsham told of a dying soldier, "so badly wounded that the surgeons had passed him by," who, completely irrational, cried out to every one around him with questions such as "Are you a Christian? Do you love Jesus?" as he exhorted them to be converted to Christ.[3]

Worse was yet to come—day after day without sufficient food, punctuated by much cold, rainy weather. Many of the Rebels seemed to suffer from lack of provisions as the Yankees did. If one had been judging from appearances, sometimes the besiegers could hardly have been told apart from the besieged. Numerous Confederate letters and diaries attest to the shortages. A member of the Seventh Florida Infantry who was keeping a diary, Robert Watson, again and again commented on the lack of food and the awful cold: "Some of the boys that were lucky enough to steal some ears of corn from the horses last night are busy grating it and making mush out of it for we are almost starved to death. We draw enough in two days to make one good meal." A few days later, Watson recorded that "it was so cold I had to sit by the fire half the night." Again, he wrote: "Nothing to eat but we are well supplied with lice. Many of the regiment are sick from drinking bad water and poorly cooked food. I think we will all be sick soon if they don't give us more food." Some two weeks later conditions apparently had not improved for Watson, who, noting that the weather was "very cold with a heavy frost," continued to deplore the lack of food. He had "nothing to eat for the roads are so bad that the wagons can't get over them," and he added that he was so hungry that he could not sleep.[4]

Watson's comments are echoed in a letter by G.E. Goudelock, a Rebel in the Second Arkansas Regiment of Patrick R. Cleburne's division, who wrote to his wife about the short rations and the cold, rainy weather and attested that he had been "barefooted about two months." A Confederate in the Second Tennessee Infantry, W.E. Yeatman, referred to "the miserable time at Missionary Ridge," recalling "the diet of cush," which he described as "moulded cornbread too hard to bite cold, softened by boiling in tin cans." R.A. Jarman, a Mississippian stationed on Lookout Mountain during November, wrote that "rations became very scarce" and that "one day our issue of rations consisted of three crackers and about two tablespoons of sugar," while a Tennessean later claimed that "in all the history of the war, I cannot remember more privations and hardships than we went through at Missionary Ridge." According to this account by Sam R. Watkins, "when the army was most dissatisfied and unhappy, we were ordered into line of battle to be reviewed by Honorable Jefferson Davis. When he passed by us, with his great retinue of staff officers. . . , cheers greeted them, with the words, 'Send us something to eat, Massa Jeff. Give us something to eat, Massa Jeff. I'm hungry! I'm hungry!' "[5]

And still another Confederate, suffering from the cold, learned that a female relation had somehow, "very carelessly," lost a pair of boots, filled with gloves, which was intended for him. J.W. Harris was so enraged that he wrote his mother concerning the offending person: "I don't care whether I ever see her again or not. I have never had anything to annoy me as that did. . . . I will soon need the boots and gloves badly, and there are none to be had out here. I have been in a bad humor ever since I heard of it. . . ." From deploring his lack of sufficient clothing, Harris next dwelt on the scarcity of food, indicating that he feared he would soon be reduced to only one meal per day. James L. Cooper, Twentieth Tennessee Infantry, stated that he almost starved during the month of October, saying that once, for three days, he had only a spoonful of sugar daily. And J. Stoddard Johnson, Chief of Orders Department, Army of Tennessee, one day in November wrote in his journal, "Rations are scarce and complaints great. The troops have been several days without meat." On another day he wrote: "There is a great scarcity of corn and provisions. Much complaint." Just as with the Yankees, Rebel accounts abound with stories of hardship and suffering during the siege of Chattanooga.[6]

Some of the Confederates looked to a higher power for deliverance; others deserted the cause and went home, with desertions picking up noticeably in the fall of 1863. Most, however, stayed on, suffered, and endured; and many vented their wrath upon General Bragg. Sensing that the general had frittered away a great opportunity to crush the Yankees following the bloody triumph at Chickamauga, the miserable soldiers, like many of their generals, focused their recriminations upon the most visible (and vulnerable) object of authority. "Everyone here curses Bragg," wrote John W. Harris, and if he is removed "it will put our troops in much better spirits," because it was only "through Bragg's imbecility" that the Rebels failed "to ruin the whole Federal army; there was never such a chance."[7]

Robert J. Boyd Thigpen of the Forty-second Alabama would have agreed with Harris. Writing to a friend on November 15, he said that the soldiers had "always cursed Mississippi and wished they were in Tennessee with Bragg. We are all here now and I . . . think that forty nine of every fifty would like to be back in Mississippi." In a letter dated October 16, W.R. Montgomery, Third Georgia Battery, spoke hopefully of a rumor that his unit might be transferred to Mobile, because he would like to get away "from under General Bragg for I . . . do not like him." Montgomery continued to say that he did not believe Bragg was "competent to fill the place he holds." A soldier in the Second Arkansas was appalled that, "in spite of the lack of confidence in Bragg, Davis left him in command of the Army of Tennessee." And another Confederate recorded in his diary that "the general sentiment is undoubtedly that Bragg should resign his command, none of his subordinates having any confidence in him."[8]

Unquestionably, many Confederates at Chattanooga would have heartily approved the sentiments expressed in an Atlanta newspaper. "Bragg remains as the incompetent head of the greatest army of the Confederacy, placed at the post of vital danger," the editorial stated, lashing out at Jefferson Davis for not removing the general from command. The president was described as having "toyed with the danger that hangs over us . . . , that today threatens the center and heart of the Southern Confederacy." Having made a few minor changes "which mean nothing and effect nothing," the president of the Confederacy departed, "serene upon the frigid heights of an imperturbable egotism, . . . deaf to the universal call of the country." Returning to Bragg, the paper noted that Napoleon said the art of war consisted in knowing how to separate to subsist, and how to unite to fight, but "the art of Bragg has been to unite to starve, and to separate to be whipped."[9]

Some soldiers, as might be expected, were having their troubles with officers other than the commanding general. One Rebel was highly perturbed by his company captain ("he has become quite a tyrant lately and we all dislike him," reads a diary entry). Another entry, October 29, 1863, speaks for itself: "Several of us were drilled today for swearing. I was one of the number. Our captain has got very pious and particular lately. I told him that when I joined the Confederate Army that I did not intend to become a Methodist preacher and if he thought that he could make a preacher or hypocrite of me by punishment that he was mistaken, for the more he punished the worse I would be for I was neither a slave nor a school boy. He thought it strange that nobody else said anything about it but me. I told him that I was talking for my rights." Again, on November 8, an entry reads: "Captain Smith offered us some brandy but we declined drinking any. He seemed very anxious to get into our good graces but he can't until he does better."[10]

Despite the supply shortages, often miserable weather conditions, and widespread discontent with General Bragg—or some lower-ranking officer—many of the men found time for various activities besides "soldiering." Every type of man seemed to be represented among the Confederates occupying the heights around Chattanooga. Like all armies, the Rebels had their card players and gamblers. Carrol H. Clark, a member of the Sixteenth Tennessee, thought some of the soldiers had no respect for anything. Parson Dewitt a Presbyterian regimental chaplain whose favorite song, noted Clark, was "Jesus, Lover of my Soul," preached every Sunday. Clark believed Dewitt's efforts were an exercise in futility. "You might as well preach to a drove of wild hogs as a lot of soldiers" Clark wrote, stating, "I have seen boys with blankets spread on the grounds, playing cards within a few steps of the Preacher while preaching."[11]

Not even war could discourage the soldiers' interest in members of the opposite sex. In fact, a good case could probably be made for the monotony and boredom of army life contributing to a soldier's libido. Writing to his niece, a Confederate named Joab Goodson in the Forty-fourth Alabama, a unit that had come from Virginia with Hood's division, reported an interesting occurrence during the train ride south: "Some of the boys amused themselves by writing billet deaux [love letters] and throwing them to some young ladies as they passed. Ruff, who you know is a great ladies man, wrote one, and threw it to a young lady at Covington, Georgia, and behold, a few days ago he received a rather lengthy reply." Goodson continued his story, writing that the woman "says she is a refugee from Charleston, and anticipates a great deal of pleasure from the expected correspondence." Goodson believed that "Ruff" had already replied, "for I saw him earnestly engaged writing yesterday; so you may look out for a bit of romance."[12]

Of course, there were those who patronized the "women of pleasure," one well-known "house of ill repute" being located near the base of Missionary Ridge.[13] Also, many Confederates, especially those on picket duty, sought divergence through trading tobacco to the Yankees for coffee, or exchanging newspapers. While on Lookout

Mountain, reported a Mississippian, "we did picket duty at the foot of the mountain, on. . .Lookout Creek, and near the railroad. While here the two picket lines at many places were not more than forty yards apart. We could see and hear them relieving their pickets and they could see us." The Confederate soldier attested that "each party kept fire at the vidette post day and night. We even met half way in the creek, where it was shallow and shoally, to swap newspapers, canteens, and tobacco for coffee. And I have seen some swap hats and shoes, and talk for half an hour at a time, but this was only when no officer was present on either side."[14] There does seem to have been at least one remarkable exception to this last statement about officers. General Grant, out one day to inspect the Federal lines, reached a spring that soldiers of both armies sometimes used. On a log by the spring was a soldier dressed in blue, his musket resting at his side. Grant asked him what corps he belonged to, and the man, rising and saluting respectfully, replied that he was one of Longstreet's soldiers. Neither man seemed alarmed. They simply paused and talked for a while before the Union commander and the Confederate private went their separate ways.[15]

From the perspective of one Federal soldier, the exchanges between the pickets seemed strange when one considered the entire situation. While the two armies faced each other "not two miles apart," he said, "their pickets, within a quarter of a mile of each other, meet daily and exchange papers, have friendly chats, no firing" being allowed. At the same time, "the main armies are both preparing for a deadly conflict, one getting heavy guns in position . . . to shell . . . , and the other fortifying to resist the attack. . . ."[16]

While the two armies waited, prepared, and suffered, the countryside foraged by both sides was being punished for miles in every direction. "The army is consuming everything in the shape of substanance [sic] in lower East Tennessee," said Confederate William Clift, who estimated that scarcely an acre of corn remained between Chattanooga and Rhea County. When Lieutenant Wilson S. Miller later led a Federal foraging party through this area, he was amazed at the wretched condition of the people in the countryside. "I never before saw women dressed entirely in rags," he wrote, adding that homes looked no better than "Northern pig pens." In Bradley County, Minerva McKamy later recalled that Federal soldiers came to the home of her sister-in-law's family, with whom she then lived, and shot the only milchcow for meat. "It was useless to plead with the

Yankees for mercy," she said, "as they had no conscience and seemed to enjoy making us suffer."[17]

Either army was a menace to the civilian population. In October 1863, devoted Southerner Myra Inman complained that Confederate troops were "acting very badly," taking corn, tearing down fences, and stealing livestock. Robert Rutledge, a soldier in Longstreet's command, reported that starvation faced many "poor defenseless Southern women and many, many poor helpless children" because of the army's activities. "Our army is getting to be as much dreaded as the low down thieving Yankees," he stated.[18]

Foraging parties often seized the opportunity to exceed their orders and secure food for themselves, by theft or otherwise. One Federal leader of such a party, realizing that many residents of the area were Unionist in sympathy, deplored these excesses: "The thieves who accompany our forage and supply trains are . . . no respectors of persons. When they discover a hen roost, sheep, or hogs, they do not stop to inquire the sentiments of the owners; neither does it concern them if they are about to take the last sheep or hog belonging to the family. . . . On the road up the Tennessee Valley over Walden's Ridge, and near the foot of the mountain on the other side," he continued, "almost every garden is found stripped and one will hardly discover a chicken or hog."[19]

Bushwhackers also plagued both sides, stripping large areas of foodstuffs and valuables, with no regard, of course, for either pro-Union or pro-Confederate sympathies. General Joseph Wheeler indirectly boosted the numbers of the bushwhackers when he released about 1,500 prisoners, after they swore not to take up arms against the Confederacy until legally exchanged. Many of these men soon formed themselves into bands and set upon a campaign of terror—burning, pillaging, and robbing as they roamed indiscriminately over the Sequatchie Valley.[20]

And, too, it was Wheeler's famous cavalry raid that brought to the Sequatchie Valley and Walden's Ridge the most violent action that that general area saw during the Civil War. A few days after the battle of Chickamauga, General Bragg gave Wheeler command of all the Confederate cavalry forces in the region, with the mission of disrupting Rosecrans's extended communications.[21] Leading his two divisions some thirty miles up the Tennessee River from Chattanooga, where they forded to the west bank, "Fightin' Joe" joined up with the men previously commanded by Forrest, on the afternoon of September 30, giving him a strength of about three divisions.

The twenty-seven-year-old, diminutive (five feet, five inches, 127 pounds) major general, who was idolized by many a common foot soldier in the western Confederacy, hoped to equal, if not improve upon, his swashbuckling ride completely around General Rosecrans's army shortly before the battle of Stones River. That reckless jaunt, covering a sixty-mile circuit, had resulted in the capture of about a thousand Federals, the burning of part or all of four wagon trains, and the acquisition of enough weapons to arm a brigade and to provide remounts for his men who needed fresh horses—not to mention the adverse psychological effect upon the Union army.[22]

Now Wheeler was to embark upon an even greater raid—the foray is still a legend in those lower East Tennessee regions—but his newly united command was far from ideal for the task. General Forrest had protested to Wheeler that his men and horses were in no condition for such a ride. Frank Armstrong, Forrest's senior brigadier, also protested, stating that his brigade was "totally unfit to start on any expedition"; and the troops themselves expressed considerable dissatisfaction, both about the expedition and about being commanded by Wheeler. Wheeler himself reported that "the three brigades from General Forrest were mere skeletons, scarcely averaging 500 effective men each. These were badly armed, had but a small supply of ammunition, and their horses were in horrible condition, having been marched continuously for three days and nights without removing saddles. The men were worn out and without rations. . . ." Nevertheless, the early part of the mission went well. Working his way over Walden's Ridge, Wheeler, on the night of October 2, decided to divide his forces, sending a detachment to McMinnville, where large Federal stores were reported to be, while he himself led some fifteen hundred men in a raid on the Sequatchie Valley, hoping to strike a large Union wagon train.[23]

At three o'clock on the morning of October 3, "Fightin' Joe" roused his men and set them in motion southward down the valley. A short distance south of Dunlap, they overtook a Federal supply train, apparently from the base at McMinnville, consisting of thirty-two wagons, each wagon drawn by six mules. Wheeler's troopers easily surrounded and captured this small train. About an hour later, at the foot of Anderson's Gap, they found what they were really looking for, an enormous Federal wagon train. General Wheeler stated that "the number of wagons was variously estimated at from 800 to 1,500." General Rosecrans would later place his loss at five hundred wagons. The head of the train was near the top of Walden's Ridge, and the tail was five miles or more down the valley toward Jasper. Colonel John T. Morgan at once directed an attack upon the Federal escort troops, but the Confederates, perhaps too eagerly anticipating their opportunity to plunder, were repulsed. Then, led by Colonel A.A. Russell's Fourth Alabama Cavalry, the Rebels broke through, and complete confusion resulted all along the Yankee train. "Such a scene of panic and confusion I had never witnessed," wrote a Confederate participant.[24]

It was the first chance in several days that the Confederates had had to fill their haversacks, and they went for the wagons loaded with cheese and other food. Wheeler and his staff rode up and down the line, literally pulling some of the men away from the Federal wagons by their heels. Riding with the troopers was a man named E.S. Bruford who admiringly referred to Wheeler as "The War Child," and called the raid "one of the most brilliant campaigns of the war." Soon after the event Bruford wrote to a friend describing the capture and plunder of the wagons: "If you could have seen the boys as they waded up to their necks in fine $50 hats, $100 boots, rivers of Champagne and liquors of all kinds, pyramids of cigars, fruits, jellies and every sort of luxury, you would have been tempted to abandon the tripod for the cavalry." Bruford thought that "any epicure in the land would have smacked his lips with a huge joy at the sight of all the good things."[25]

Eventually order was restored among the Confederate troops, but not among the Federal mules. Many of these were tangled in their harnesses, and all were in confusion. "After selecting such mules and wagons as we needed," reported Wheeler, "we then destroyed the train by burning the wagons and sabering or shooting the mules." Soon the explosions from the ammunition in the burning wagons were of such magnitude and tone that they seemed almost like artillery in action. For eight hours the destruction went on until, by midafternoon, a continuous line of burning wagons stretched up Anderson's Gap to the top of Walden's Ridge. "The destruction of the ordnance trains," wrote one of the participants, "presented a fearful spectacle. The noise of bursting shells and boxes of ammunition so resembled the sound of battle as to astonish and alarm the enemy in Chattanooga, who were in doubt as to the cause until the ascending clouds of smoke told them the food and ammunition upon which almost the vitality of their army depended were actually destroyed."[26]

While Wheeler burned the wagon train, his other column had secured the surrender of the Federal garrison at McMinnville. Following the surrender, according to Union commander Major Michael

L. Patterson, there occurred "the most brutal outrages on the part of the rebels ever known to any civilized war in America or elsewhere." The major was shocked as the cavalrymen proceeded to outfit themselves in new clothes from head to foot, taking "boots, watch, pocket-book, money, and even finger-rings, or, in fact, anything that happened to please their fancy." Patterson, observing that General Wheeler had arrived on the scene, appealed to him for aid to stop the pillaging. Wheeler only replied that he could not control his men; that they would do as they pleased. Considering the dire condition of Forrest's men, whom most of these were, and their known reluctance to obey Wheeler's orders, the general probably stated the simple truth.[27]

Wheeler had his command once more united as he rode toward Murfreesboro, now closely pursued by Federal cavalry. He then fought a running, day-by-day battle with various groups of enemy cavalry closing from different directions. Making a demonstration upon Murfreesboro, he destroyed a stockade and burned the bridge over Stones River. Destroying railroad bridges and trestles between Murfreesboro and Wartrace, he finally swept down through middle Tennessee toward Pulaski.

After his initial success, Wheeler sustained a series of sharp defeats and was fortunate to get back across the Tennessee River with a portion of his command, after he lost some 800 mules he had captured earlier. One of the Federals pursuing Wheeler, named Henry Campbell, kept a diary in which he recorded that "every few miles their column would seem to get panic stricken, for the road would be filled with guns, knapsacks, bundles, etc., thrown away in their hurry. . . ."[28]

On October 7, the raid became a near disaster at Farmington, Tennessee. Unable to coordinate a retreating defensive effort, the Rebels were driven by the Yankees, who, flushed with victory, often sabered Confederate riders in the saddle. A Confederate colonel, riding to reinforce a retreating brigade, discovered that the retreat had become a rout, reporting that he found the unit in a wild retreat, "and bearing down upon me at racing speed. It was too late to clear the way; they rode over my command like madmen, some of them stopping only, as I was informed, when they reached the Tennessee. . . . For five hours and a half, over seven miles of country, the unequal contest continued," the colonel stated. "My gallant brigade was cut to pieces and slaughtered."[29]

Although the admiring Bruford wrote of Wheeler that "amid the shower of iron and lead everywhere the War Child upon his black charger cheered on our brave boys," General Wheeler's own report clearly reveals that he was in a very tight situation. "I was obliged when near Farmington to make a fight," which the general described as "most severe, the lines being engaged at a distance of about 30 yards. We charged and repulsed them at first, but finally I found they were preparing an overwhelming force to attack. . . . Most of the troops fought most nobly, others acted shamefully."[30]

In truth, Wheeler had all but wrecked his command. For a candid summary, J. Stoddard Johnson's journal entry at Bragg's headquarters on October 29 would be difficult to improve upon: "The facts in regard to Wheeler's circuit of the enemy's rear, are becoming developed," he wrote, saying that Wheeler "inflicted a large loss on the enemy, severe and damaging. But it was a disgraceful raid. Plunder and demoralization were manifested. As soon as a train was captured, the men went to plundering. . . . Captured horses and mules were ladened with plunder and when the enemy appeared, the race was on to keep the plunder out of his reach."[31] General Manigault's account reinforces Johnson's. Noting that Wheeler's men were "never remarkable for discipline," he related that some became "almost entirely unmanageable" due primarily to "a great amount of drunkenness." Wheeler was "overtaken or headed off, had to fight his way through, and finally recrossed the river many miles below Chattanooga, where he was safe from pursuit." Several hundred of his men were killed or wounded, a good many captured, and a much larger number, alleged Manigault, "straggled or were cut off from their commands, and returned to their homes without leave, to return at their convenience, a not unusual thing with our cavalry. I am inclined to think that this raid, like a great many others, did us more harm than the enemy."[32]

By this spectacular raid—perhaps the one for which he is most often remembered—Wheeler had unquestionably done serious damage to the enemy, but by the time he got to Decatur his own force was so disorganized, exhausted, and depleted by its hard riding and fighting that it was a long time before he could get it back into fighting trim. As Wheeler's biographer suggested, the expedition had been "almost successful, almost disastrous."[33]

At Chattanooga, in the Union camp, the news of Wheeler's destruction of so many supplies evoked consternation. When the discouraging reports came in, it seemed that a bad situation had been made worse. The wagon train of the major part of a whole corps was lost. This destruction, followed by a season of heavy rains that made it even harder to move in more wagons, was little short of a disaster to the Union army occupying the small city.

Perhaps when the Federal soldiers in Chattanooga gazed upward at the Confederates on the heights all around them, some may have reflected upon the unlikelihood—to all appearances—of so many struggling for so little. Chattanooga was not venerable for its age. Far from being an old Southern community, like Charleston, Nashville, or New Orleans, the city had technically come into the possession of the United States less than a quarter of a century before the Civil War began, only after the Cherokee Indians were ejected in the late 1830s.

The name of the city was of Indian origin, of course. Actually, *Chattanooga* was the aboriginal name for Lookout Mountain, and the word is said to be one of the Cherokee's half-anglicized terms, derived from *Chatta* (crow) and *nooga* (nest), but often given a more impressive meaning of "eagles' nest" or "hawks' nest." The name *Chattanooga* has also been explained as a phonetic rendering of "Chadona-ugsa," a Creek phrase that means "rock that comes to a point."[34] In the days before the American Revolutionary War, Spanish Catholic priests from St. Augustine, Florida, established a mission and school for Indians on the ridge to the east of Lookout Mountain. The religious outpost caused the height to be called Mission Ridge (and many Civil War soldiers so designated it), later corrupted into Missionary Ridge. Another explanation for the name is that the Indians established the ridge as the point beyond which Christian missionaries would not be permitted to cross.

Chattanooga had attained some importance as a trading post by the 1830s, although it was then known as Ross' Landing, after John Ross, a one-sixteenth Indian who was chief of the Cherokees. Then came the discovery of gold in north Georgia, and soon a U.S. army detachment had arrived at Missionary Ridge, under General Winfield Scott, charged with the task of moving the Cherokees west of the Mississippi. One of Scott's subordinates was a young lieutenant fresh from the West Point class of 1837, Braxton Bragg.

By Civil War days Chattanooga had grown to be a town of about 5,000 citizens, still very small by any standard, especially compared to Nashville's 20,000 or Richmond's 40,000. Certainly, Chattanooga was not significant for its size.

The most important structure in the city was the Crutchfield

House, described by historian Glenn Tucker as "a rambling hostelry of three stories at Ninth and Broad Streets." The hostelry was conducted by Tom and William Crutchfield, both of whom were Union men. When war came, the Stars and Bars soon flew from atop the Crutchfield House, despite the sentiments of the owners. The town became a Confederate military depot, and the *Chattanooga Daily Rebel* reported news of the war. All this had changed by the fall of 1863; the Stars and Stripes floated above the Crutchfield House—even though the Federal army found itself under siege.[35]

If the soldiers thought about the role of the city, they probably soon realized that Chattanooga was important not for the town itself but because it is a natural passageway between North and South. This is true because of the Tennessee River. Even more significant, however, were the railroads. To the northeast lay the East Tennessee Railroad to Knoxville, Bristol, and Lynchburg. From the west came the Memphis and Charleston from North Alabama, and the Nashville and Chattanooga from Middle Tennessee, with connection to Louisville and the Ohio River. To the southeast ran the Western and Atlantic to Atlanta. From Atlanta were rail connections with Virginia through the Carolinas, as well as with the munitions and iron centers of central Georgia and Alabama.

Thus, with the Union in possession of Chattanooga, the Confederacy's rail communications were sorely damaged. Moreover, the Union potential for making war on the Deep South from such a staging base as Chattanooga was almost unlimited. The North, fully geared to mass production of war materials, could outstrip the South on a gigantic scale, and the rail lines into Chattanooga made it the natural jump-off point for waging total war against the southeastern Confederacy. Chattanooga, if the Federals could hold it, was the key to splitting the South along a second corridor, Nashville-Chattanooga-Atlanta, just as Fort Donelson, Shiloh, New Orleans, and Vicksburg had earlier split the Confederacy along the general line of the Mississippi. And now U.S. Grant, with "Baldy" Smith's plan, was moving to open "the cracker line" at Brown's Ferry, which promised to insure the Federal grip on the strategic city.

10. Lookout Mountain viewed from the Union works. *Harper's Weekly Magazine.*

5

Brown's Ferry and Wauhatchie

Generally a great battle is conceived as a struggle of many thousands who fight and suffer and die; like the bloody engagement at Eylau in Napoleonic times, where the Russians and the French battled to a tactical draw; or like the World War I British attack on the Germans at the Somme, where 60,000 casualties were taken by the British in a single day; or the largest armored battle of World War II when the Russians and Germans fought at Kursk. But once in a great while, and perhaps when least expected, the awful drama of war narrows to a very small focus, to a relative handful of men, and the story of a great struggle takes a decisive turn through the successful execution of a simple, daring plan—and the fearful momentum of war begins to swing from one army to the other. So it was at Brown's Ferry.

The assault at Brown's Ferry came early on the morning of October 27, under the direction of Grant's chief engineer officer, "Baldy" Smith. Preparations had begun two days earlier when the brigades of Brigadier Generals William B. Hazen and John B. Turchin were detailed for the mission, with three batteries under Major John Mendenhall assigned to support the infantry. The key to the success or failure of the expedition would be the performance of Hazen's brigade, or rather a portion of it, which had been assigned the most hazardous task. Hazen's After Action Report succinctly stated the goal and the method of achieving it, as explained to him by General Smith, "which was to organize fifty squads of one officer and twenty-four men each, to embark in [pontoon] boats at Chattanooga and float down the river . . . a distance, by the bends of the river, of nine miles, and land upon its left bank, then occupied by the enemy, making thereafter, immediate dispositions for holding it, while the remaining portions of my brigade, and another one, should be speedily sent over the river in the same boats to re-enforce me; the movement was to be made just before daylight. . . ."[1]

The other brigade to which Hazen referred was Turchin's command, of course. Along with several hundred of Hazen's men and Mendenhall's batteries, Turchin would move on a hidden road across the neck of Moccasin Point, arriving near Brown's Ferry ahead of Hazen's flotilla. Encamped in the woods out of sight, these men would be ready to cross to the left bank of the Tennessee as soon as the boats had landed their original occupants. General Hooker would be leading a third and still larger contingent, approaching Brown's Ferry from Bridgeport. Leaving one division at Bridgeport, Hooker would march with three divisions to the relief, if necessary, of Hazen and Turchin.

A swift, surprise assault was called for. Although Hazen's boats would be within range of Confederate pickets along the bank of the river for about seven miles of the nine-mile journey, this was considered an acceptable risk. Even if they were spotted by the enemy, the chances of succeeding with the daring attack still appeared good. As General Smith himself explained: "It was deemed better to take this risk than to attempt to launch the boats near the ferry, because they would move more rapidly than intelligence could be taken by infantry pickets, and, in addition, though the enemy might be alarmed, he would not know where the landing was to be attempted, and therefore could not concentrate with certainty against us." Smith believed in his plan, but, at the same time, perhaps no one knew better than he that it might fail. His After Action Report does sound one ominous note: "The artillery was . . . to move down and go into position as soon as the boats had begun to land, to cover the retirement of our troops in case of disaster."[2]

Since the success of the mission largely depended upon surprise, the maintenance of secrecy was imperative. Only a handful of officers besides Grant, Thomas, Smith, and the brigade commanders actually knew the plan. These few were men such as Colonel Timothy R.

Stanley of the Eighteenth Ohio, under whose charge the pontoon boats were placed, and Captain P.V. Fox, First Michigan Engineers, who would direct the positioning of the bridge across the Tennessee. Most of the soldiers chosen to participate in the assault had no idea what their objective might be, only that the undertaking would be important and dangerous.

One of the attacking regiments would be the Sixth Ohio Infantry, whose regimental historian later provided a record of the order that came down from brigade headquarters two days before the mission. It stated: "Regimental commanders will at once organize parties of picked men as specified below, each squad to be in charge of an officer selected especially for efficiency and courage." As soon as organized, each regimental colonel was to "furnish these headquarters with complete roles of squads, which may include the names of men on picket, if they are known to be effective. Commanders of parties will at once muster and drill their squads." The Sixth Ohio was instructed to "furnish seven squads of twenty-five men each, including officers and non-commissioned officers. . . . Regimental commanders will at once take command of these squads, leaving the officer next in rank to command the remainder of the regiment." Lieutenant Colonel E. Bassett Langdon, First Ohio, was detailed to command the remainder of the brigade and to report at brigade headquarters.[3]

Except for rumors, always plentiful in an army, no one heard more of the secret expedition until midnight of October 26, when the men selected were ordered to prepare, in the words of the Sixth Ohio's E. Hannaford, "to move at once, without blankets, but with a full supply of cartridges." The soldiers fell in quickly and, according to Hannaford's account, "marched to the brigade rendezvous, and thence through the town to the river, where a flotilla of clumsy flatboats and barges were waiting, manned by oarsmen from Colonel Stanley's Eighteenth Ohio."[4] Most of the troops embarked promptly, although Lieutenant Colonel James C. Foy, Twenty-third Kentucky, reported that his large party of seventy-five men, which Hazen had assigned to spearhead the landing, found their over-size boat "with considerable water and some dozen or more pieces of heavy iron in it, that had to be unloaded before we could start." The boat also had to be pulled up the river some three hundred yards in order to get in proper position for casting off; further delaying Foy's departure was the discovery that only fifty men could fit in the crude craft, even if it was considerably larger than the other boats. The remainder were sent to General

Hazen, to be either transported in his boat or dispersed among the others.[5]

At 3 A.M., October 27, the improvised flotilla of more than fifty pontoon-transports cast off and started silently drifting downstream from the Chattanooga wharves. Screened from the light of the moon by a fortunate mist, they depended upon the strong current for power; there was no need for oars, except for steering. C.C. Briant of the Sixth Indiana left a description of the movement. "The men were to lie down in the boats, and not a word to be spoken above a whisper," he wrote. The boats were "allowed to float perfectly quiet and without noise, and not a man moved, except the fellow who did the guiding of the boat and he lay flat down and used only a small paddle." If it sounded simple, James Foy again found that he had a problem, for "the men who were left to work the boat knew nothing about it, and Captain T.J. Williams had to take the steering oar and pilot us down."[6]

Hugging the tree-fringed right bank opposite the enemy, the boats moved swiftly. Rebel pickets could be spotted "taking their ease before blazing fires," according to a Federal's account of the river journey. If any Confederate lookouts saw the boats—and the Sixth Indiana's C.C. Briant claimed they did, "but seeing no men about them supposed them empty boats, drifting with the current, and gave the matter no further attention"—they did not raise an alarm. The river passage was marred only by two incidents, one man being knocked into the river by a tree branch, and another somehow falling overboard. The first was rescued by another boat, but the latter was reported drowned.[7]

Just before daylight, as reveille began to sound in some Confederate camps, the first assault boats neared Brown's Ferry. The left bank of the Tennessee, here a steep ridge, rose perhaps one hundred and fifty feet from the river's edge. The ridge was broken at Brown's Ferry by a narrow gorge, through which ran the road from the ferry west to Raccoon Mountain. The landing was to be made at two points, one the gorge at the ferry and the other another gorge approximately a third of a mile downstream. About 4:30 in the morning, the Federals had kindled signal fires that now burned brightly on the right bank of the river to help guide the boats in identifying the proper landing sites as they swept across the river for the assault.

The boats had been divided into two groups: one, under the direction of Lieutenant Walter B. McNeal, headed for the landing at

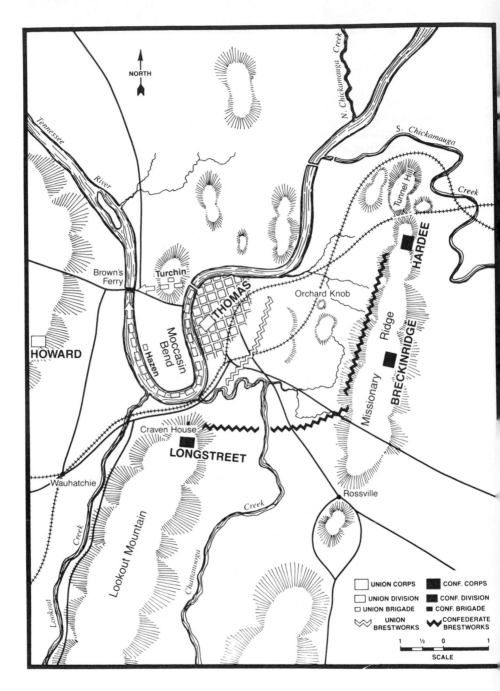

NORTH

N. Chickamauga Creek

S. Chickamauga

Creek

Tennessee

River

Tunnel Hill

HARDEE

Brown's
Ferry

Turchin

THOMAS

Orchard Knob

BRECKINRIDGE

HOWARD

Moccasin
Bend

Hazen

Missionary

Ridge

Craven House

LONGSTREET

Wauhatchie

Rossville

Creek

Lookout Mountain

Creek

Chattanooga

Lookout

	UNION CORPS		CONF. CORPS
	UNION DIVISION		CONF. DIVISION
	UNION BRIGADE		CONF. BRIGADE
	UNION BRESTWORKS		CONFEDERATE BRESTWORKS

1   ½   0   1

SCALE

Map 3. Assault on Brown's Ferry. *Map by J.L. Moon, Jr.*

Brown's Ferry, while the second wave, under Captain Ebenezer Grosvenor, made for the gap below the ferry. There were some anxious moments near the ferry when events did not develop quite according to plan, some of the boats landing a little below the point where the ferry road strikes the river and attracting Rebel picket fire before reaching the shore. Lieutenant Colonel Foy's After Action Report stated: "I am sorry to say that some of our men returned the fire. I had them to cease immediately. I had given orders before starting that this would be only a small party, and we were to receive their fire and march on and take possession. . . ." Enemy picket fire proved little more than a minor nuisance as the troops swarmed ashore, scrambled up the steep bank, and realized that the Confederate pickets had fled after firing only a few shots; some of the drowsy ones had, in fact, been captured.[8]

The Confederates should have been prepared to give the Federals a very tough battle for this strategic ground. Being taken by surprise, although deplorable, was more understandable (and forgivable) than not having enough troops at hand to make a real fight for the bridgehead. If the Union assault force had struck two days earlier, they likely would have been confronted by all five regiments of E. McIver Law's brigade. This brigade had been effectively blockading Haley's Trace, the road from Chattanooga to Bridgeport, which passed near the point of Raccoon Mountain on the opposite, or right, bank of the Tennessee River, by firing across the water upon the Federal wagon trains as they passed. Two of Law's regiments had been employed both as sharpshooters against the Yankee communications and in picketing the left bank of the river back to the bend near the foot of Lookout Mountain. The pickets were intended to prevent an enemy force from cutting off the sharpshooters. Law held his other three regiments in reserve at a point convenient for reinforcing any part of the line. "As the line was long and necessarily weak," Law explained, "my principal security for holding it was in having a sufficient reserve to foil the enemy, if he should attempt a crossing, by throwing it upon him before he could strengthen himself on this side."[9]

There was nothing wrong with Law's thinking. Such a deployment of his brigade seemed to be the most reasonable move for the general to make. The Confederates should have assigned more than a brigade, however, to guarantee their grip on such important terrain. If they were going to continue depriving the Union forces in Chattanooga of all but a bare minimum of supplies, the Rebels had to hold

Lookout Valley. Yet, when the Yankees swarmed ashore at Brown's Ferry about five o'clock in the morning of October 27, the Confederates no longer had even brigade strength with which to meet the assault!

Three of Law's regiments, by orders from division headquarters, had been withdrawn to the side of Lookout Mountain on October 25. Little wonder that the Rebel effort to throw back the Yankees, though gallantly launched, quickly turned into a defeat. Attempting to counter-attack the Federal beachhead in the gray dawn were the Fifteenth Alabama and the Fourth Alabama, the former led by Colonel William C. Oates, one of several young officers in Longstreet's corps who showed an aptitude for command. Fearful that he would be attacked, Oates had requested earlier that General Longstreet send him at least one more regiment that night. Also, he sent the same request to Micah Jenkins, acting division commander. Then the colonel was suddenly aroused by a private, dispatched from the captain of the pickets at Brown's Ferry, reporting the enemy had landed, driven off the pickets, and was busily strengthening his position. At once Oates had the long roll beaten to awaken the troops at hand (five companies were strung out along the river as pickets) and soon moved as rapidly as possible toward the Federal position. Approaching the river, the colonel could hear the invaders entrenching a defensive perimeter.

"I then detailed two companies," Oates remembered, "and ordered [the captains] to deploy their men at one pace apart and instruct them to walk right up to the foe, and for every man to place the muzzle of his rifle against the body of a Yankee when he fired. Away they went in the darkness." The tactic proved effective, as both companies succeeded in driving the Federals on their front out of the fledgling fortifications. But the Union line to the Confederate right quickly opened a heavy fire on the Rebel flank. Oates deployed another company on his right, only to find the Confederate position still outflanked. "I put in one company after another," he wrote, until all six were deployed, "and still I could not cover the enemy's front." Momentarily, the Fifteenth Alabama enjoyed success on the left side of the line, where three companies got inside the Yankee defenses and drove them toward the river, capturing the ridge north and west of the Brown's Ferry Road. The Rebels on the right, however, were quickly halted and raked by flanking fire. Worse, the Federals now got reinforcements from across the river.[10]

General Hazen described the action as seen from the Union side of the fight, acknowledging that the Confederates "came boldly up, along nearly our entire front, but particularly strong along the road, gaining the hill to the right [north] of it, and would have caused harm to the party on the road had not Colonel Langdon, First Ohio Volunteers, commanding the remaining portion of the brigade, arrived at this moment. . . ."[11] Outflanked and facing superior numbers, the Confederates were soon forced to give ground.

The Fifteenth Alabama's Colonel Oates, who had dispatched a courier down the river to bring his other companies as speedily as possible, saw the battle rapidly turning in favor of the Yankees. Trying to encourage his men, Oates was shot through the right hip and thigh. "It struck a blow as though a brick had been hurled against me," he recalled, "and hurt so badly that I started to curse as I fell, and said 'God d---,' when thinking that possibly I was killed, and that it would not seem well for a man to die with an oath in his mouth, I cut it off at that d--- and did not finish the sentence. All this flashed through my mind as I fell," avowed the colonel. With the help of two other soldiers, Oates managed to escape capture as the Confederates withdrew toward Lookout Mountain.[12]

Meanwhile, the Federals continued to pour across the river, General Turchin's brigade following Langdon's men over. "So soon as the skirmishers were thrown out from each command," reported "Baldy" Smith, "the axes were set at work felling an abatis, and in two hours the command was sufficiently protected to withstand any attack which was likely to be made. So soon as the last of the troops were across, a bridge was commenced and . . . completed at 4:30 P.M."[13] Surprise and superiority of numbers are very difficult to offset without some inherent advantage, such as a well-prepared defensive position, or vast firepower. The Confederates had only pluck.

Sometime later, as Colonel Oates lay on the floor of a house— despite the protests of the female owner, "Don't bring that nasty rebel into my house"—enjoying a drink of whiskey while a brigade surgeon bound up his wound, General Law arrived with the other three regiments of his brigade and the Texas brigade. "I told him that he was too late . . . to accomplish anything; that a heavy force had already crossed the river," wrote Oates. "I suggested that he ride up on an eminence nearby, from which he could overlook the . . . greater part of the valley. . . . He went up, but soon returned, and said I was quite right; that they had laid a pontoon bridge and had then at least a corps in the valley."[14] Moreover, although unknown to either Law or Oates, dis-

11. Landing for the Assault at Brown's Ferry. *Harper's Weekly Magazine.*

patches sent forward on the afternoon of October 27 by General Hooker announced that he was approaching Wauhatchie and would arrive in person the next day with his divisions.

The Union army's first significant move since coming under siege at Chattanooga was over. The fight had been no more than a sharp skirmish. It had lasted barely thirty minutes. But the capture of Brown's Ferry signaled the beginning of the end for the Confederates at Chattanooga. And, above all, the responsibility for the loss must rest upon Generals Bragg and Longstreet.

Longstreet did not even inform Bragg on the morning of October 27 that Brown's Ferry had fallen to the Federals. Rather, the information came from General St. John Liddell, sent by Bragg to the top of Lookout Point on reconnaissance after the sounds of firing were heard in the early morning. Liddell, when he looked down upon Yankees at the ferry and a pontoon bridge being built, said that he "could not understand the indifference on our part, at this unmistakeable lodgment of the enemy," and that General Bragg, when informed, "was very much incensed. . . ."[15]

Apparently, almost inexplicably, Longstreet either failed to understand the importance of controlling Lookout Valley or did not appreciate its vulnerability until too late. Bragg seems to have paid little atention to the area (probably depending far too much upon Longstreet) before the Union assault at Brown's Ferry, after which he was deeply disturbed—"the loss of our position on the left," he wrote Longstreet, "is almost vital; it involves the very existence of the enemy in Chattanooga." Bragg wanted to know what Longstreet intended to do about the loss.[16]

Longstreet, however, despite several warnings—particularly from E.M. Law and William C. Oates—that the Federals were moving from Bridgeport, curiously continued to look elsewhere than Brown's Ferry, convinced that the real enemy threat was in another sector, a move against his rear via occupying Lookout Mountain some twenty miles to the southwest. To army headquarters Longstreet wrote on October 27: "The enemy's design seems to be to occupy this bank of the river for the purpose of shortening his line of communication, and possibly for the purpose of creating a diversion near the point of Lookout Mountain whilst he moves a heavier force up to occupy the mountain via Johnson's Crook." Then followed a sentence showing how completely Longstreet had misinterpreted the Brown's Ferry attack. "The latter move and object," affirmed the general, "seems to

12. Bridging the Tennessee River. *Harper's Weekly Magazine.*

me to be more important; essential indeed—than any such partial move as his present one."[17]

While Longstreet worried about an enemy movement to the southwest and Bragg stewed, Hooker's infantry was marching from Bridgeport, watching the vast eminence of Lookout Mountain gradually loom larger and larger. Reaching Wauhatchie, a point on the railroad about a mile and a half from the northern tip of Lookout, Hooker decided to leave John W. Geary's division, 1,500 men, at that position to protect his rear. He then continued his march northward with Oliver O. Howard's two divisions, some 5,000 soldiers, under Adolf von Steinwehr and Carl Schurz, linking up with the Federal bridgehead at Brown's Ferry on October 28.

Hooker knew that Confederates atop the mountain had been watching his divisions tramp through Lookout Valley. Rebels by the score were plainly visible as the Yankees gazed upward. Hooker, who possessed the self-esteem of an actor, probably enjoyed the attention. Tall, well built, with a handsome, ruddy complexion that probably stemmed from too much hard liquor rather than from exercise, Hooker was a forty-nine-year-old general who knew that he made a good appearance. Perhaps even Hooker would have been a bit surprised, though, if he could have known that both Bragg and Longstreet were watching him.[18]

Actually, of course, the Confederate generals were watching more than Hooker: they were observing the northward advance of the blue infantry column. A messenger from the west side of Lookout had interrupted them in the midst of a stormy discussion to say that a large Union force was marching up the valley through Wauhatchie toward Brown's Ferry. Longstreet later wrote that Bragg was skeptical and began reproving the courier, who replied: "General, if you will ride to a point on the west side of the mountain, I will show them to you."[19] Bragg and Longstreet rode to a vantage point on the mountain from which they saw for themselves the ominous truth. Bragg, still outraged, as he had been since the previous morning, returned to his headquarters that evening with General Liddell, who wrote that Bragg "was very restless and complained with bitterness of Longstreet's inactivity and lack of ability; asserting him to be greatly overrated, etc."[20]

On this point, one is inclined to sympathize with Bragg. The Confederate commanding general, on October 27, had ordered Longstreet to dislodge the Federals from their bridgehead at Brown's Ferry.

Yet the general from Virginia remained inactive all that day and the next. At 6 P.M. on October 28, an exasperated Bragg told Longstreet: "Since 11 P.M. last night your whole corps was placed at your disposal for the movement indicated against the enemy. It is still at your disposal. . . . The movement should be prompt and decisive. Every hour," the message continued, gave "the enemy great advantage. . . ." At last Longstreet did something, although he apparently misunderstood what Bragg intended; he decided to attack the smaller Union force at Wauhatchie rather than the enemy at Brown's Ferry. Later, he tried to blame Bragg for the resulting fiasco, claiming that Bragg would not give him enough men to make the attack successfully. This was not true. Several times during the night of October 28 (as if once were not enough) Bragg sent word that all three of Longstreet's divisions could be used in his attack. In a 7:30 P.M. communiqué, Bragg even informed Longstreet that, while he thought three divisions sufficient, he had also instructed John Breckinridge to hold a division of his corps, which was closest to Longstreet, "in readiness to be subject to your orders."[21]

Longstreet, probably because of his disastrous bungling, never acknowledged the significance of the Union occupation of Brown's Ferry. Amazingly, in his official report, not penned until March 25, 1864, he alleged of Brown's Ferry: "That the point was not essential to the enemy at Chattanooga is established by the fact that he supplied his army at that place some six weeks without it."[22]

If Longstreet was embarrassed by the Federal operation at Brown's Ferry, his effort at Wauhatchie, late on the night of October 28, was a debacle. The plan called for Law's brigade, reinforced by Jerome Robertson's brigade, to occupy the valley road about midway between Brown's Ferry and the position of the Federal rear guard at Wauhatchie. These troops would prevent any of Hooker's main force from reinforcing Geary's division. While Law blocked the road, the Yankees at Wauhatchie would be attacked by Hood's old division, now led by Brigadier General Micah Jenkins.

There is much confusion associated with the early-morning engagement of October 29 at Wauhatchie. That Longstreet intended to make the attack with a single division (perhaps depending upon the surprise of a night assault) is indicated by a note the general sent to Bragg before nightfall of October 28. Certainly the note is not consistent wih the later account in his memoirs that he waited until midnight, expecting Lafayette McLaws's division to be sent to him.[23]

After all, if Longstreet wanted the division of McLaws, he himself could have sent for it anytime on that day. Bragg had already placed it at his disposal. As Bragg complained, "Longstreet's inactivity" does seem manifest.

Probably Longstreet, groping around in Lookout Valley near midnight with Jenkins, and unable to locate the Federal rear guard among the dozen or more knolls rising 50 or 100 feet high, decided to call off the attack. He did return to his headquarters. Perhaps Jenkins did not understand that the attack was cancelled. More than likely, however, Jenkins decided to attempt the mission anyway with his lone division. After the failure, Longstreet, who of course despised Bragg, well might have thought his best excuse was a lack of sufficient troops, for which he tried to place the blame on Bragg. Regardless of what general scenario is projected from the known facts, the situation does not enhance Longstreet's reputation.

Brigadier General Micah Jenkins, destined to die six months later in the Battle of the Wilderness, was from Edisto Island, off the South Carolina coast. In 1854, he had graduated first in his class at the South Carolina Military College, today The Citadel. He fought at Manassas as the colonel of the Fifth South Carolina Infantry, steadily rising as the war progressed. Having led Hood's division since Chickamauga, Jenkins intended to be recognized. No doubt he thought he saw a good opportunity for personal advancement as he launched the attack on the Federals at Wauhatchie.

The leader of the Union rear guard was also an ambitious man. Brigadier General John White Geary had served in the Mexican War and become the first mayor of San Francisco and then territorial governor of Kansas. After seeing Civil War action in minor engagements, Geary had been at Chancellorsville and Gettysburg. Surviving the war, he would serve two terms as governor of Pennsylvania before suffering a fatal heart attack in 1873.[24]

Geary was surprised by the suddenness and the aggressiveness of Jenkins's attack, but his men gave an excellent account of themselves in defending their ground. The Federal general, in his After Action Report, stated that "the enemy precipitately hurled his main body, without skirmishers, upon my left," their attack being met "with intense and well-directed fire." He put down the time of the first volley as half past midnight. The Union line of battle, still quoting General Geary, "was the corner of a square," with the left side perpendicular to the Nashville and Chattanooga Railroad, while the right side of the line was parallel with the railroad. From left to right, the Yankee alignment consisted of the One Hundred and Thirty-seventh New York, the One Hundred and Ninth Pennsylvania, the One Hundred and Eleventh Pennsylvania, the Seventy-eighth Ohio, and the One Hundred and Forty-ninth New York. The ninety-degree angle in the line was where the One Hundred and Eleventh Pennsylvania and the Seventy-eighth Ohio linked up.[25]

In the midst of the position held by the One Hundred and Eleventh Pennsylvania was a log house in which fourteen persons were said to be present, huddling together in the cellar, and not a one harmed in spite of the house itself being demolished in the course of the engagement.[26] After the initial concentration on the Union left, the Confederates gradually extended their attack to the center and right flank. Although the Rebels had superior numbers, about 4,000 in Jenkins's command, they found it difficult to coordinate their efforts in the dark. A Federal soldier later said that it was difficult in the darkness to distinguish friend from foe, that one could see no more than a few feet. Consequently, he concluded, "the fire of the men was directed by watching the explosion of the enemy's muskets."[27] In this confusing situation, perhaps the defenders had an advantage in being able to remain in one place. At least they knew where they themselves were located and thus were not as likely to shoot one another as were the Rebels. Also, the four guns of Joseph M. Knap's battery, named for the man who had organized it and given it four cannon, were located about fifty yards in the rear of the Federal position and elevated just enough to fire safely over the heads of the Federal troops. These guns raked the Rebel lines again and again, shooting spherical cases with short fuses. The Confederates had no artillery.[28]

As the fighting intensified on the Federal right flank, their artillery fire became devastating to the Confederates. "Pick off the artillerists" was heard repeatedly along the Rebel line, according to General Geary. Describing the action on the Federal right, Geary wrote: "The fire upon our right commenced from a piece of woods to the right of the railroad upon our skirmishers, covering the right, and advanced. One piece of Lieutenant [Edward] Geary's section was turned to the right. . . ." (Artillerist Edward Geary was the general's son.) Continuing with his report, the general stated that two companies of the One Hundred and Eleventh Pennsylvania, with the skirmishers, were hastily positioned behind the railroad embankment. Here "they checked the enemy's advance, who were much distressed and met with considerable loss by the combined efforts of the piece of artillery, with its excellent execution, and the indomitable behavior of my center, held by the One Hundred and eleventh Pennsylvania, which faced, in portions, two directions to resist the enfilading fire. It was under this fire," said Geary, "that my men fell rapidly and the battery suffered a most unparalleled loss."[29]

Captain Charles A. Atwell, of the battery, fell mortally wounded, and Lieutenant Geary was killed instantly. Men and horses were so devastated that only two guns could be manned after this attack and command of the battery rested solely upon Major J.A. Reynolds, chief of artillery of the Twelfth Corps, the only artillery officer left unscathed. The small battle continued to rage along the whole line, but on the left flank the overlapping right flank of the Rebels compelled the One Hundred and Thirty-seventh New York to recess a portion of their line until part of the regiment was fighting almost back-to-back with the other part.[30]

The Federals were nearly out of ammunition by three o'clock in the morning. A limited supply was available, of course, from the dead and wounded, but very soon the Yankees would be forced to defend themselves with the bayonet if reinforcements did not arrive shortly. Then, suddenly and rather unexpectedly, it was all over. "At half past three o'clock they ceased firing on our left," reported General Geary, "their hostility manifestly having grown weaker during the last fifteen minutes, and, firing a few volleys at our center, which were promptly responded to, they retired, leaving the field in our possession, and our lines in the same position as when the battle opened."[31]

After a strong initial encounter, the Confederate attack had gradually deteriorated, losing momentum and, in the dark, lacking coordination. The next day Micah Jenkins wrote about it, deploring the odds against him and calling the fight "terrible."[32] It was, indeed, a hard, brutal fight, although Jenkins actually enjoyed numerical superiority. Probably, in the night, he truly did not realize that fact; certainly he was never able to maintain control over the wild affair at Wauhatchie. There is also a story that the Confederate effort was victimized, in part, by a chance stampede of Yankee mules. The Union teamsters became frightened that they were about to be overrun by the Rebels and abandoned their mule teams. The terrified mules broke loose and stampeded, as luck would have it, toward the Confederates. Some of the Rebels, in the blackness of the night, supposed that a cavalry charge had been launched at them, and they too "stampeded," fleeing before the onrush of the mules.

Among the many points of disagreement about Wauhatchie is this mule story. According to General Grant, who was not present at the engagement, the mules did dash directly toward the enemy and disperse them. Captain James L. Coker, acting assistant adjutant general on the staff of Colonel John Bratton, who was present and seriously wounded in the fighting, denied the mule-charge story and said the Rebels retired in good order.[33]

Whatever the truth of the matter (and probably there was at least a germ of truth, in that some Confederates were terrified by stampeding mules), many soon accepted the story as indisputable fact. The alleged incident gave rise to the "Charge of the Mule Brigade," a parody on Alfred Lord Tennyson's famous account of the British light horse at Balaclava during the Crimean War. One is tempted to picture its composer, an anonymous infantryman of the Twenty-ninth Ohio, inspired by a convivial glass—or perhaps several glasses—as he conceived the stanzas:

> Half a mile, half a mile,
>   Half a mile onward,
> Right towards the Georgia troops,
>   Broke the two hundred.
> "Forward, the Mule Brigade,"
> "Charge for the Rebs!" they neighed;
> Straight for the Georgia troops
>   Broke the two hundred.
>
> "Forward, the Mule Brigade."
> Was there a mule dismayed?
> Not when the long ears felt
>   All their ropes sundered;
> Theirs not to make reply;
> Theirs not to reason why;
> Theirs but to make them fly.
> On! to the Georgia troops,
>   Broke the two hundred.

Through three more stanzas the tale continued before concluding with:

> When can their glory fade?

O! the wild charge they made!
All the world wondered.
Honor the charge they made,
Honor the Mule Brigade,
Long-eared two hundred.[34]

Whatever the precise facts about the mule charge may have been, the decisive event in dooming the Confederate attack was the arrival of the Federal reinforcements dispatched by Hooker from Brown's Ferry. Marching to the relief of Geary came the division of Carl Schurz, ordered toward Wauhatchie when Hooker heard the sounds of heavy firing in that direction soon after midnight. Hooker also alerted von Steinwehr to stand ready to move out, if he should be needed. General Schurz's division, "after some delay, occasioned by losing the road and getting into a swamp," according to General Oliver O. Howard's report, succeeded in pressing up against the Rebels who were blocking the road and gradually overpowered them.[35]

Confederate General Law, who had protested that his seventeen hundred men were insufficient for such a task, was positioned on the range of hills bordering the Brown's Ferry-Wauhatchie road. The Federals encircled his flank and forced him to pull back, although he held out for some two hours, giving Micah Jenkins time to extricate his division from a losing situation. Yet Jenkins, who certainly thought of Law as a rival, criticized him for withdrawing too soon and letting Federal reinforcements through. Law reported that he ultimately pulled back in a "leisurely manner," only after being convinced, from more than one source of information, that Jenkins's retreat was well underway and that Colonel Bratton was actually at the bridge over Lookout Creek. "Believing that the object for which my position was occupied had been accomplished, I withdrew," he wrote.[36]

About two hours before sunrise it was all over. The Confederates had withdrawn across Lookout Creek and would make no further effort to reclaim the area. A striking discrepancy occurs in participants' accounts with respect to the nature of the night—from pitch black to illuminated by a full moon in a clear sky[37]—but for the Confederates, unquestionably, it was a dark night. The October 28 journal entry of J. Stoddard Johnson had well forecast the situation: "The enemy had strengthened and reinforced his position at Brown's

Ferry. Longstreet writes that he will put a brigade in rear of the enemy at dark and attack him. Should this effort to dislodge him fail, I think we shall have to abandon this position."[38]

For General John W. Geary, despite the triumph of his outnumbered command, it was also a dark night. Deeply mourning the loss of his son, the tormented general experienced a Calvinistic sense of punishment—that through the tragedy he would somehow be drawn closer to God. To his wife, Mary, not the mother of his dead child, Geary wrote on November 2 of "the almost impenetrable gloom which hangs around me since the death of my beloved Son. . . . Poor dear boy, he is gone, cut down in the bud of his usefulness, but I trust in this chastisement, I may learn to love My Dear Saviour, Jesus Christ, with unalloyed devotion, and . . . I may be brought near to Christ. . . . Oh, my God, I feel this chastisement for the pride I took in him. . . ."[39]

6

Our Position, It Strikes Me,
Is Objectionable

The Confederate loss of the route to Bridgeport gave the Federals a line of supply across Raccoon Mountain to Brown's Ferry. And it enabled Grant to receive reinforcements. For several weeks General Bragg had known that Sherman's corps was moving to Chattanooga with twenty thousand men or more. By the first of November, the Confederate commander knew also that Rosecrans had been relieved and Grant was coming, if not already present with the Union army. And, of course, Bragg knew that Hooker's divisions were already at Chattanooga. Clearly the siege had failed and the Union was gathering superior forces. General Liddell wrote that the enemy "gradually moved up to the base of Lookout Point—which we had entrenched on the slopes to keep him back. Hardee now took command of the left wing and strained every point to maintain himself. Danger was thickening fast around Bragg," although, said Liddell, the general "seemed singularly indifferent."[1]

November 1 proved to be a beautiful Sunday, clear and bright after the dark, cold, and stormy weather of many recent days. About noon, artillery fire was directed from Lookout Mountain toward some Federal trains, but most of the Wauhatchie road, and certainly Brown's Ferry, was out of range. J. Stoddard Johnson continued to worry as he succinctly stated the Confederate situation in his journal: Part of the army lay west of Chattanooga Creek, "a swollen stream," while the center was "composed of one corps and two divisions, on an extended, single line." In a bit of understatement he wrote, "Our position, it strikes me, is objectionable."[2]

Indeed it was undesirable. Like Johnson, General Liddell was disturbed about the position. He said that he called Bragg's attention to the wretched condition of the roads and bridges to the rear, "which might enable him in case of necessity to secure a safe retreat," but the commanding general "merely assented to the fact and wished me to examine them and report to him." Liddell said he complied at once, only to discover that his report "had no weight" with Bragg. "I thought," Liddell continued, "he was infatuated with the hopeless anxiety to get Chattanooga, causing hm to overlook the gathering storm."[3]

Having lost his greatest ally, famine, the Confederate commander needed to take action—particularly since he could not expect any reinforcements and knew that the enemy would soon be receiving Sherman's troops. Yet, as Glenn Tucker well stated the situation, Bragg "did not undertake to invest Chattanooga by regular approaches, by storming, or by any measure whatever that might lure the Northerners from their position so that he might meet them again in open battle. He merely waited. . . ."[4] In other words, he did essentially the same thing he had been doing all through October—waiting while other generals, some of them desperately, groped for a suitable plan of action.

When Jefferson Davis visited the army, he had pressed Bragg concerning his plans, apparently not convinced that trying to starve the Federals into submission was the best strategy. Davis wanted something more aggressive. Bragg had then suggested the possibility that the Army of Tennessee be strongly reinforced by troops from Lee, after which he would cross the river north of Chattanooga, flanking the Yankees out of the town and forcing them into a major engagement. Actually, the plan was Beauregard's, who had suggested the strategy a few days earlier in a letter to Bragg, warning that the authorship of the plan must be kept secret, or else President Davis would be prejudiced against it because of his dislike of the colorful Creole.[5]

"If my opinion for once could be listened to, I would say again, act entirely on the defensive in Virginia," wrote a rather exasperated Beauregard to Bragg in a letter dated October 7. Beauregard said that

25,000 men from Lee's army, and 5,000 or 10,000 more from Joseph E. Johnston's forces, should be sent to Bragg immediately "to enable you to take the offensive forthwith, and cross the Tennessee to crush Rosecrans before he can be reinforced to any large extent from any quarter." Thus, Beauregard projected that Bragg "could attack and defeat the enemy's reinforcements in detail before they could be concentrated into a strong army." If this were not done, Beauregard feared that Middle Georgia and Atlanta would soon be lost, and the Confederacy "now cut in two would then be cut in three!" While Confederate troops concentrated in southeastern Tennessee, Lee, if necessary, "could fall back within the lines around Richmond, until a part of [Bragg's] army could be sent to his relief. I fear any other plan will sooner or later end in our final destruction in detail."[6]

The plan was vintage Beauregard. Just as before Shiloh, saturated with Napoleonic concepts, the general was again proclaiming the necessity of concentrating all available forces in the Western theater. Here lay, the Creole still thought, the most promising opportunity for the Confederacy. Nor had Beauregard forgotten to call upon the Almighty, characteristically imploring, "Let us then unite all our efforts in a last deadly struggle and, with God's help, we shall yet triumph!"[7]

The major problem with the strategy—and otherwise Davis seemed to like it—was that the president felt he could not afford to reduce Lee's army by the more than 30,000 reinforcements that Beauregard and Bragg wanted. Beauregard had sent his brother, Armand, to personally present his plan to Bragg. Armand, probably wisely, did not meet with Davis, allowing Bragg to deal with the president. Afterward, he reported to his brother that General Bragg "submitted your last document, in his name, to the President, urging its importance. . . . The President admitted its worth and was inclined to adopt it, only he could not reduce General Lee's army." Then Armand continued with an unwarranted optimism, saying that "reinforcements from all other quarters would be hurried up as soon as possible" and that Bragg "entertained every hope of having under his command a very large army, able to undertake a successful campaign on a large scale."[8]

Longstreet, too, had a plan; one Davis liked better, if for no other reason than that Longstreet did not ask for any reinforcements. The strategy was very similar to the Beauregard-Bragg proposal and seemed to promise more gain with less effort. Longstreet suggested a change of base to Rome, Georgia, followed by a strike in force across the Tennessee River at Bridgeport, Alabama. The move would sever the Federal supply route completely and place the Confederates between the Yankees in Chattanooga and the reinforcements coming to join them. The Union would have to abandon its defensive position and fight or retreat. If a battle ensued, the Federals probably would be on less favorable ground and, in any case, the Confederates would be taking the initiative with a good chance to retain the momentum lost after Chickamauga. The preliminary change of base to Rome was to insure that the Federals would be surprised when the Rebels struck. According to Longstreet, President Davis not only approved the plan but also, before he left, ordered the army to change base to Rome.[9]

Davis was assured by Bragg that, as soon as the troops could be readied to advance, the crossing of the Tennessee on the Union right would be undertaken. But, as a dreary October wore on, abundant with rain, Bragg seemed less than enthusiastic about Longstreet's plan. In fact, he likely never favored it, and he reported to the president that rain had delayed his preparations for the crossing. With a decided preference for defensive warfare, at least in the Chattanooga setting, Bragg procrastinated while continuing to indulge in the war with his own generals. The long, drawn-out controversy with Buckner, bitterly contested by both men, was raging, while relations with Longstreet, never good, were becoming worse.[10]

On October 29, the president, although he still preferred operating against the Federal right, reminded Bragg that "the period most favorable for actual operations is rapidly passing away" and proposed an alternative plan if the strike across the Tennessee at Bridgeport could not be made. "In this connection it has occurred to me," wrote Davis, "that if the operations on your left should be delayed, or not be of prime importance, that you might advantageously assign General Longstreet with his two divisions to the task of expelling Burnside and thus place him in position, according to circumstances, to hasten or delay his return to the army of General Lee."[11]

Perhaps, other than a possible court-martial of Buckner, sending Longstreet to Knoxville was one of the most pleasant thoughts that crossed Bragg's mind during all the weeks of the Chattanooga siege. It made no military sense, of course, unless one was blind, as Davis and Bragg apparently were, to the Union concentration at Chattanooga. But Bragg seized the chance "to get rid of him," as he admitted to General Liddell about Longstreet; and he confided to Davis his "great relief" to be sending Longstreet to East Tennessee.[12] General Grant

13. General P.G.T. Beauregard. *Library of Congress.*

thought the Confederate president had consciously taken a step to separate two incompatible generals and caustically remarked: "Mr. Davis had an exalted opinion of his own military genius. . . . On several occasions during the war he came to the relief of the Union army by means of his superior military genius!"[13] Whether or not Grant was right about Davis wishing to separate the generals, it is clear that Bragg wanted Longstreet out of the way.

"It was folly in Bragg to do this," commented General Liddell, "reducing his own strength" when he had to meet "the accumulation of all the Western armies against him. . . . But," he continued, "Bragg was headstrong and too often unreasonable. . . ." Bragg did hope that the defeat of Burnside would force Grant to detach part of the Chattanooga command to relieve him. However, the fact remains that Bragg was dividing his force in the face of an ever stronger enemy. Bragg would have only about thirty-five thousand infantry at the most— hardly twenty-five thousand, according to Liddell—confronting an enemy believed to be seventy or possibly even eighty thousand strong. And even if Burnside was defeated, Grant would not necessarily be compelled to retreat from Chattanooga. His communications line would remain intact via the river and railroad into Middle Tennessee.[14]

That motives of a personal nature were strongly behind Bragg's decision to detach Longstreet is convincingly detailed by Connelly, in *Autumn of Glory*, who notes that other commanders, like Carter Stevenson, were more accessible for such a campaign. Stevenson's division, with two cavalry brigades, had been sent into East Tennessee in mid-October. Also, Bragg had just reinforced General Stevenson with another infantry division, B. Franklin Cheatham's, whose unit was temporarily under John K. Jackson. In sum, by the first of November, Bragg already had about eleven thousand infantry and cavalry in the area where Longstreet was being assigned, and Stevenson's men were familiar with the country. Longstreet knew very little about East Tennessee and had no maps or scouts who knew the territory. He also had a shortage of transportation, having left his wagons in Virginia, as previously noted. Neither were mules and horses sufficient for moving Longstreet's artillery. Finally, Longstreet occupied the extreme left of Bragg's position at Chattanooga. Troops from Breckinridge or Hardee on the center and right, respectively, could have been detached more easily.[15]

But what did Longstreet, who had wished to conduct an independent campaign, think of the East Tennessee project? Longstreet said he first heard about it through camp rumors. Eventually he was summoned to Bragg's headquarters, along with Hardee and Breckinridge, to be formally briefed. At that time, according to his account, Longstreet had a counter-proposal. Believing that to detach so large a portion of the army's strength must certainly be fatal, he proposed that if Bragg would withdraw his entire command from the heights around Chattanooga and take up a good defensive position behind Chickamauga Creek, then conceivably a strong column could make a quick strike against Burnside, defeat him, and return to Bragg before any more enemy reinforcements might reach Chattanooga. Not impressed, Bragg ordered Longstreet to proceed against Knoxville with two divisions, Alexander's artillery and Wheeler's cavalry. Any further discussion "was out of order," said the commanding general.[16]

Hardee's version, however, does not agree with Longstreet's. Writing in April 1864, Hardee claimed Longstreet never suggested that Bragg place the army in a strong defensive position behind the Chickamauga until his command could return from defeating Burnside. Nor did Hardee recall anything about Longstreet returning to Chattanooga after the projected defeat of Burnside. In fact, according to Hardee, Longstreet made no proposal beyond renewing his project for an attack across the Tennessee River at Bridgeport.[17]

Longstreet took the train, running badly off schedule, to Sweetwater, Tennessee, en route to Knoxville. While his corps was in the process of moving out of the Chattanooga area on November 5, Longstreet sent Bragg a statement of his understanding of the mission and asked if it was correct. He said that his concept was that "I should gain possession of East Tennessee." Probably, he continued, he would have to break rail communication with Chattanooga. If he was successful, then Bragg could launch his own attack against Grant or move to the East Tennessee valley and join him. Longstreet, seemingly, was not concerned with returning to the Chattanooga area. Bragg's reply confirmed that the objective was to "get possession of East Tennessee" and mentioned nothing about the Virginia general returning to Chattanooga.[18]

The best chance for Longstreet's movement to succeed was through a rapid strike before General Burnside had time to concentrate his forces. But this turned out to be impossible. With trains running irregularly and wagons and teams in short supply, not until November 9 did Longstreet's infantry negotiate the sixty miles to Sweetwater. The situation did not improve. Previously assured that rations would be on hand when he reached Sweetwater, Longstreet

now learned that the commissary depot had been sent back to Chattanooga when General Carter Stevenson left the area. Halting for four
days to find food, he felt he needed more troops also and requested
General Bragg to send reinforcements, stating, "As soon as I find a
probability of moving without almost certain starvation, I shall
move, provided the troops are up." Obviously, Bragg's repeated
urgings for Longstreet to move faster had become irritating. For his
part, Bragg informed Longstreet that his estimate of enemy strength
"is deemed larger than the facts justify."[19]

On November 12, Bragg's temper seemed about to reach a boiling
point. He dispatched a message saying to Longstreet: "Your several
dispatches of today astonish me!" He told the Virginian that "transportation in abundance was on the road and subject to your orders. I
regret that it has not been energetically used. The means being fur-
nished, you were expected to handle your own troops, and I can not
understand your constant applications for me to forward them."[20]

While Bragg and Longstreet engaged in acrid exchanges, General
Burnside was calling in all his scattered troops, with the exception of
those at Cumberland Gap, preparing to follow Grant's instructions to
simply hold Longstreet in check so that Grant might gain time.
Altogether Burnside had about 20,000 troops with him; when Longstreet finally arrived before Knoxville on November 17, he found the
Yankees well positioned and entrenched. Rightly believing that he
had more strength than did the Confederates, Burnside confidently
waited while Longstreet's East Tennessee campaign slowly turned
into a fruitless enterprise. Soon Longstreet would be telling Bragg that
he must send another infantry division if he hoped for favorable
results.

At Chattanooga, on the Union side, Grant had been feeling much
more comfortable since opening up "the cracker line" through
Bridgeport. To Halleck he wrote: "If the Rebels give me one week
more time I think all danger of losing territory now held by us will
have passed away and preparations may commence for offensive
operations."[21] Grant's plan awaited only the arrival of Sherman, for
whom Grant had grown anxious well before Longstreet ever left
Chattanooga. Impatient of the railroad repairs that Halleck had
ordered Sherman to accomplish on the Memphis and Charleston line,
Grant told the red-haired Ohioan to drop everything and "hurry
eastward with all possible dispatch toward Bridgeport."[22] The message, according to Sherman, was delivered by an adventurous fellow
named Pike, who paddled down the Tennessee River in a canoe,

14. General James Longstreet. *Chickamauga-Chattanooga National Military Park.*

shooting rapids and racing past Rebels who occasionally fired at him. Sherman admired the man's daring and asked him what he wanted to do next; Pike replied, "something *bold!*" After the war, perhaps unable to accept domestication, Pike shot himself. Grant told Sherman that upon reaching Bridgeport he would be in position to block a Confederate attempt to turn the Union right flank. Apparently Grant had no "inside" information about Rebel thinking but was merely preparing to respond to a possible and logical movement to cut his supply line and flank the Federals out of Chattanooga.[23]

Meanwhile, in Chattanooga, Grant was being pressed by Washington to do something to aid Burnside at Knoxville. No sooner had the administration learned of Longstreet's departure from Chattanooga than, in Grant's words, they became "more than ever anxious for the safety of Burnside's army and plied me with dispatches faster than ever, urging that something should be done for his relief. . . . I, as well as the authorities in Washington, was . . . in a great state of anxiety for Burnside's safety. Burnside himself, I believe, was the only one who did not share in this anxiety," stated Grant. "Nothing could be done for him, however, until Sherman's troops were up."[24] Grant did not believe that sending part of his army to Knoxville would do anything more than add to Burnside's supply problem, which was precarious. What Grant wanted to do, instead, was attack Bragg's right flank. If the assault did not succeed in driving the Rebels from Missionary Ridge, he reasoned that it probably would so alarm Bragg that the Confederate commander would recall Longstreet.

But while he waited for Sherman to arrive, Grant was becoming depressed. And when he became depressed he tended to overindulge with alcohol. John Rawlins claimed in a letter to his fiancée that Grant's problem made Rawlins's presence essential because of "the free use of intoxicating liquors at Headqurters, which last night's developments showed me had reached to the General commanding." Rawlins added, "I am the only one here (his wife not being with him) who can stay it. . . ."[25]

It is impossible to know how frequently the Union commander was drinking at Chattanooga. Likely it was not as big a problem here as during the famous binge that occurred in the Vicksburg campaign. Clearly, Grant's indulgence did not interfere with his conduct of operations. That he was impatient is understandable. Also, in this case, it was unfortunate. If he had only waited a little longer to attack, two more divisions would have departed from the Rebel line along the heights, detached by Bragg to strengthen Longstreet!

15. General William J. Hardee. *Chickamauga-Chattanooga National Military Park.*

7

The Perfect Order of a Holiday Parade

Actually, the fight did not start the way that General Grant intended, nor did it begin as early as he planned. On November 7, having learned that Longstreet had marched against Burnside at Knoxville, Grant ordered Thomas to make "an attack on the north end of Missionary Ridge with all the force you can bring to bear against it, and, when that is carried, . . . threaten, and even attack if possible, the enemy's line of communication between Dalton [Georgia] and Cleveland [Tennessee] . . . . The movement should not be made one moment later than tomorrow morning."[1] The general hoped that such an attack would compel the Confederates to recall Longstreet.

Grant was on the verge of a colossal blunder. Fortunately for the Union army, the advice of Generals George H. Thomas and William F. Smith finally prevailed. "The order staggered Thomas," recalled General Smith in an article penned after the death of Thomas.[2] If Thomas was dismayed, Smith was only slightly less disapproving of Grant's plan, essentially an adaptation and a major extension of his own. "I think I may safely state that I did not propose at that time, in view of the condition of the army of the Cumberland, to suggest anything that would bring on a general battle unless under the guns of our forts at Chattanooga," Smith wrote. "The plan proposed by me, as chief engineer, was only a *threat to seize* the north-west end of

106

Missionary Ridge . . . with the idea that such a feint might force the recall of Longstreet."[3]

Immediately after receiving Grant's attack order, General Thomas set to work to have it revoked. He sent for Smith and, under the correct impression that the order was related to Smith's plan, told that general, as Smith remembered, "If I attempt to carry out the order I have received, my army will be terribly beaten." Then, probably also aware that Smith's rapport with Grant was better than his own, Thomas said: "You must go and get the order revoked."[4] Smith related that he then asked Thomas to accompany him up the river for a personal examination of the terrain. The two generals left at once for an intensive reconnaissance on the Union army's left flank.

"Going to a hill opposite the mouth of the South Chickamauga Creek," Smith recounted, the two "spent an hour or more" and "looked carefully over the ground on which Thomas would have to operate, noted the extreme of Bragg's campfires on Missionary Ridge, and then, [became] convinced that Thomas with his force could not outflank Bragg's right without endangering our connection with Chattanooga." Smith concluded by saying that, upon returning, he "went directly to General Grant, and reported to him that after a careful reconnaissance . . . I was of the decided opinion that no movement could be made in that direction until the arrival of Sherman's forces."[5]

That night, Grant countermanded the order for Thomas to attack. In his official report Grant explained that "after a thorough reconnaissance of the ground . . . it was deemed utterly impracticable to make the move until Sherman could get up. . . ." However, Grant's words in a telegram to Halleck could well be taken as thinly disguised criticism of Thomas: "I have never felt such restlessness before as I have at the fixed and immovable condition of the Army of the Cumberland."[6] With the passage of time Grant certainly was ungenerous and seemed to become, after Thomas lay in his tomb, as Smith later noted, "so unjust to the memory of the late Major General George H. Thomas. . . ."[7] In his memoirs Grant said he directed Thomas to "take mules, officers' horses, or animals wherever he could get them, to move the necessary artillery. But," in Grant's choice of words, Thomas "persisted in the declaration that he could not see how he could possibly comply with the order. Nothing was left to be done but to answer Washington dispatches as best I could, urge Sherman forward, although he was making every effort to get forward, and encourage Burnside to hold on. . . ."[8]

Excuses may be offered for Grant—for example, he was irritable due to pain from a bad fall off his horse; he was being pressured by "the authorities at Washington," who plied him with dispatches "faster than ever, urging that something should be done" for the relief of Burnside; and perhaps Grant remembered the fate of Major General Don Carlos Buell, an officer who ignored East Tennessee and was removed from command—but in the final analysis Grant did Thomas a serious injustice. Ironically, if not for Thomas, Grant well might have made one of the worst mistakes of his career. "When it is remembered," wrote General Smith in a bit of understatement, "that eighteen days after this, Sherman, with six perfectly appointed divisions failed to carry this same point of Missionary Ridge, at a time when Thomas with four divisions stood threatening Bragg's center, and Hooker with nearly three divisions was driving in Bragg's left flank (Bragg having no more strength than on the 7th), it will not be a matter of surprise that the order [to attack] staggered Thomas."[9]

Whether pleased or not, Grant's order delayed the attack for a good number of days. As the end of the third week in November approached, Grant prepared to try again. Sherman had arrived on November 15, his troops would soon follow;[10] the army was well supplied, and Grant issued his plans for battle to begin. The date assigned for attack was November 21.

Not surprisingly, because it is the case with most preliminary battle blueprints, his plans were altered several times. Problems with shifting troops, weather conditions, and changing intelligence about enemy forces and intentions are some of the reasons for the modifications. Only in the broadest sense did the plan not change.

Bragg's right, as Grant saw it, was his strategic flank. The Confederate supply line ran up the railroad east of Missionary Ridge to the right flank. And Longstreet had used the railroad to Loudon in moving against Burnside at Knoxville. Grant planned to attack against the Rebel right, therefore, with Sherman's army making the main effort. Sherman would cross the Tennessee River at Brown's Ferry, march behind Stringer's Ridge north of Chattanooga, and secretly take cover in the woods opposite the mouth of South Chickamauga Creek. If the Confederates atop Lookout Mountain spotted his crossing at the Ferry, Grant hoped they would conclude that reinforcements were being sent to Burnside at Knoxville. Sherman would then cross the Tennessee just below South Chickamauga Creek, launch a surprise attack against the north end of Missionary Ridge (Tunnel Hill), and carry the ridge to the railroad tunnel before the Rebels could react. Secure atop the ridge, Sherman's Army of the Tennessee would extend its line to the left, moving across the creek to threaten the railroad at Chickamauga Station and hoping to get astride Bragg's line of retreat.[11]

General Thomas, meanwhile, would hold the center and right flank of the Yankee front and cooperate with Sherman, only attacking when the proper time arrived, that is, after Sherman had rolled up the flank. Then Thomas's Army of the Cumberland, moving to the left, would connect up with Sherman, and the two would sweep the Confederates from the ridge and the valley. "An assault on the center before either flank was turned," asserted General Smith, who, of course, was present, "was never seriously contemplated. . . ." General Hooker, on the Union right flank, with a relatively small force, would hold Lookout Valley and simply threaten Lookout Mountain at the point where it strikes the Tennessee.[12]

As a diversionary move, one division of Sherman's army was to march up Lookout Valley, on the extreme right, and threaten a pass across Lookout Mountain. This feint to turn Bragg's left flank was to be made in daylight, in sight of the Confederates. After dark the division would retrace its march, cross the Tennessee at Brown's Ferry, and rejoin the main body of Sherman's army for the attack on Missionary Ridge. Thus, from first to last, the key roles were to be performed by Sherman's Army of the Tennessee, which would lead the attack and set the pace.

On November 17 Sherman's leading division left Bridgeport for a march of thirty-five to forty miles and an intended rendezvous with battle at daylight on the twenty-first. Harassed by bad roads, rain and mud, and three frail bridges, the troops were soon way behind schedule. By November 20, the head of Sherman's army had only reached Brown's Ferry. Realizing the impossibility of Sherman's troops attaining the jump-off position in time for an attack on the twenty-first, Grant postponed the operation. Rain continued to fall on November 21, and the time of attack was again delayed.

At this point General Thomas suggested to Grant that Hooker's command be strengthened for an attack on Lookout Mountain—a plan originally favored by Thomas. He had some good reasons for this strategy. If the Rebels were pushed off the mountain, then Thomas's center and right flank would no longer be separated by the Moccasin Bend of the Tennessee River. Also, a trouble-free supply route between Bridgeport and Chattanooga would be doubly assured. And the Union army would be in good position to pressure the Confederate left flank. Hitting this flank might be just as advantageous as hitting the right, for success on either flank of the Rebels would threaten their railroad and line of retreat into Georgia. Thomas was worried, also, that the Confederates would discover Grant's battle plan for turning their right flank, especially since they could see Sherman's troops crossing the Tennessee at Brown's Ferry. But Grant rejected his advice. While Grant could not have been pleased by the delays, the nervousness of Washington authorities, and the reports of fighting at Knoxville, he held to his plans for Sherman to launch the main attack.

On the night of November 22, however, a deserter entered Union lines with a report that Bragg was withdrawing. Now Grant thought he understood the meaning of a puzzling earlier communiqué from Bragg, received under a flag of truce on the twentieth, which read: "General: As there may still be some non-combatants in Chattanooga, I deem it proper to notify you that prudence would dictate their early withdrawal." General Bragg, thought Grant, was trying to cover the dispatch of reinforcements to Longstreet by a message indicating an imminent attack. With reinforcements, Longstreet might capture Knoxville quickly and then return to Chattanooga.[13]

Wishing to learn if Bragg, for whatever reason, had weakened his line on Missionary Ridge, Grant directed Thomas to conduct a reconnaissance in force and determine if the Confederates were withdrawing. If Bragg was falling back, Grant wanted to attack him at once. Actually, Bragg had ordered the divisions of Buckner and Cleburne to reinforce Longstreet.

Thus General Thomas opened the three-day struggle for Chattanooga. Preparing for any eventuality, and not merely for a reconnaissance in force, Thomas organized a movement as strong as Grant had planned to use in his main attack. He designated five divisions, if necessary, for the mission, with Howard's corps massed in the rear as a reserve. The movement began in the late morning on Monday, November 23. The Federal objective was the fortified Confederate outpost line. Running roughly north and south, this line lay about a mile and a half to the east, just about halfway from the Union position to Missionary Ridge. Confederate pickets, which of course would be first encountered, were slightly east of the Western and Atlantic Railroad. The Confederate line of rifle pits was strengthened by barricades of logs and stone. The most imposing points on the line were two bald knobs, especially the more northerly eminence, which rose about one hundred feet above Chattanooga Valley and was called both Indian Hill and Orchard Knob. The latter name became the better known and is the designation by which this engagement is popularly called. Occupying the line were hundreds of Confederate soldiers, but they obviously were no match for the thousands being marshalled against them—and they were taken by surprise.

General Thomas, from all accounts, both Union and Confederate, put on a great military show. More impressively and importantly, he thereby mounted a surprise attack, with 25,000 men, in full view of the watching Confederate army. When Rebel prisoners were later questioned, they admitted thinking it was all a grand review and general drill.[14] That Confederates watched the deployment of Union troops with an air of enjoying a pageant is hardly surprising when one realizes that even some of the Yankees participating did not suspect what was about to happen. "The boys of the Sixth Indiana will remember that we thought we were only out for the purpose of brigade drill," recalled a soldier of the regiment who participated in the attack.[15]

Some drill it must have been! Troops in line and column covered the broad Chattanooga Valley, the steps of thousands beating equal time. Flags were flying. Bayonets glistened. The sharp commands of company officers and the clear notes of bugles sounded. The drums were beat. And then, about two o'clock, suddenly the Yankees moved forward, Wood's division in the lead, with Sheridan's division, on Wood's right, advancing soon afterward in support. The other divisions were close, if they were needed.

When the Rebel pickets started firing, John Ely, a soldier in the Thirty-sixth Illinois, said that "an amusing little incident occurred which caused a good deal of shouting and laughing among the troops. As our skirmishers were advancing and exchanging shots with the Rebel pickets, there were three grey hounds, that had been staying with some of the boys. . ., and while the two . . . armies were busy with the work of death, they were as busy running rabbits and their sharp, quick yelps sounded strangely in contrast with the din of musketry."[16]

Frank Wolfe, a Federal officer, "excited by the novelty of the scene and the danger," admitted that he watched the dramatic spectacle, "merely to experience what a fight was like, and having once thoroughly enjoyed the luxury," he had little ambition for more. "It was beautiful," wrote Wolfe, "to see column after column march, the skirmishers deploy," and then came the charge and the sharp cracking of rifled-musketry.[17]

Quickly and decisively, the Confederate line was overwhelmed. Brigadier General Arthur Manigault described the action from the Rebel viewpoint across the way. "At that time my picket line occupied a front of about 800 yards. . . . The 24th and 28th Alabama regiments . . . held the . . . line" and "numbered together about 600 men on duty, both of them being small regiments." The enemy's "first line was checked by our fire," Manigault continued, "but the second line coming to their assistance, together they moved forward in spite of our fire, which was not heavy enough to deter them. . . . Both regiments behaved well, particularly the 28th which resisted obstinately, . . . many of them fighting hand to hand; but the odds against them were irresistible, and Lieutenant Colonel Butler, 28th Alabama, Commanding, in order to save his regiment, was forced to give the order to retire. The other regiment, . . . had already given way. Had they contended much longer, they would have been killed or captured to a man, as the lines to their right and left were broken, and the enemy were getting to their rear. The 28th lost a good many, the 24th fewer—in all about 175 men." Manigault, who observed from "the top of the ridge with my glass," concluded his account of this action by observing that "having obtained possession of our picket line and [Orchard Knob] the enemy seemed satisfied, and pushed forward no farther. Our skirmishers retired about 350 or 400 yards and halted."[18]

General Manigault's description seems straightforward and, in substantive matters, consistent with the record of General Thomas in his After Action Report. Thomas said: "The formation being completed about 2 P.M., the troops advanced steadily and with rapidity directly to the front, driving before them first the Rebel pickets, then their reserves, and falling upon their grand guards stationed in their first line of rifle pits, captured something over 200 men, and secured themselves in their new position before the enemy had sufficiently recovered from his surprise to attempt to send reinforcements from his main camp."[19]

Brigadier General Thomas J. Wood's division—organized with Hazen's brigade on the right, Willich's on the left, and Beatty's in reserve in rear of Willich's left—both led the assault and engaged in the bulk of the fighting. General Wood was very proud of his command's performance, as his After Action Report makes obvious. "My division seemed to drink in the inspiration of the scene," he wrote, "and when the 'advance' was sounded moved forward in the perfect order of a holiday parade." Then the general began to reminisce. "It has been my good fortune to witness on the Champ de Mars and on Longchamps, reviews of all arms of the French service, under the eye of the most remarkable man of the present generation. I once saw a review, followed by a mock battle, of the finest troops of El Re Galantuomo. The pageant was held on the plains of Milan, the queen city of Lombardy, and the troops in the sham conflict were commanded by two of the most distinguished officers of the Piedmontese service, Cialdini and another, whose name I cannot now recall. In none of these displays did I ever see anything to exceed the soldierly bearing and the steadiness of my division, exhibited in the advance on Monday afternoon, the 23rd."[20]

When General Wood proudly signalled "I have carried the first line of enemy entrenchments," General Thomas, who stood with Grant on the eastern parapet of Fort Wood, signalled in reply: "Hold your position and I will support you."[21] Thomas at once ordered troops into line on Wood's left flank. Sheridan occupied the line to the right. Also, a six-gun battery was put into position on Orchard Knob, and General Grant soon moved his headquarters up to this forward hill.

The line of the Union advance had moved about a mile closer to the Confederate positions and had thrust a formidable salient toward Bragg's center. It was an excellent vantage point for observation of further developments—and a better starting point from which to launch an assault on Missionary Ridge, if such were ever to seem feasible. Also, Grant was convinced the Rebels were not withdrawing.

Having concentrated on the defense of his flanks, Bragg apparently suffered a surprise when this action occurred on the center. The effect on Bragg was partially good and partially bad for the Federals. The good part for the Yankees was that, during the night of November 23, Walker's Rebel division was withdrawn from the line between the eastern base of Lookout Mountain and Chattanooga Creek and placed on Missionary Ridge, a mile or more from the north end of the ridge. The transfer of this division weakened the Lookout Mountain defense and helped assure a Union success there on the next day. The bad part was that, although Bragg stopped the transfer of Bushrod

Johnson's and Pat Cleburne's divisions to Longstreet's command at Knoxville, Cleburne's troops, composing one of the very best divisions in the Confederate army, would be placed, and just in the nick of time for the Rebels, right in the path of Sherman's attack on the northern end of Missionary Ridge—an assault intended, of course, to be the decisive movement of the battle.

By dusk the day's work was done and the divisions of Thomas's army were settling down for the night. So too were the Confederates. "It would be hard for anyone to imagine my surprise when, about dusk," related General Manigault in a most intriguing account in his memoirs, "I received an order to report to [Brigadier] General [James Patton] Anderson . . . and was informed by him that I must at once make an attack, and recover the hill which my picket force had lost—as if I only had lost ground, and the line . . . on each side had not also been driven in. I must say that I have seldom been more taken aback." Manigault inquired what troops would be supporting him and was informed that Anderson's own brigade, now commanded by Colonel William F. Tucker, would be on his left, while Brigadier General Zachariah C. Deas's brigade was assigned to his right. As Manigault remembered it, Anderson told him: "The orders have been given them to advance with you and to conform to your movements. They are in readiness, and as soon as you are, communicate with them, and then move forward."

Having so said, Anderson, according to Manigault, went into his tent to supper, while Manigault rode to his brigade. "I gave the necessary orders, and instructed my regimental commanders as to what was expected of us, and how they were to guide themselves, and, everything being in readiness," continued Manigault, "I sent word to the two brigade commanders on my right and left that I was ready to advance, and would do so as soon as I received an intimation from them that they were also ready." By then it was dark, with only a few prominent objects visible against the sky, but, since the ground was familiar, Manigault felt confident that he could guide the center of the Rebel line straight to Orchard Knob. "As to our ability to recover it," the general stated, "that was another matter, and I had a good many forebodings as to the result of our effort, but . . . my orders, whatever I may have thought of them, were imperative."

Obviously, Manigault thought that Confederate prospects for recovering the lost position were bad. They quickly became worse. Shortly after the general had dispatched his messengers to the cooperating brigade commanders, one returned with Colonel Tucker and the other brought a message from General Deas, "each reporting that their orders had just been changed, and that instead of their brigades advancing, only their skirmish lines were to do so, and that these were awaiting [Manigault's] orders."

Manigault, understandably, was shocked. "Thinking that there must be some mistake . . . I determined to see General Anderson again, scarcely believing it possible that he intended to sacrifice my brigade, as would assuredly be the case if I were sent forward with 1,400 or 1,500 men, alone against certainly not less than six or eight thousand, supported by many pieces of artillery, already crowning the hill. I thought it folly as originally planned," asserted the general, "but as the arrangement now stood, I regarded it as madness and the most reckless stupidity."

Riding at once to division headqurters, Manigault, as he later noted, "found the Commander still at supper." Stating the cause of his delay in advancing, he requested a clarification of the orders. Anderson "informed me that he had changed his original plan . . . and that I would immediately make the attack alone." Infuriated at being ordered to do what he considered the impossible, Manigault remembered that he then replied: "General Anderson, are you aware that my command does not exceed fifteen hundred men, and that . . . under such circumstances it is beyond all reasonable ground of hope that the venture can result in success, whilst the great likelihood is that my brigade will be annihilated or captured?"

Anderson responded that Manigault exaggerated the numbers of the enemy and insinuated, alleged Manigault, "a backwardness on my part, not very creditable to me." Manigault replied that he intended to obey the order to attack, but, since he did not expect to return from the assault, he felt compelled to protest within the hearing of a couple of officers standing nearby against "the rashness and recklessness" of Anderson's order, "which would cost so many lives and men, to no purpose," and which was "perfectly impracticable." About this time, as Manigault, "in a state of high indignation," turned and mounted his horse to leave, Colonel James Barr, Jr., commander of the Tenth Mississippi and acting as the division officer of the day, rode up and began speaking to Anderson.

Manigault said he caught some fragments of their conversation, Barr estimating the Federal force, which Manigault was about to attack, at "not less than ten thousand" and expressing his opinion that Manigault's whole division would be inadequate for the work. Manigault wrote that he did not linger to hear more, but galloped back to his command, "and was giving some last instructions to several officers," when General Anderson's adjutant general rode up "in great haste, and informed me that the General countermanded the order, and that the troops would return to their quarters. There was a general sigh of relief," continued Manigault, "and many a 'Thank God!' . . . as the order was extended, and the different regiments dismissed for the night. There was scarcely an officer or man," the general concluded, "who did not regard himself as saved . . . from death, injury, or a Yankee prison." Manigault credited Colonel Barr with having spared him and his command.[22]

Not surprisingly, there is no mention of this episode in the *War of the Rebellion* records. A number of Confederate After Action Reports never appeared in the publication, including J. Patton Anderson's, Manigault's, and those of the other brigade commanders in the division. Manigault's report, a copy of which is in the P.K. Yonge Library of Florida History at the University of Florida, mentions nothing of this incident. Anderson's report, in the William P. Palmer Collection of the Western Reserve Historical Society, simply states: "General Manigault was directed to advance from his brigade, a force sufficient to retake the knobs, but while he was making necessary dispositions to execute the order, the project was abandoned by direction of the General commanding."

Manigault's detailed account of the affair in his memoirs is strongly compelling. His narrative, unlike so many, was written immediately after the war, when the events described were still fresh in his mind. He was a man of high character, and his memoirs where they can be checked, seem extraordinarily accurate. Also, his "track record" for military competency is impressive; but Anderson's is less so. Apparently, the episode is one more example of how the Confederates, throughout the campaign, were prone to blunder.

8

Tell Cleburne We Are To Fight

Hindsight provides the historian with a seemingly invincible tool for analyzing past events, especially when coupled with modern technology. General Sherman, of course, never examined Missionary Ridge from a Boeing 727 at twenty thousand feet on a clear day. Looking northeast as the plane passes south of Chattanooga on its route from Atlanta to Nashville, flying at a comfortable pace for observing the terrain, the historian can readily appreciate Sherman's problem in attacking the right flank of the Confederate Army. The northern extremity of Missionary "Ridge," near the Tennessee River, actually is not a ridge at all; rather it has expanded from the thin, rugged line that characterizes most of its length to a confusing eruption of eminences and hilly outcroppings. Little wonder that Sherman at first did not find the main force of the enemy. Storming up a knoll unoccupied except for Rebel pickets, the Yankee infantry then discovered that the Confederates were entrenched on another rise farther to the south, the real northern end of the ridge, called Tunnel Hill.

The Union commanders should not be blamed for lack of reconnaissance. On November 16, Sherman, Grant, Thomas, and Smith had all viewed the general area where the attack was to be made, although, for security against detection, their observation post was a long distance from the ridge. In his memoirs, Sherman described how they "got on a hill overlooking the whole ground about the mouth of the Chickamauga . . . and across to the Missionary Hills near the Tunnel. Smith and I crept down behind a fringe of trees that lines the river-bank, . . . where we sat for some time, seeing the rebel pickets on the opposite bank, and almost hearing their words."[1] Having carefully studied the terrain, Sherman then shut his long glass with a snap, turned to Smith, and confidently said, "I can do it!"[2]

From their vantage point on the north side of the Tennessee, it would have been very difficult, probably impossible, to determine that the ridge was not continuous and that a series of knobs existed just south of the river, separated from Tunnel Hill by a steep-sided ravine. The only maps Sherman possessed were faulty and showed the ridge to be continuous. Amid the many uncertainties of war, this mistaken concept of terrain is hardly surprising.[3]

Sherman's planning and execution of the river crossing were excellent. After initial delays in bringing his troops from Bridgeport—caused in part by torrential rain and bad roads and in part by the general's questionable decision to move the supply trains in the rear of each division as usual, rather than sending all the soldiers and artillery first—Sherman sent one division marching up Lookout Valley to threaten the Confederates' southern flank, while with his other three divisions he set out for the real objective on the northern flank and disappeared behind the hills west and north of Chattanooga. Although his main movement, as feared, was observed by Rebels atop Lookout Mountain, the Confederates also thought Sherman had reappeared from behind the hills when they mistook troops reinforcing Thomas, which had crossed the river directly to Chattanooga, as belonging to the Army of the Tennessee.[4]

By evening of November 23, Sherman's troops were well concealed in the woods near the Tennessee River, eating supper while their general inspected the one hundred and sixteen pontoon boats constructed by his one-time law partner, Dan McCook, now colonel of the Fifty-second Ohio Infantry. Hidden near the mouth of the North Chickamauga Creek, which emptied into the Tennessee about seven or eight miles northeast of Chattanooga, the crude boats would carry thirty men each—ready to cross the Tennessee by surprise if possible, by force if necessary. They would land near the mouth of South Chickamauga Creek, which flowed into the Tennessee some four miles below their starting point.[5]

Captain S.H.M. Byers, Fiftieth Iowa Infantry, was one of the Yankees waiting to make the crossing. "No fires or lights were permitted and no noises allowed," recalled the captain. "We were at supper when the order came to row over the river and assault at midnight." Thereupon, Byers said, he laid down his knife and fork and stopped eating. "A strange sensation came over me," he continued. "Yes, we had seen fighting, but . . . something told me that . . . some calamity was in store for me." Pondering his personal fate while thinking about the mission that he and the others would soon attempt, Byers stated that "the critical situation and the vast consequences dependent upon success or failure were known to us all as we lay in the shadows that evening, waiting . . . to move over the dark river and assault the heights of Missionary Ridge."[6]

Midnight came. The crossing began with Sherman first sending a single boat of thirty men dropping swiftly with the current, their oarsmen pulling for the other side of the Tennessee. Silently and safely across, these soldiers got in behind the Rebel pickets, surprising and capturing them. Explained Captain Byers: "The boys, crossing above [where the main force crossed] and calling out the 'relief,' deceived and captured all but one." But Byers, and hundreds of other Federals, did not know of this success when they began quietly filing into the pontoon boats about 2 A.M., and they wondered if the enemy would open fire as they neared the opposite bank.[7]

"Be prompt as you can, boys; there's room for thirty in a boat," said a slim man who stood nearby on the bank in the darkness. The encouragement, in a hushed voice, came from Sherman. Some troops were startled when they realized that the general was right beside them.[8]

Within fifteen minutes a thousand or more Yankees were afloat in the swift current, striking for the Rebels' side of the Tennessee. In the middle of the river some soldiers were aware of a boat heading for the north bank, but in the darkness most probably did not realize that it carried the captured Confederate pickets. In thirty minutes or less, hundreds of Federals were scrambling up the bank on the opposite side of the Tennessee, creeping along through the thickets with a spade in one hand and a rifle in the other. In the darkness and the still of the night, they wondered what might happen at any moment. As word spread that a Rebel picket had escaped, they spent anxious, sleepless hours, many expecting the Confederates, in force, to suddenly open fire.[9]

It was not to be. Except for the captured pickets, there were not any Rebels near the Federal crossing. Both above and below the mouth of South Chickamauga, Union soldiers landed unopposed, rapidly entrenching their position as they had been instructed. A steamer named *Dunbar*, seized and repaired downriver, came up from Chattanooga and was soon aiding in ferrying more men across from the north side of the Tennessee.[10]

By daylight of a gloomy, overcast morning, much of the apprehension of the Federal troops had been relieved. Already numbering several thousand, the force steadily continued to swell, as the thuds and clinks of spades signalled the lengthening and improvement of a mile-long line of rifle pits. "An old Quaker came down to expostulate with us for ruining his farm by such digging," remembered a Yankee. "The scene was ludicrous, and the boys gave a derisive little cheer for 'Broad-brim.' " By noon a pontoon bridge, 1,350 feet in length, planned and constructed under the immediate supervision of General William F. Smith, was in place, and the remainder of Sherman's troops came across the river in a short time. A pontoon bridge had been built at the same time over the South Chickamauga, near its mouth, and this bridge provided communication with the two regiments on the north side of the creek. Sherman was profuse in extolling this engineering achievement: "I have never beheld any work done so quietly, so well, and I doubt if the history of war can show a bridge of that extent . . . laid down so noiselessly and well in so short of time. I attribute it to the genius and intelligence of General William F. Smith."[11]

Three divisions strong, Sherman now moved to the attack. The time was about one o'clock. The Yankee formation, advancing in a drizzling mist, had Brigadier General Morgan L. Smith's division leading on the left, its flank covered by South Chickamauga Creek (hereafter referred to simply as Chickamauga Creek); next in line to the right came Brigadier General John E. Smith's center division, which was echeloned back, as was also Brigadier General Hugh Ewing's division on the far right. Opposed only by outposts from Pat Cleburne's division, the Federals' cautious movement met slight resistance. According to the estimate of a Yankee soldier, the Confederates were only 200 or 300 strong and "retired hastily and in some disorder. . . ." General Sherman, in his After Action Report, stated that his "skirmishers crept up the face of the hill, followed by their supports, and at 3:30 P.M. we gained, with no loss, the desired point."[12]

16. General William T. Sherman. *Library of Congress.*

In actual fact, Sherman had gained two high points, neither being the "desired point," Tunnel Hill, which he soon discovered was separated from his three divisions by a deep ravine. Instead of pushing on to the tunnel, however, Sherman ordered his troops to halt and entrench for the night. At that moment, General Cleburne had only a part of one Rebel brigade, Brigadier General James A. Smith's Texas command, entrenching between Sherman and the tunnel. Sherman has sometimes been harshly criticized—"the blunder of the battle," proclaimed one general—for calling a halt to his advance.[13]

Perhaps Sherman was wise not to push farther. Undoubtedly, he could have so contended, with well-reasoned, impressive arguments. First, of course, he was not aware that the enemy confronted him with only a portion of a brigade. As far as he knew, the tunnel might be strongly held, a possibility that may have seemed more likely after a firefight on the Yankee flank. "The enemy felt our left flank about 4 P.M.," Sherman reported, "and a pretty smart engagement with artillery and muskets ensued. . . ." Judging from Cleburne's report, Sherman exaggerated the intensity of this flank affair.[14] Sherman, however, contended that "cost us dear, for General Giles A. Smith was severely wounded and . . . the command of the brigade devolved on Colonel [Nathan] W. Tupper. . . ."[15]

Sherman's position then lay approximately one and a quarter miles from Tunnel Hill. On a short November day darkness came soon after four-thirty, and it seemed even earlier on this day, which was heavily overcast, with rain falling sharply at times. The distance, elements, and time made it impossible to arrive at the tunnel much before dark. If the Confederates, in strength, did attack his right flank, which would be nearly two miles from the support of General Thomas's left flank, there was a possibility that Sherman's entire line might be rolled up and driven back against Chickamauga Creek, totally cut off from the rest of the Union army. If unmolested by the Rebels, to select a tactically sound position and entrench it in the dark would be difficult, although not impossible. Probably these would have been the considerations, some of them at least, weighing most heavily in Sherman's mind.

Nevertheless, the general's decision to stop for the night, to this author, seems highly questionable. Because Sherman's troops had been across the river in some force since early morning, their numbers steadily swelling throughout the day, and still the enemy had not attacked, this should have suggested to Sherman the possibility that

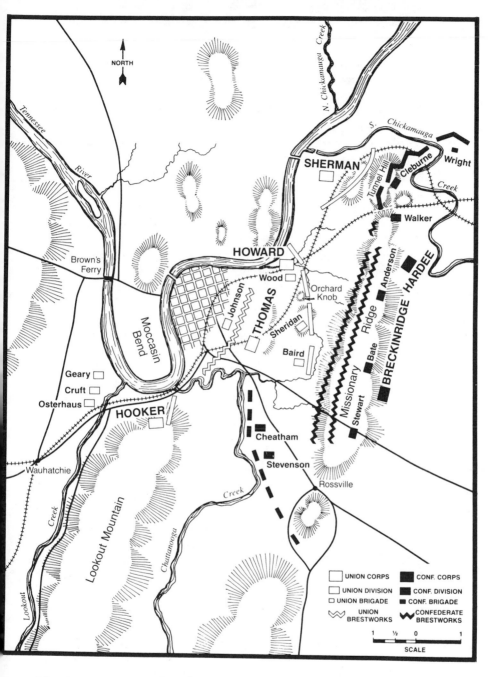

Map 4. Missionary Ridge: Sherman's Attack, Morning, November 25, 1863.
Map by J.L. Moon, Jr.

the Rebels were not present in strength. If he thought the enemy might be enticing him into a trap—and certainly a commander's alertness for this strategy is imperative—then an immediate reconnaissance in heavy force was Sherman's best move. If his worst fear, Confederate masses pouring down from the ridge, did materialize, he would still have a formidable command occupying high ground, well situated for repelling an attack. If, as was indeed the case, there were hardly anything to stop him, then, once atop the northern end of Missionary Ridge, the Union would have the Confederates in an untenable position.

Surprise, always one of the most important elements in war, had been with Sherman in crossing the river. But he was excessively cautious and failed to exploit this advantage to the fullest. Always war involves risk, and here the risk was minimal, while the possible gain would be decisive—securing, at little cost, the keypoint of the entire battle area.

While Sherman seems to have made the wrong decision in halting for the night, he also apparently misled General Grant, failing to make it clear that he was not on Tunnel Hill. That evening Grant wrote to Thomas, saying: "General Sherman carried Missionary Ridge as far as the tunnel, with only slight skirmishing. His right now rests at the tunnel and on top of the hill; his left at Chickamauga Creek."[16]

Actually, Cleburne's Confederates, not Sherman's Federals, were trudging rapidly into position above the tunnel. Ironically, they were coming, in part, because of Grant's actions the previous day.

On the morning of November 23, upon Bragg's order, Cleburne had been at Chickamauga Station, in process of transporting by rail both his own and Simon Buckner's division (now commanded by Bushrod Johnson) to reinforce Longstreet at Knoxville. By noon most of Johnson's division, except for A.W. Reynolds's brigade, was entrained and rolling along the Western and Atlantic road toward Loudon. But when Grant sent Thomas's Army of the Cumberland snappily marching out to occupy Orchard Knob, Bragg became convinced that the Union army was about to give battle. Also, apparently for the first time, the Confederate commander was seriously concerned for the security of his northern flank rather than for the southern. At once Bragg sent a dispatch to Cleburne, stating that his front had been attacked and ordering an immediate halt to the movement of reinforcements for Longstreet.[17]

In fact, Cleburne received three quick dispatches, commanding him to "move up rapidly" to army headquarters with whatever troops were at hand, while instructing that those already on the trains be stopped at Charleston. Reporting in person at Bragg's headquarters, Cleburne was ordered to place his troops as a reserve behind Missionary Ridge in the rear of the army's right center. There they remained through the night. Late in the morning of November 24, Bragg learned that Sherman had crossed the river. Cleburne reported, "General Bragg informed me that the enemy had crossed the Tennessee River, both above and below the mouth of the Chickamauga, and directed me to send a brigade and a battery to the East Tennessee & Georgia railroad bridge over the Chickamauga to guard that point." The bridge, representing a line of retreat, had to be held, as Bragg later said, "at all hazards." Cleburne sent Lucius E. Polk's brigade and Henry C. Semple's battery to do the job.[18]

It was sometime between two and three o'clock in the afternoon before General Bragg did anything more about the threat on his northern flank. Then he instructed Cleburne to hurry to the right with his three remaining brigades and batteries and seize the rising ground near the mouth of the Chickamauga. One of Hardee's staff officers, said Bragg, would be waiting near the tunnel and show Cleburne the position.

Galloping forward ahead of his command, Cleburne soon found Major D. H. Poole of Hardee's staff, only to be appalled when he learned what was expected of his three brigades. Hardee wanted Cleburne to occupy a detached knoll north of the ridge with one brigade and with the remainder of his soldiers to stretch southward along Tunnel Hill all the way to the right of William H.T. Walker's division, located three-quarters of a mile south of the tunnel. Quickly realizing that his troops would be spread out for about two miles, Cleburne sent Major Poole to inform Hardee that he only had three brigades and could not cover such a long line.

Hardly had the staff officer departed when Cleburne received word from one of his signal corpsmen, Private Henry Smith, that the Yankees, in line of battle, were advancing on the detached hill north of the main ridge. The head of Cleburne's division, James A. Smith's Texas Brigade, had then just arrived, traversing much of the rugged ground at a double-quick pace. Cleburne at once attempted to beat the Federals to the detached ridge, sending Smith quickly toward the objective point. Too late by only a few minutes, General Smith, as he moved into the valley, was fired on from the hill, Sherman's Yankees having already crowned the top. Nothing remained for Smith to do except, as Cleburne had instructed in such event, pull back and form on top of Missionary Ridge north of the tunnel. Smith placed his two left regiments, one under Colonel Roger Q. Mills and the other under Colonel Hiram B. Granbury, on Mills's right, facing the detached ridge, while Major William A. Taylor's regiment lay on Granbury's right and was thrown back toward the east to protect the flank. All three regiments began to dig in.[19]

Just as at Stones River, where Bragg ignored a potential threat to his whole position—a hill on the northern flank—until the enemy had taken command of it, so again the Confederate commander was too late in appreciating the menace to his right flank posed by Yankee possession of the detached knoll north of Tunnel Hill.

Now Cleburne rode rapidly over the ground, quickly examining the complicated terrain in the fast-fading twilight and deciding upon his line of defense. Mark P. Lowrey's brigade was placed on the west face of the ridge, south of the tunnel. Immediately over the tunnel Cleburne positioned a battery of Napoleon guns under Lieutenant Thomas J. Key. Concerned for his right flank, and for Polk's isolated brigade at the bridge over Chickamauga Creek, Cleburne changed his first intention of positioning Daniel C. Govan's brigade on the left of Lowrey, which would have completed a continuous line southward to Walker's division. Instead, Govan's regiments were placed on a spur that jutts out from the eastern side of Missionary Ridge for a distance of about a thousand yards just north of the tunnel. Govan's skirmishers soon pushed out to their front and right until they reached Chickamauga Creek. Hardee arrived shortly to approve the line. Evidently Hardee also worried about the right flank. He shifted two of Lowrey's regiments and some artillery into position in rear of that flank and ordered the burning of a nearby bridge over the badly swollen Chickamauga.[20]

By then it had been dark for some time and Cleburne fully expected the army to fall back from the ridge. Having heard about "the disaster at Lookout," Cleburne's own choice of words in describing the Federal success earlier in the day on the mountain, the division commander knew that the weak Rebel southern flank was now in grave danger of being turned at the Rossville Gap through Missionary Ridge. That factor foremost, plus the imbalance of troops—the reduction of Bragg's force by detachments while Grant's numbers increased—plus the expected pressure against Cleburne's own position and outnumbered troops all dictated one course to Cleburne: a withdrawal beyond the Chickamauga. "Accordingly," the general reported, "I had sent my ordnance and artillery across that river, with the exception of the two pieces of cannon planted beyond my right flank."[21]

But time passed and no withdrawal order came. Cleburne's apprehension mounted steadily. Finally, about nine o'clock, unable to restrain his anxiety, Cleburne turned to Captain Irving A. Buck, his assistant adjutant general. As Buck remembered it, Cleburne said: "Go at once to General Hardee's quarters, ask what has been determined upon, and say that if it is decided to fight it is necessary that I should get my artillery into position."[22]

Reaching corps headquarters, Buck learned that General Hardee had been summoned to a council of war at Bragg's quarters. Tramping still farther along the ridge, the captain reached Bragg's headquarters before the council adjourned and in time to hear General Breckinridge, who Buck thought had urged strongly that the army stand its ground and fight, remark, "I never felt more like fighting than when I saw those people shelling my troops off Lookout today."[23]

Cleburne had guessed wrong. "Tell Cleburne we are to fight," General Hardee said to Captain Buck; "that his division will undoubtedly be heavily attacked, and that he must do his very best." Perhaps Buck felt that the last admonition was unnecessary. Whatever he thought, the captain wrote that he replied, "the division had never yet failed to clear its front, and would do so again." In company with Hardee, he then rode north along the ridge's crest, noting, in the stillness of the night, the sparse campfires burning low along the rifle-pits at the western base. Remarking about the thinness of the line, and the possibility that the Yankees might assault the Confederate center, Buck noted that Hardee "observed that the natural strength of the position would probably deter such an attempt; and that the enemy had been massing on the flanks, where the heaviest work was to be expected."[24]

About midnight Buck returned to Cleburne with his report. The division commander wasted no time. "I now ordered my artillery and ordnance to join me at daylight," Cleburne reported, "sent to my train for the axes belonging to the division in order to throw up some defenses, and rode out myself to make a moonlight survey of the ground and line of retreat."[25]

The additional reconnaissance was not without reward. Cleburne discovered a hill on the north bank of the Chickamauga, between his right flank and the railroad bridge, which he said "completely commanded my line of retreat." He ordered Polk to send two of his regiments and a section of artillery to occupy the hill at once. And he was soon making some other adjustments in the positioning of his troops. The night was abnormally dark and somber due to an eclipse of the moon. There were soldiers who saw this as an evil omen, but Cleburne's only mention of the eclipse involved the delay it caused him: "I was determined to construct a slight [defensive] work in front of my line," he wrote. "I was prevented for some time by an eclipse of the moon, which rendered the morning very dark, but at length, distributing our few axes, we went to work."[26]

The thirty-five-year-old general from County Cork, Ireland, once a British soldier, already had proved he was unsurpassed as a division commander in the Confederate Army. Energetically and characteristically, he prepared to demonstrate that fact yet again.

While Cleburne worked to strengthen the Rebel position, across the valley in the Yankee camp some of the soldiers seemed strangely enamored by a certain glamor with which, in the darkness, they imagined themselves somehow associated. "Pickets were thrown out and skirmish firing was kept up until late into the night," wrote Edwin Payne of the Thirty-fourth Illinois Infantry. "The positions of these two lines were such that the flash of the guns from both sides was plainly visible from our camp. It was a unique and romantic sight. . . . Our whole camp remained outside of quarters long into the night, thrilled with the awful glory of the spectacle."[27]

9

This Feat Will Be Celebrated

Eight miles away on the far right, southwest across Chattanooga and the Moccasin Bend of the Tennessee River—while Sherman's army attempted to gain a lodgment on the Rebel northern flank—another and different kind of action had been progressing, under the direction of Major General Joseph H. "Fighting Joe" Hooker. Disappointed with his original battle role to merely hold Lookout Valley and "make a demonstration" against Lookout Mountain while Sherman did the real attacking, the vibrant Hooker was elated by Grant's change of plan late on November 23. High water had broken the pontoon bridge at Brown's Ferry, and Brigadier General Peter J. Osterhaus's division, unable to join up with Sherman, had been ordered to report to Hooker in Lookout Valley. With this additional strength, Hooker was then instructed to take the point of Lookout Mountain if he could, preparatory to descending into Chattanooga Valley east of the mountain.

The result, on the misty, fog-enshrouded slope of Lookout, popularly would be called "the Battle Above the Clouds." Apparently it was Brigadier General Montgomery C. Meigs, efficient, practical, quartermaster general of the Union Army, who, observing the scene from Orchard Knob, first designated the struggle by that romantic name.[1] The title appealed so much to the soldiers and the press that it became permanent. Critics have often scoffed, pointing out that no fighting took place on top of the mountain, or that there were no clouds to fight above.[2] Perhaps some have been too cynical. A murky, gloomy curtain of weather did enclose the mountain during the day, making most of the fighting invisible to those who watched from afar. Glenn Tucker contributed a sensible summation, writing, "since a fog is merely a low-lying cloud, and since the fog shrouded the mountainside, the title, one of the most renowned of the war, was not altogether a fantasy. . . ."[3] Whether history or fantasy, "the Battle Above the Clouds" involved hard work, heavy skirmishing, and, for some of the thousands who participated, bleeding and death.

"On some fine morning General Hooker is going to take Lookout," had been a standing joke in the Union camps for a long time, related a Federal soldier in the Sixtieth Regiment of New York State Volunteers. "No one regarded it as anything more than a joke," he continued, since the mountain was considered impregnable.[4] But now, suddenly, that morning—and certainly it was not so fine—had come. At daylight, November 24, the Yankees were forming in line with one day's rations, blankets, and sixty rounds of ammunition to make an attack on Lookout. Many could hardly believe the order. "The men had not breakfasted," wrote a soldier in the One Hundred and Forty-ninth New York, "and this announcement took away their appetites."[5]

The troops marshalling for battle under Hooker's command were more than 10,000 strong; interestingly, they consisted of one division from each of the three armies on the field at Chattanooga. "We were all strangers," according to General Hooker, "no one division ever having seen either of the others."[6] The key role in the attack, not surprisingly, was given to Hooker's own Army of the Potomac division, led by Brigadier General John W. Geary, whose men had fought on Culp's Hill at Gettysburg and, more recently, of course, in the struggle at Wauhatchie, so important to the maintenance of the Union supply line and a consequent reversal of martial momentum. Geary had three brigades in his division, led by Colonels Charles Candy, George A. Cobham, Jr., and David Ireland. The division was reinforced by Brigadier General Walter C. Whitaker's brigade of Charles Cruft's division, Army of the Cumberland. Whitaker's brigade was quite large and mustered almost as many troops as Geary's entire division. The remainder of Cruft's division (Colonel William Grose's brigade) would come on the ground just a little later in the morning, accompanying Hooker's third division, which was Osterhaus's unit from the Army of the Tennessee. Late in the day Brigadier General William P. Carlin's brigade would also be sent to Hooker, crossing Chattanooga Creek near its mouth.

The terrain confronting Hooker's command was the dominant feature of the whole region. For miles in any direction nothing compared with rugged, steep, heavily timbered Lookout Mountain, topped at the northern end by a rocky, almost sheer cliff. At the cliff base, approximately halfway up the mountain, was a plateau of arable land, farmed by Robert Cravens, a man who had built a comfortable house on the site, with a view overlooking Moccasin Bend of the Tennessee River. In the vicinity of the Cravens house would occur the most severe fighting of the battle.[7] The Confederates were holding Lookout Mountain to guard against an enemy approach from Trenton. Sherman, in fact, had sent Ewing's division toward the town earlier as a diversion; the division rejoined his command, of course, before the attack on the northern end of Missionary Ridge.[8]

About eight o'clock in the morning, Hooker sent Geary's division, supported by Whitaker's brigade, up the valley on the west side of Lookout Creek. Crossing the railroad at Wauhatchie Junction, these troops massed behind a hill, further screened from view by a heavy mist, and suddenly appeared two and a half miles from the mouth of the creek, quickly overpowering the Rebel pickets. More than forty Confederates were captured, and the Yankees were soon across the creek in strength. Geary then climbed the mountain until the head of his column reached the base of the cliff. Turning north, the division proceeded horizontally along the western slope toward the point of the mountain, and in the general direction of the Cravens house. Cobham's brigade was on the right, hugging the side of the mountain, with Ireland's in the center, Candy's on the left, and Whitaker's in support to the rear. Even if unopposed, the Yankees had undertaken no easy job, scrambling and climbing over and around ravines, ledges, and boulders on a treacherous slope. Whitaker reported that the advance "over the steep, rocky, ravine-seamed, torrent-torn sides of the mountain" became "laborious and extremely toilsome."[9]

While Geary climbed the mountain, Cruft's other brigade, under Colonel William Grose, seized a bridge over Lookout Creek, only about a mile from its mouth. Crossing with Osterhaus's division, these Federals faced a sharp skirmish with Rebel defenders. But, far outnumbered, the Confederates soon retreated up the mountain. The three Union divisions were moving to join on a common line, with

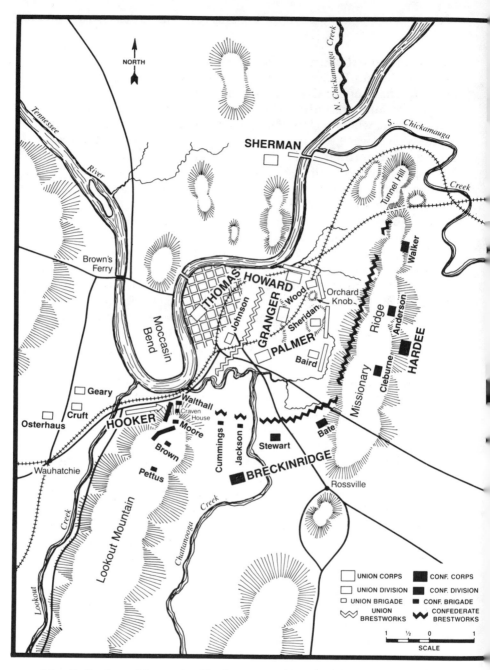

Map 5. Lookout Mountain: Hooker's Attack, November 24, 1863. *Map by J.L. Moon, Jr.*

the objective, in Geary's words, of "sweeping every Rebel from [the mountain]."[10]

Artillery supported the advance. Two batteries fired from a low-lying ridge west of Lookout Creek, at a range of less than three-fourths of a mile. Two pieces were firing from a position closer to the Tennessee River. And across the river, Union batteries on Moccasin Point were also firing in support of the Yankee troops.[11]

Clearly the Rebels were taken by surprise. Atop the mountain a Confederate, recently returned from North Alabama and a visit with his wife—interestingly, a woman whom he had courted several years ago on Lookout—walked to the point in the early morning, watching the Yankee cannons firing from Moccasin Bend. His name was Robert D. Jamison, Company D, Forty-fifth Tennessee Infantry, and he and his companions mirrored the lack of preparation among the Confederate defenders. Amused by the cannon shots which did not reach to the mountain top, "we would holla [sic] to them," Jamison said, "to 'put in more powder,' and other ludicrous remarks. . . . We were enjoying the fun of our fancied security, when suddenly we heard the rattle of small arms. . . ." At once ordered to arms, Jamison claimed that "a number of our men were drunk, or pretended to be," from whiskey which had been sold to them by a member of Company I.[12]

The Confederates had a lot of problems, not the least of which was being outnumbered about four or five to one. Walker's division had recently left to strengthen the Missionary Ridge position. Also, command responsibility for the defense of Lookout had been shifted to Major General Carter L. Stevenson, Lieutenant General Hardee being ordered to the right flank of the Confederate army. Stevenson took over after dark on the evening of November 23, and his After Action Report well summarizes his difficulties: "Having thus . . . been placed in command at night, at a most critical period, over a wing of the army, with whose position and disposition . . . I had enjoyed no opportunity of making myself acquainted, I at once used every exertion to gain the necessary information by sending every officer of my staff and devoting the whole night myself to riding over and examining the lines." However, Stevenson concluded (and anyone who has tramped around on Lookout Mountain, even in the daytime, can well imagine that the general's statement is no exaggeration), "the distance and the . . . situation" were "most unfavorable for personal observation. . . ." Obviously, Stevenson was inadequately prepared to exercise command when the battle began the next morning.[13]

Still another problem plagued the Rebels. Once the fight was underway, according to the reports of three brigade commanders, Edward C. Walthall, John C. Moore, and Edmund W. Pettus, all of whom were heavily involved, the division commander, Brigadier General John K. Jackson, contributed nothing beyond sending messages that the Confederate "position must be held."[14] Some of the time he could not even be found by staff officers, and apparently he spent much of the day safely atop the mountain. True, he was in command of an improvised division composed for the emergency, but this hardly justified Jackson's conduct.

The Confederates, even with the reduced number available, plus the other difficulties, made a much tougher fight than might have been expected under the circumstances. Facing west and north, they had a line of log and stone breastworks constructed at the same elevation as the Cravens house. If one were standing atop the mountain, at the point and looking down, the left flank of the Rebel position could have been seen extending several hundred yards, perhaps a quarter of a mile or more, to the left (or south) of the point. This line of defensive works was held by Brigadier General Edward C. Walthall's brigade, about 1,500 strong, and reached, on the right flank, to the vicinity of the Cravens house. To Walthall's right, and situated slightly below the Cravens farm elevation, was Brigadier General John C. Moore's brigade, approximately 1,200 strong. Continuing the Confederate line to the right, Moore's troops extended around the mountain's northern base to the eastern slope. The Confederates had a second line of prepared defenses about four hundred yards east of the Cravens house, upon which they could retire if enemy pressure became too great. Walthall's and Moore's troops, bearing the brunt of the battle, would receive no reinforcements until well past one o'clock in the afternoon.[15]

On top of the mountain were two brigades, commanded by Brigadier Generals Edmund W. Pettus and John C. Brown. At the bottom of the mountain's eastern slope were Brigadiers Cumming's and Jackson's brigades, neither of which would see action in the Lookout Mountain fight. The battle was underway for a long time before anything resembling a coordinated defensive effort on the part of the Rebel brigades could be achieved. Efficient command control under an energetic division leader was simply nonexistent.

The sudden Federal advance across Lookout Creek began with a big "bag" of Confederate pickets. Both Moore and Walthall had a large number of their total force on the picket line (over a third of Walthall's brigade). Moore's pickets were strung out, right to left, from the mouth of Chattanooga Creek on the east to Lookout Creek on the west, where Walthall's men continued the sentinel line leftward along the east bank of Lookout Creek to the railroad bridge. There the line went up the mountainside to the plateau. Each brigade's picket line covered more than a mile. Although the Confederates had spotted portions of Geary's Federal column moving up Lookout Valley in the early morning, the dense fog made any estimate of numbers highly speculative. And many of the pickets had spotted nothing, totally surprised as Geary's command swept in on them from the south. When the right wing of Geary's division (Cobham's brigade) reached the plateau beneath the point of the mountain, that unit stopped while the center and left kept advancing, swinging around the northern base of Lookout on a wide swath that resulted in the capture of a large number of Walthall's pickets. One who escaped claimed that he jumped off two ledges, each nearly twenty feet high, in his dash for freedom.[16]

As the left of Geary's division came around, it connected with the right of Osterhaus's division, supported by Grose's brigade. The advance of these Union forces, having crossed Lookout Creek closer to its mouth at the Tennessee, prolonged Geary's line on the lower slope, moving it along the Chattanooga road at the base of the mountain. Their angle of attack, while also sweeping up some of Walthall's pickets, fell upon even larger numbers of Moore's outposts. One of the Rebels fortunate enough to escape said that the pickets' "first intimation . . . of the presence of the enemy . . . was their appearance in force on the side of the mountain" to the rear. General Moore reported that most of his pickets were captured, placing the number at 225.[17]

Confederate gun crews on the summit of the mountain at first contested the advance of the greatly superior Union force with well-directed fire. But soon, as the range decreased, the artillery pieces could not be depressed sufficiently to avoid overshooting their targets. Then the gunners lighted the fuses of their shells and hurled them over the side of the mountain. Beyond minor annoyance, however, this effort accomplished little. On the other hand, the Union batteries were laying down a destructive artillery barrage along the line of General Walthall's brigade, first primarily with the guns west of Lookout Creek, supported by those north of the Ten-

17. Moccasin Bend from the top of Lookout Mountain. *Chickamauga-Chattanooga National Military Park.*

nessee; later, as the Rebels gave ground, fire from the latter became the most effective.[18]

The weight of the Yankee attack, of course, went against Walthall's single brigade, which blocked the narrow passage around the northern face of the mountain. The greatest pressure, both initially and continuously, was applied to his left flank. Falling back slowly and fighting over the rocks and ravines, "with the hope," Walthall later reported, "that support (for which I had sent to General Moore) might reach me," Walthall tried to strengthen his left flank with sharpshooters. He ordered the colonel of the Twenty-fourth Mississippi, William F. Dowd, to deploy four companies of sharpshooters several hundred yards to the rear and up the slope of the mountain. Union reports indicate these Rebels were a factor with which the Yankees had to reckon.[19]

The Confederates fought stubbornly; however, Walthall had no support, and the Federals were advancing along the entire length of his brigade, threatening to envelop the right flank as well as the left. Once, according to the reports of Walthall and Dowd, the Yankee front line was severely punished, wavering and even falling back. But soon it re-formed, moving "steadily and irresistibly forward," admitted Walthall, "pressing heaviest upon my extreme left."[20]

Again the Rebels retreated, this time back beyond the position of their sharpshooters. "The enemy were within ten paces of us," related William Dowd, "when the order was given to fall back. When I reached the line occupied by the sharpshooters of Captain [J.D.] Smith, nothing but a handful of the companies of Captain [M.M.] Rowan and Captain [J.W.] Ward were left, the most of them having been killed, wounded, or captured." This Confederate account seems to confirm that General Geary's sometimes flamboyant report hardly exaggerated when, speaking of his successful advance, the general explained that, "keeping my right firm against the . . . mountain . . . whenever the center attacked the enemy in front, my right was continually on his flank, and outflanked, with withering enfilading fire, his every position, which . . . compelled him to yield . . . as long as we continued to advance."[21]

By twelve-thirty or one o'clock, Walthall's men had been driven back some four hundred yards east of the Cravens house, taking position in a portion of the line of works there prepared. The fog was very dense, making it "almost impossible," remarked General Pettus, "to distinguish any object at a distance of 100 yards." Now

General Moore's brigade began arriving to reinforce Walthall, although Moore was unable to see Walthall's men, located off somewhere to his left. Approaching the entrenchments, Moore was astonished to see Federal troops already occupying a part of the trenches. Fighting furiously to drive the Yankees back, Moore continued, "We were thus compelled to enter the entrenchments under the fire of the enemy in front and a very heavy fire from the Moccasin Point batteries within short range." Nevertheless, Moore's brigade seized and held the ground.[22]

Finally, Edmund Pettus's brigade, coming down from the mountain top, arrived on the scene. According to the brigadier's account, the time was twelve-thirty when he received the order to move his command to the site of battle. His brigade thus could not have gone into action until almost an hour later. Coming down the mountain, Pettus said, he "found Brigadier General Jackson at the point where the road to the Craven [sic] house leaves the road leading down the mountain" and was directed to reinforce the troops fighting at the Cravens house. By then, unknown to Jackson of course, the Rebels had already been driven back east of the house. Upon reaching Walthall's command, Pettus suddenly found himself in the midst of a furious fight, complicated by a pall of acrid gunsmoke and fog. Walthall greated him with the appalling news "that he had lost a large part of his command; that his ammunition was nearly exhausted, and that he could not hold the position. . . ."[23]

Relieving Walthall's brigade at once, Pettus's men quickly became engaged in a fierce firefight with the Federals trying to press their advance. As soon as his brigade was positioned, Pettus sent a staff officer to the right, groping through the fog to locate General Moore's brigade. When Pettus at last ascertained that Moore's left flank lay about a hundred and fifty yards off to the right, he then "extended intervals to the right so as to connect with his line." For the first time in the battle, a Rebel line of two brigades had been joined up. "These facts were communicated by me to Brigadier General Jackson," reported Pettus, "with the request that he would come forward, look at the line, and give us orders. . . ." Jackson, according to Pettus, did not come, but "sent orders that the position must be held."[24]

Certainly Pettus and Moore were trying to hold their ground, and in the face of repeated Yankee assaults, characterized, so General Geary said, by "an animation that disdained restraint. . . ." The

Federal commander added, "the ardor of our men surprised . . . the enemy, and we punished him severely. . . ." Evidently Geary's account was not all braggadocio. Rebel General Moore's After Action Report described "the enemy repeatedly charging, but repulsed, two of their color bearers being shot down by our men in the trenches while attempting to plant their colors on the embankment. I have never before seen them fight with such daring and desperation."[25]

The Federals were pushing all along the Confederate front, especially, as all through the day, against the Rebel left at the base of the mountain cliff. Moore's brigade was weak, and many of his soldiers were low on ammunition. Again, the worried Pettus sent a staff officer to request help from his division commander. So, too, did General Moore. The latter's aide returned saying that he could not find Jackson. Pettus's staff officer, Captain [John S.] Smith, located Jackson atop the mountain, reportedly conferring with General Stevenson about the best way to withdraw. The message he sent to Pettus was to hold his position "as long as possible."[26]

Meanwhile, General Walthall had re-formed the remnant of his brigade, resupplied it with ammunition, and returned to the fight, taking position to reinforce the critical left flank. Obviously, something had to be done to neutralize Union pressure on that flank if the Confederates were going to maintain their ground. At Walthall's suggestion, Pettus said, he detailed the Twentieth Alabama Regiment with orders to press forward and upward on the left. The mission was to control the higher ground at the bluff, from which the Federals were firing with good effect. "Promptly and in gallant style" is how Pettus described the advance of the Twentieth Alabama, as they scrambled forward, drove the enemy back, occupied the higher ground, and held it throughout the remainder of the battle.[27]

At last the Rebel position had been stabilized. Although General Jackson remained atop the mountain, the Confederates carried out his instruction to "hold the position as long as possible," maintaining it all afternoon, and, in the words of Walthall, "until long after nightfall." Walthall only fell back then, after being relieved by another brigade. His After Action Report evidences a distinct bitterness: "At no time during this prolonged struggle, . . . did I have the benefit of my division commander's personal presence. . . . After I was relieved, and while awaiting orders to move, I saw him for the first time on his way, as he told me, to see the general-in-chief."[28]

The deep feelings of General Walthall did not subside easily. He, along with Pettus and Moore, was openly critical of Jackson's conduct in the days and weeks following the battle. Upon the appearance of their reports, Jackson, perhaps unusually sensitive because of critics dubbing him "Mudwall," in contradistinction to the late "Stonewall" Jackson, began a fiery correspondence with the brigade commanders, particularly Walthall. For a time, the possibility of a duel—or even several duels—seemed not unlikely. Major General W.H.T. Walker, at first sympathetic with Jackson, reportedly advised that general to "Call them out, sir! Call them out!"—apparently meaning that Jackson should challenge all three in turn. As Walker learned more of the situation, however, his ardor for Jackson to fight duels seemed to cool. At last he was advising Jackson to "drop the matter," which ultimately was the solution.[29]

About two o'clock in the morning of November 25, while the brigadiers brooded, all the Confederate forces on Lookout Mountain, as well as those in Chattanooga Valley, were withdrawn to defend Missionary Ridge. Whether the Rebels could have maintained their position on the mountain that long if Hooker had chosen to keep driving is a moot point. After about four o'clock in the afternoon of 24 November, with ammunition running short and Chattanooga Valley obscured by the darkness of an approaching storm, the Union general thought it best, except for a few patrols sent out to annoy the Rebels, to rest his men for the next day.

It was a miserable night on the mountain slopes. Men were wet from the storm and the wind was very cold. Weary soldiers and heavily laden pack mules toiled up and down over the ragged rocks and fallen timber, replenishing empty cartridge boxes and hungry stomachs as well. As the men prepared for another strenuous day of fighting, bivouac fires burned brightly, revealing to the rest of the army in front of Missionary Ridge the extent of Hooker's progress on the mountain.

Anticipating that the enemy would be gone by morning, Hooker went to the front early. Details from several regiments were dispatched to scale the cliffs and take the peak of Lookout. Of course it was not known for sure that the Confederates were gone, and volunteers were requested for the bold undertaking. From the Eighth Kentucky Regiment six men volunteered. The soldiers who climbed soon became competitors for the honor of planting their regimental flag atop Lookout Rock. "To the Eighth Kentucky," reported a triumphant General Hooker, "must belong the distinction of having been foremost to

18. U.S. troops atop Lookout Mountain. *Harper's Weekly Magazine.*

reach the crest and at sunrise to display our flag from the peak of Lookout, amid the wild and prolonged cheers of the men whose dauntless valor had borne it to that point."[30]

The verbose and dramatic General Geary, whose After Action Report on the fight at Lookout Mountain covers eleven long pages in the *War of the Rebellion* records, was highly pleased with his part in the battle. To his wife, Geary wrote: "I have been the instrument of Almighty God . . . . I stormed what was considered the . . . inaccessible heights of Lookout Mountain. I captured it. . . . This feat will be celebrated until time shall be no more."[31]

General Grant was not so impressed. Later he said: "The battle of Lookout Mountain is one of the romances of the war. There was no such battle and no action even worthy to be called a battle on Lookout Mountain. It is all poetry."[32] Grant's appraisal is ungenerous, even unfair, to Hooker and his soldiers. While General Geary clearly exaggerated, he was closer to the truth, perhaps, than Grant. Navigation of the Tennessee River and control of the railway to Chattanooga were assured; more important, the entire Confederate line on Missionary Ridge was now in a very difficult position, and the Rebels probably should have retreated and never tried to defend it.

General Hooker certainly was piqued by Grant's failure to share the glory by giving him proper credit. He also resented the closeness of Sherman and Grant. Consequently, Hooker became as unfair toward Sherman as he thought Grant had been toward him. Writing a "confidential" letter to Secretary of the Treasury Salmon P. Chase, which was dated December 28, 1863, Hooker related: "You will perceive that the strategy and tactics of the campaign were to throw it into the hands of Sherman, to my exclusion . . . [Sherman's] attack on the left, after I had taken Lookout, which was well known to all the army, can only be considered in the light of a disaster. Sherman is an active, energetic officer, but in judgment is as infirm as Burnside. He will never be successful. Please remember what I tell you. It was natural for Grant to feel partial to his old companions, and do all in his power to enhance their renown. . . . He aimed for the battle to commence and end on the left, while it commenced and ended on the right. I am informed that he has since said, 'Damn the battle; I had nothing to do with it.' "[33]

10

Whiskey Was Not Enough

Wednesday morning, November 25, dawned hazy but soon turned clear and beautiful, a marked contrast to the previous day. General Grant, still holding to the chief feature of his plan, to hammer Bragg's right flank, sent orders that Sherman should attack at break of day. About seven o'clock Sherman pushed skirmishers forward and a heavy picket firing began, followed soon after by the lines and artillery. He did not launch a real attack, however, before ten or ten-thirty in the morning. Meanwhile, Cleburne noted with evident aggravation, heavy enemy fire on his working parties prevented the Confederates from erecting any defenses whatever in front of a battery on top of Tunnel Hill.[1]

Doubtless Cleburne's position was not developed to the general's total satisfaction. Nevertheless, working with Hardee, who had arrived about two or three in the morning for a second inspection, Cleburne had the Confederate troops, after a few more transfers and modifications of position, well distributed to make a determined defensive stand. General Hardee directed Cleburne to take his post at the tunnel, exercising command over everything in that vicinity, both to right and left.[2]

More Confederate soldiers were now at hand. Carter Stevenson's division, coming around from Lookout Mountain to take position on Cleburne's left, released two of Cleburne's regiments for deployment elsewhere. And, finally, Cleburne had fully grasped the ridge's confusing contour. Still worried that the Yankees would turn his right flank, he shifted Lowrey's two regiments from the west side of the ridge, near the tunnel, to a spur projecting from the ridge's east side. This spur was just north of the one already occupied by Govan's troops. Here Lowrey's men were reunited with the brigade's two other regiments, which had spent the night in rear of the division's right flank. The steep north side of this second spur, now held by Lowrey's entire brigade, was washed by Chickamauga Creek.

Cleburne had also readjusted James A. Smith's Texas brigade, positioning his three regiments higher, near the crest of the ridge, and changing the angles of their line. From Smith's left, which rested about one hundred and fifty yards north of the western entrance to the tunnel, Colonel Mills's regiment stretched northward nearly to the highest point of Tunnel Hill. On top of the hill Swett's Mississippi battery of four Napoleon guns, commanded by Lieutenant H. Shannon, was stationed. Next in line, continuing from left to right, were Colonel Granbury's Seventh Texas, with Major Taylor's regiment on Granbury's right flank. But, instead of continuing northward, the brigade's line, from Swett's battery at the hill's apex, angled sharply to the east. Thus Smith's flank was secured, the right side of his line thrown back to within about two hundred yards of Govan's brigade. This made each brigade close enough to assist the other if necessary.[3]

Artillery (Douglas's Texas battery, commanded by Lieutenant John H. Bingham) was strategically placed on Govan's line to rake the flank of any Federals charging the north front of Smith's brigade. And, with Lowrey's brigade holding the northern spur extending to the Chickamauga, complemented by Polk's regiments covering the high ground across the creek, as well as the railroad bridge to the rear, Cleburne's right flank was greatly strengthened. Over on his left flank—the ground now held by Stevenson's division—John C. Brown's brigade covered the area north of the tunnel, with Alfred Cumming's brigade next in line to Brown's left. The right flank of Cumming's command rested upon the top of the tunnel, from which his troops extended southward along the ridge toward Walker's division. All these Rebel troop dispositions were well conceived to gain full defensive advantage of the natural terrain on the north end of Missionary Ridge. The man primarily responsible for their selection was, of course, Pat Cleburne.[4]

Like Cleburne, General Sherman, who never seemed to sleep for long, had also been up early, beginning to examine the ground before sunrise. Moving from left to right, Sherman observed that "quite a valley" lay between the Federals and the Confederates atop Missionary Ridge. The sides of the ridge were steep, the west face only partially cleared and the rest covered with forest. The Union approach, for several hundred yards to the west side, would be across open fields before reaching the cover at the base of the ridge. As the battle developed, however, this open ground presented no major problem for the Union because Cleburne, wisely, had chosen not to contest seriously the Yankees' advance until they started scaling the ridge. Too, when the assault began, the batteries from Stevenson's division, which might have enfiladed the Federals by firing from sites on Cleburne's left, were still not in position.[5]

Launching the main attack on Tunnel Hill were two brigades of Brigadier General Hugh Ewing's division. "I guess, Ewing, if you're ready you might as well go ahead," Sherman reportedly said to his brother-in-law, between puffs of his cigar. "Keep up formation till you get to the foot of the hill," he continued. "And shall we keep it after that?" inquired Ewing. Pushing the division commander by the arm as he talked, Sherman responded that he might go up the hill "if you like—if you can"; but, Sherman cautioned, "don't call for help until you actually need it."[6]

As bugles sounded the advance, Ewing had Brigadier General John M. Corse's brigade in a center position, tramping straight toward the front of Tunnel Hill. On Corse's right flank was Colonel John M. Loomis's brigade, moving along the west base of Missionary Ridge toward the tunnel, supported by two brigades from Brigadier General John E. Smith's division following in the rear. Over on the Yankee left flank marched the division of Brigadier General Morgan L. Smith, hoping to move on the ridge's east base and cut the railroad line to Chickamauga station.[7]

Directly in the path of the mass of Federals advancing across the valley toward Tunnel Hill were Confederates from the Twenty-fourth Texas Cavalry (dismounted), led by Captain Samuel T. Foster. The men had been standing picket duty since three o'clock in the morning. Foster claimed that one of his men, as soon as it was light enough to see anything, had fired the first shot of the day aimed at a Yankee soldier. After several hours of brisk picket firing, Foster saw Corse's full Union brigade advancing in battle formation, preceded by a double line of skirmishers. "Fall back slowly," Foster said he instructed his pickets; "but keep firing from tree to tree as we fall back." Gradually retreating for perhaps three-quarters of a mile, the captain stated that "the Yankees pressed us very hard," and also, by this time, the Rebel pickets had discovered that their brigade was not where they had left it. Adding that during this prolonged retreat "we killed several [Yankees] that we could see fall," Foster and his pickets at last found Smith's Texas brigade high on the crest. Scrambling over the dirt and log entrenchments that had just been thrown up, they took their place in the line.[8]

Union artillery now played back and forth across the Confederate positions on Tunnel Hill, while Confederate batteries laid down an artillery barrage on the advancing Federal lines. Rebels on the high ground, rifled-muskets ready, many tense and anxious for the engagement to begin in earnest, endured silently as the Yankees approached. "Nearer and nearer they came until we could see the glittering steel and the flash of the officers' swords in the sunlight," wrote one Confederate. "Nearer and nearer they came until lost to sight at the base of Missionary Ridge." Lying down, hugging the ridge closely, the Rebels grimly waited for the determined Yankees, crawling slowly over the rocks, struggling upward through the underbrush, to ascend the steep, heavily wooded, six-hundred-foot slope of Tunnel Hill. When the Federals came in sight again, now at close range, the most severe and prolonged fighting of the battle quickly erupted.[9]

Corse's brigade, led by "our eager general," as the brigade's second-in-command described Corse, pushed, according to Sherman, within eighty yards of the Confederate entrenchments. There Corse found some cover along a secondary crest of the ridge, at the works earlier abandoned by the Rebels. He called for his reserves and asked for reinforcements, which Sherman reported were sent forward. In a short time Corse mounted a strong assault, personally leading the Fortieth Illinois, One Hundred and Third Illinois, and the Forty-sixth Ohio straight into a galling musketry and canister fire. The Union soldiers charged "with a fearlessness and determination that was astonishing," reported Colonel Charles C. Walcutt.[10]

Confederates, if not astonished, were surely impressed by the Federals' tenacious onslaught. General Cleburne reported that the artillerymen of Swett's battery, at the apex of Tunnel Hill, "stood bravely to their guns under a terrible cross-fire, and replied with canister at short range, but still the enemy advanced." The brigade was rushing forward into, as a Yankee in the Sixth Iowa described it, "a terrific storm of musket balls and canister, shot at short range."[11]

19. General Patrick R. Cleburne.

20. Colonel (later General) Hiram B. Granbury.

The attackers were within fifty steps of the battery, Cleburne thought, when Confederate infantry, to both right and left of the cannon, rose from behind their breastworks and charged. Engaging the Federals in a grimy, bloody, hand-to-hand fight, the Rebels drove them back to cover at the abandoned works. In this counter-assault both Roger Mills and James Smith were wounded, and Colonel (later General) Hiram B. Granbury took command of the brigade. The leader of the Union brigade, General Corse, had also fallen, severely wounded, and was replaced by Colonel Walcutt.[12]

In less than half an hour the Yankees had re-formed and made a second assault with equal fury—"another desperate charge," Cleburne called it—against the front of the Texas brigade. The Federals were swept by fire not only from the front but also on their left flank, as Douglas's battery enfiladed them from Govan's position. Too, Lowrey's extreme left regiment leveled a long-range volley on that flank. A few men did reach the Rebel works but were quickly killed. Again the Federals were driven back, "repulsed and hurled bleeding down the slope," as Captain Buck described the struggle, "only to reform and charge again. . . ." Buck thought Cleburne "seemed omnipresent, watching and guarding every point, and providing for any contingencies. Once or twice," Buck related, "counter-charges were made by the Confederates, Cleburne leading or accompanying them."[13]

As the fighting raged in front of Swett's four Napoleon guns, the Federals obstinately focusing on the artillery, so many officers and sergeants in the battery were killed or wounded that command fell to a corporal, F.W. Williams. And Colonel Granbury had to make a detail from the infantry to keep the guns firing.[14]

As always, men carrying the flag drew marked attention. Captain Foster of the Twenty-fourth Texas, now shooting at the enemy from behind the breastworks, watched as a Yankee color-bearer went down with the flag. Another man picked it up, said Foster, "and down he went, and then another—until away they all go leaving three dead, in trying to carry that flag." (General Loomis would report that every color-bearer in his brigade was shot down.) Foster also saw one man helping another who was wounded, but both men were shot down together, as "a great many dead were left on the ground, and wounded ones crying for help."[15]

About noon a short lull occurred in the battle. Cleburne took advantage of the break to strengthen his front, shifting the Second, Fifteenth, and Twenty-fourth Arkansas (consolidated), under Lieutenant E. Warfield, from Colonel Govan's left flank to the top of Tunnel Hill in rear of Swett's Battery. Also, concluding that Douglas's guns had proved too light for effective action from their position on Govan's line, Cleburne moved two of Swett's twelve-pounders to strengthen this enfilading fire. To replace the guns sent off, Cleburne ordered Lieutenant Key's battery of four light field pieces to move up to the apex of the hill and placed Key in charge of all the artillery on Tunnel Hill.[16]

Meanwhile, the Union right flank brigade of General Loomis, which had been advancing toward the tunnel, with supporting brigades from John Smith's division in the rear, had "made good progress" during the march—according to General Sherman's After Action Report. Actually, aside from marching a bit farther than Corse's brigade, if that be deemed progress, nothing particularly noteworthy had been accomplished. Moving with a double line of skirmishers in front, and the left flank hugging the western base of the ridge, Loomis crossed several hundred yards of open fields where his troops were exposed to artillery fire from over the tunnel and on the ridge. Approaching the railroad track leading to the tunnel, and not far from the base of the ridge, the Federals could see a white house belonging to a man named Glass, with log barns and slave quarters nearby.[17]

The area and the buildings were contested by two Confederate regiments, the Thirty-ninth and Fifty-sixth Georgia from Cumming's brigade. These Rebels, spotting the enemy approaching, had just scrambled down the ridge, one regiment on each side of the railroad. Upon orders from General Hardee, they were to hold the buildings if possible but burn the structures if forced to retire, so that the Federals could not use them for shelter.[18]

A brisk firefight broke out at once, although at long range. It lasted for some time, the Yankees gradually applying more pressure, especially with artillery, after bringing up a section of a battery to support the advance of their left flank. This threat to the Rebel right mounted steadily. Also, their ammunition would soon need replenishing. Slowly and in good order the two Georgia regiments withdrew, climbing back up the ridge but failing to burn the houses—"owing to some misconception of orders," reported General Cumming. The Thirty-ninth's colonel, J.T. McConnell, immediately requested permission to take his regiment down again to fire the buildings. Permission was denied, but, a little later, four companies led by Captain W. P. Milton did receive authority to return. About one o'clock, probably a little before, they finally succeeded in burning the houses.[19]

Following the fight with the Rebels at Glass's property, the Yankees of Loomis's brigade were notified that General Corse was about to make an assault on the north front of the ridge. Advancing to cooperate, they moved simultaneously, more or less, against the west slope. Soon encountering a heavy, direct fire of rifled-musketry, the troops halted, going to the ground and seeking whatever cover the rugged ridge presented.

By the time of the lull around noon, the advance of the Yankee right flank had presented no real challenge to the Confederate grip on the tunnel. Too, when Loomis turned and began to struggle up the side of the ridge, the Rebels, taking advantage of interior lines, could quickly shift troops from another point if necessary. And this they did. About one o'clock, or soon thereafter, when again the battle began to heat up, the Thirty-ninth Georgia, with ammunition replenished, and accompanied by the Thirty-fourth Georgia, moved north along the crest to strengthen the left flank of Cleburne's division. Riding ahead at the front of his regiment and scouting for an effective position, the Thirty-ninth's Colonel McConnell was shot in the head and killed. (A Yankee examining the ridge a day later would remark upon the large number of Rebel dead who had been "shot through the head.")[20]

While Cleburne worked feverishly to toughen his front against "another grand attack," the Federals tenaciously girded to renew their assault, bringing up more troops to support the brigades led by Walcutt and Loomis. The latter, concerned for his left flank, which was without any immediate support, ordered forward two regiments from Colonel Adolphus Buschbeck's brigade of Howard's Eleventh Corps, which had been placed at Loomis's disposal. Leading the way came the Twenty-seventh Pennsylvania Infantry, commanded by Lieutenant Colonel Joseph B. Taft, who would die in the afternoon fighting. Charging first across open ground at double-quick time, and then up the ridge under a heavy fire of musketry and canister, the regiment drove the enemy back, rushing even beyond Loomis's flank and to within a few yards of the Confederate works. Almost exhausted, these troops threw themselves upon the ground; but, even so, some men immediately opened fire on the Rebels. Joining the Twenty-seventh in the charge was Company B, Seventy-third Pennsylvania. The remainder of the Seventy-third, however, continued to occupy the area of the burning buildings at the base of the ridge.[21]

Despite their ardor for battle, clearly demonstrated in this aggressive assault, the Pennsylvanians, going so far up the ridge, as well as bearing too far to the left, had not provided the cover Colonel Loomis sought for his exposed flank. Giving them credit for "a spirited and gallant" attack, Loomis also noted that it was "without my order" that the Pennsylvanians' assault went nearly to the ridge's crest, and he reported further that "while this attack was in progress the enemy made an assault on my left with a strong column down Tunnel Hill road." The Confederates were making some excellent tactical, offensive-defensive maneuvers; standing on the defensive, but effectively exploiting opportunities to keep the Federals off-balance by carrying the fight to them. Loomis's exposed flank now in grave danger, the colonel immediately called on John Smith's supporting division.[22]

Smith sent his Third and Second Brigades, the Third leading, under command of Brigadier General Charles L. Matthies, whose Ninety-third Illinois regiment climbed the ridge first. "Resting once in the ascent we gained the top of the hill about one thirty P.M.," said Lieutenant Colonel Nicholas C. Buswell, the regiment's second-in-command. "Advancing our line within twenty paces of the enemy's breastworks of logs and stone, behind which was planted a battery that poured grape and canister into our ranks continually," Buswell observed, "the engagement grew into a fierce battle." The Ninety-third's commander, Colonel Holden Putnam, whom General Matthies had ordered to "move up cautiously," was, according to Buswell, "holding the colors in one hand and waving his sword with the other, all the time cheering on his men," when he was shot in the head and killed instantly during the early stages of this fight. And General Matthies soon went down also. "I was turning around to caution my men to fire low and sure," he reported, when "I was struck by a bullet . . . which felled me to the ground." Regaining consciousness shortly, Matthies sent for Colonel Benjamin D. Dean, Twenty-sixth Missouri, who assumed command of the brigade.[23]

Meanwhile, coming up on the left flank of the Ninety-third Illinois—precisely on the opposite flank from where ordered—was the Tenth Iowa, while the Twenty-sixth Missouri formed on the right of the Illinois regiment. Clinging to the side of a heavily wooded, ragged ridge, which they had never seen before, and facing a galling enemy fire, the Yankee regiments, not surprisingly, were somewhat intermingled. Apparently, the Twenty-seventh Pennsylvania, at least part of it, now lay between the Tenth Iowa and the Ninety-third Illinois. The Federal line was neither continuous nor located along the same elevation. Markedly jagged in appearance, there were also places on the "line" where clusters of men were isolated, remaining in one position on the slope for hours, perhaps throughout the battle, and, in some instances managing to place a destructive enfilading fire on the Confederate positions.[24]

Two regiments of Colonel Green B. Raum's Second Brigade were also climbing up the ridge in rear of the Third Brigade. On the left was the Eightieth Ohio, with the Seventeenth Iowa on its right, the latter coming up immediately in rear of the Ninety-third Illinois. But the Confederates, better organized, with less, more easily traversable ground to cover, were also marshalling additional troops at the threatened point. General Cumming's two remaining regiments, the Thirty-sixth Georgia and the Fifty-sixth Georgia, were shifted from near the tunnel to the top of the hill. Cleburne placed the Fifty-sixth Georgia, whose Colonel J.T. Slaughter was wounded while positioning his regiment, behind the breastworks near the cannon, at the highest point of the hill—the angle in the line that Cleburne rightly considered his weakest point. The other Georgia regiment was located to the left, along the western crest.[25]

Now, in the early afternoon, the battle's tempo seemed to reach a crescendo of noise and fury. Under partial cover of Smith's abandoned works, the Federals were laying down a constant, heavy fire on Smith's north front, particularly the artillery. Cleburne said the fire was concentrated on "a space of not more than forty yards" and seemed like "one continuous sheet of hissing, flying lead." Simultaneously attempting to charge up the west face of the ridge, some of the Yankees worked their way very close, right under the crest of the Confederate position. "Here the enemy lay down behind trees, logs and projecting rocks, the first line," according to Cleburne, "not twenty five yards away," and opened fire. In some instances the Yankees had a deadly cross-fire on the Rebels and were constantly disabling men near the apex of the hill.[26]

Lieutenant Key depressed his guns to the utmost, firing shell and canister down the hill into the face of the Federals. Some of Colonel Warfield's men found it impossible to fire effectively down the ridge, due both to the danger from the Yankee fire and to the angles and natural shelters of the hillside. Their solution was to hurl stones and roll or drop large rocks, even boulders, upon the enemy. Also, there were artillerists who lighted shells and rolled them down the ridge into the Federals. General Hardee, from a hill south of the tunnel, now had some pieces of artillery trying to dislodge the Yankees with a flank fire, but their right flank was protected by a slight intervening projection of the ridge.[27]

And so the battle raged, a continual heavy firing from both sides, with occasionally a charge, and possibly a counter-charge, at some points along the ridge. "The fight had lasted unceasingly for an hour and a half," Cleburne said in his After Action Report. Warfield's regiment, still holding to its exposed position near Swett's battery, had many men disabled and many almost out of ammunition. Then a few welcome reinforcements, the First and Twenty-seventh Tennessee regiments from Maney's Brigade, Walker's division, came up, led by Colonel Hume R. Field, and took position on Warfield's right flank.[28]

The Federals, some of them, were also experiencing ammunition problems. There were many instances where men could only keep firing by appropriating the ammunition of their fallen comrades. And some Yankees had charged again and again. Confederate Captain Foster claimed that six times they came at his position, "like they were going to walk right over us," only to be turned back.[29]

Probably for both sides it now seemed, sometime around three or three-thirty in the afternoon, that such an intense, prolonged melee must soon reach a climax, one way or another. Certainly it appears, from After Action Reports, that such a sense of imminent crisis was felt by some Confederates. Lieutenant Colonel Warfield expressed his opinion, according to Cleburne, that the Rebels were wasting ammunition and, even worse, were "becoming disheartened at the persistency of the enemy." He suggested that a bayonet charge might prove decisive. General Cumming thought so too and, in fact, offered to lead the assault. Cumming reported that the rank and file of his regiments "seemed to be moved by a desire to engage the enemy in a hand-to-hand conflict." Also, he said, several officers thought a bayonet charge, in strength, would drive the Federals down the ridge. Cleburne agreed immediately.[30]

The charge was made with the strength of a brigade front. Two of the regiments were Cumming's own Thirty-sixth and Fifty-sixth Georgia. Cumming had been told of an opening in the breastworks, forty or fifty yards wide, directly in his front, and through there he determined to make the assault with two of his regiments, one in front of the other, then fanning out once past the opening. At the signal to charge, the troops would move at a double-quick time, break over the Yankee position, engage with the bayonet, and only fire when the enemy should begin to give way. On Cumming's left, the troops of Mills's regiment would also join in the assault.[31]

The gray line rose and swept forward cheering, but when they hit the opening in the breastworks, the passage was too narrow. Only about a third of a regimental front could pass through, the men on the flanks climbing or crawling over the soldiers in the ditches and the breastworks. The resulting confusion and disorganization were made worse by a rapidly increasing volume of Yankee musketry fire, concentrated at once on the now highly visible enemy targets. Fortunately for the Rebels, regimental officers quickly re-formed the ranks; the men surged forward and met the Federals in a short hand-to-hand encounter. Overwhelmed, the Yankees fell back over the slope of the ridge from which they had been firing.

Then the charging Confederates, somewhat disorganized by the sharp fight and the broken terrain, found themselves swept by Federal flanking fire. They immediately pulled back up the ridge. The Yankees cautiously closed behind, working their way over the rugged ground to take up again the position from which they had just been driven.

In about ten or fifteen minutes, reorganized, the Confederates charged again. Repulsed once more, they re-formed and charged a third time. Another short, desperate, hand-to-hand fight—men bayonetted or clubbed their opponents, and one Rebel soldier said he saw the colonel of his regiment smash a Yankee in the head with a stone—and the Union infantry, this time, fled down the ridge. The action was decisive.[32]

The weight of the Confederate bayonet charge apparently went against the Ninety-third Illinois and the Twenty-seventh Pennsylvania, hitting hard the right flank of the Illinois regiment. Directly behind the Ninety-third lay the Seventeenth Iowa, which had advanced up the ridge with the Eightieth Ohio on its left flank and skirmishers from the Fifth Iowa deployed on the right. Suddenly, front-line soldiers from the Ninety-third Illinois began scrambling and sliding down the hill, breaking through the lines of the Seventeenth Iowa; then, reported the Seventeenth's Colonel Clark R.

Wever, "the whole right of the Third Brigade (Matthies) gave way and fell back through the Seventeenth Iowa and the Eightieth Ohio." Evidently undaunted by the fleeing soldiers dashing pell-mell through their ranks, the two reinforcing regiments pressed forward, nearly to the crest of the hill, only to be met "by a heavy force of the enemy," closing in, according to Wever, on the right flank and rear, moving at double-quick time. In trying to fall back to the left, and even before receiving the full fury of the Rebel onslaught, the Federal regiment began to crumble. Finally, said Colonel Wever, "the whole line (including a portion of Matthies', which had remained on the hill) gave way and retreated in confusion. . . ."[33]

Many of the triumphant Confederates followed the Federals all the way to the base of the ridge before the Tenth Missouri Infantry, waiting in reserve position, advanced to cover the retreat and checked the pursuing enemy. The brigades of Walcutt and Loomis, although they tried to keep up the fight, were finally compelled to recognize that the struggle had gone against the Union. Loomis, who had never pushed as high up the slope as some of the other units, nevertheless eventually fell victim of the general collapse, and he recalled his brigade about four-thirty and bivouacked for the night. As for Walcutt, when the Federals on his right retreated, the brigade, "with volley after volley," beat off Rebels planning a bayonet charge from that direction. Fighting continued "in a greater or lesser degree" until dark, he reported. But there was no longer a chance of carrying the Confederate position, and Walcutt, too, eventually pulled back down the slope.[34]

Rebels thought they now understood why the Yankees had sometimes charged so furiously and recklessly. Some of the Union troops were captured and, according to the account of Captain W.W. Carnes, found to carry canteens containing whiskey. Canteens of the dead and wounded on the ridge were also examined, said P.D. Stephenson of the Thirteenth Arkansas, who claimed they "were filled with whiskey."[35]

More than likely some of the Federals had tried to brace themselves for the day's awful ordeal by imbibing freely, but obviously the whiskey was not enough to bring about a victory. The major problem of the Yankees was that they never found a way to use their superior numbers effectively. Cleburne had his right, or northeastern, flank so well secured, holding the dominant terrain everywhere on that wing, that Morgan Smith's division never mounted a serious threat against it. Then, at the height of the afternoon fight, the Union troops failed to make their greatest effort against the weakest point of Cleburne's line. Instead of the apex of the ridge, where the sharp angle of the Rebel position invited an effective cross-fire, and where the Federals had concentrated their morning attack, the Federals marshalled soldiers on the western side of the hill. Here the Confederate line was naturally stronger. Making the situation worse for the Federals, the brigades of Buschbeck, Matthies, and Raum came up the ridge either in a somewhat helter-skelter fashion or one behind the other. Thus Raum's brigade never got into action until Matthies's preceding brigade, which advanced to the front line, had been overwhelmed. While the Federals had many more troops in the general area of Tunnel Hill than the Confederates, they were never able, at the actual points of fighting, to take advantage of these potentially overpowering numbers.

Succinctly put, the ground on the northern end of Missionary Ridge favored the defense if the line was properly positioned. Cleburne had deployed his troops well. By placing his line farther up the hill from its original posting and angling it from the apex of the ridge sharply back to the east, he had both effectively anchored his right flank and shortened his front, so that fewer defenders were needed. Also, he had made it possible to reinforce threatened points more quickly; finally, his position drew the Yankees into an increasingly cramped situation near the crest of the narrow ridge, rendering it impossible for them to deploy their full superiority of force.

About the same time that Confederates atop the ridge launched the attack that drove many of the Federals down the western slope, other Rebels attacked at the base of the ridge, falling upon parts of the Fifth Iowa and the Seventy-third Pennsylvania, which were holding the area of the burned houses on the Federal right flank. The Fifth Iowa was overwhelmed, apparently by a Confederate rush on both the front and the flank. Colonel Jabez Banbury first spied Lieutenant John Wright, an aide to General Matthies, rushing toward him yelling "Retreat!" and he realized that the main line on the ridge to his left had collapsed. "I gave the order to retreat," the colonel said, "but the enemy was now upon us demanding our surrender, and I regret to say many of the men were compelled to submit. . . . Those who escaped did so through a shower of balls, and yells from the enemy to halt."[36]

Captain Byers of the Fifth Iowa gave an intriguing account of this action. He was convinced that the Confederates who flanked the regiment on its right had come through the tunnel from the east side of the ridge. He wrote: "Some one cried, 'Look to the tunnel!' There, on the right, passing through a tunnel in the mountain, and out of the railway cut, came the gray-coats by hundreds, flanking us complete-ly. . . . They were through by the hundreds, and a fatal enfilading fire was cutting our line to pieces." Byers's dramatic account of later years was also echoed by another Federal who, in his regimental history, asserted that the Rebel flanking force came through the tunnel.[37]

The idea makes a good story, perhaps one might even say a roman-tic story, but it probably never happened. In the first place, not any Confederate After Action Report mentions such a spectacular move-ment, which is indeed surprising if it actually occurred and was so successful. Nor do the Federal reports. The only accounts seem to be from Union veterans writing years later. Secondly, to come through the tunnel in order to flank the Federals was neither necessary nor sensible, unless some reinforcements had arrived at the eastern base of the ridge, which was not the case. For any of the Confederate troops present, a trek through the tunnel would have been unnecessarily long and time-consuming. Soldiers from along the western slope could have been deployed for action at the base of the ridge much more rapidly than those on the eastern side could have first descended to the tunnel level and then awkwardly jogged along the uneven footing of the railroad bed passageway. Even if troops on the eastern side of the hill were used for the attack, they could have hiked across the crest of the narrow ridge more quickly than they could have scram-bled down to the tracks and come through the tunnel. Apparently Sherman's After Action Report was correct about this attack when he explained that the Confederates had "massed in great strength in the tunnel *gorge*" and, being unobserved, had "suddenly appeared on the right and rear" of the Union troops.[38]

About other matters, General Sherman appears to have been a bit frustrated, as well as simply mistaken. "Column after column of the enemy was streaming toward me," he dramatically wrote in his After Action Report. "Gun after gun poured its concentric shot on us from every hill and spur that gave a view of any part of the ground held by us." About three o'clock, upon a signal from Grant to "Attack again," Sherman later said that he "thought 'the old man' was daft!" He sent a staff officer to inquire if there had been a mistake. Informed that

Grant had replied that there was no mistake, the staff officer remembered that Sherman blurted: "Go signal Grant. The orders were that I should get as many as possible in front of me and God knows there are enough. They've been reinforcing all day." And, still again, in his report, Sherman declared, "our attack had drawn vast masses of the enemy to our flank. . . ."[39]

Sherman was wrong. The brigades of Brown and Cumming from Carter Stevenson's division, earlier stationed on the Lookout Mountain flank, were in position on Tunnel Hill when Sherman launched his attack in late morning. Other than the two regiments of Maney's brigade, which came from Walker's division to help Cleburne in the afternoon fight—and surely could not accurately be described as "vast masses"—there were no troops shifted to Tunnel Hill from other parts of the line. Cleburne wrote that "the brunt of this long day's fight was borne by Smith's (Texas) brigade and the Second, Fifteenth and Twenty-fourth Arkansas (consolidated) of Govan's brigade, together with Swett's and Key's batteries." The remainder of his division, Cleburne concluded, were only engaged in "heavy skirmishing."[40]

The fact was that Sherman—with two corps of the Army of the Tennessee, Howard's corps of the Army of the Potomac, and Jefferson C. Davis's division of the Army of the Cumberland all at his disposal, as well as Absalom Baird's division of Cumberlanders sent by General Grant (whom Sherman said he did not need)—could not drive Cleburne's division, assisted by only two other brigades and two regiments, off the ridge. It is understandable that Sherman, thinking about shifting some of his problem elsewhere, was inquiring "Where is Thomas?" and calling repeatedly for Thomas to take up the assault.[41]

While Sherman's columns futilely hurled themselves against the northern end of the ridge, Hooker's soldiers were supposed to be moving through Chattanooga Valley, toward Rossville Gap and the Confederate southern flank on the ridge.

Hooker began the day energetically. Soon after ten o'clock in the morning he received orders to post two regiments on Lookout Mountain, return Carlin's brigade to Johnson's division of Thomas's Army of the Cumberland, and march with the remainder of his three divisions to Rossville Gap. Well before noon Hooker's entire command was on the road, and by one-thirty they had reached Chattanooga Creek, having covered about three-fourths of the distance to the gap.

But here he halted and bogged down. Confederates had destroyed the bridge over the creek as they retreated from the mountain during the night.

General Hooker estimated that he would be delayed about half an hour. Leaving his trains and artillery until a bridge could be built, the general only crossed his infantry. As it turned out, however, even the infantry crossing consumed about three hours—most of the rest of the afternoon.[42]

11

All Hell Can't Stop Them

Now the fight came to the center of Missionary Ridge. This struggle would be the decisive battle—the climax of the long, frustrating Chattanooga campaign. But, realistically, no one in the Union army, whether a private or a general, should have expected that the final moments of the fray were at hand. Premonitions, possibly, there may have been for a few; yet what was about to happen could not have seemed likely, not in quite the manner that the spectacular event suddenly and rapidly unfolded.

In fact, an all-out assault on the center of the ridge was never seriously contemplated by the Yankee high command. Any attack that might be launched by General Thomas's Army of the Cumberland was conceived as complementary, to follow in the wake of decisive action on the Confederate flank. The whole Rebel position looked strong, but, from the Federal lines, the center appeared to be the toughest section. Brigadier General Thomas J. Wood, commanding a division of the Army of the Cumberland, succinctly summarized the thinking at departmental headquarters: "It was conceded that a direct frontal attack of the enemy's works on Mission Ridge could not be made with a reasonable prospect of success . . . ."[1]

Wood's account is supported by General William F. Smith. "The original plan of the battle of Chattanooga," said Smith, "was to turn Bragg's right flank on Missionary Ridge, thereby throwing his army away from its base and line of retreat . . . . The assault on the center before either flank was turned was never seriously contemplated, . . . and was made without plan, without orders . . . ." Sherman would "make the grand attack," testified Brigadier General Joseph S. Fullerton, and "the Army of the Cumberland was simply to get into position and cooperate."[2]

General Grant did not order an assault on the center of Missionary Ridge, and it is to his credit that he did not do so. Grant had no reason to expect the mismanagement of which the Confederate high command had been guilty. Rather, the Union commander's instructions on the afternoon of November 25 were for General Thomas's troops to charge and carry the rifle-pits at the foot of Missionary Ridge. Nothing more was intended. And again, the record of General Wood is pertinent. He said that Grant told him that the Army of the Cumberland "ought to do something" to help Sherman, adding: "I think if you and Sheridan were to advance your divisions and carry the rifle pits at the base of the ridge it would so threaten Bragg's center that he would draw . . . troops from the right to secure his center and [that would] insure the success of General Sherman's attack." Wood said that he replied he would be glad to try.[3]

Yet, some have left another impression—that Grant even foresaw and engineered the charge up the ridge; that the general's battle plan, from first to last, worked to perfection, exactly as anticipated. Sherman strongly contributed to this legend. Soon after the battle, in effervescent style, Sherman wrote Grant, with reference to General Bragg, that "no man could have held his army after our combinations were made." Again, later, he commented, "it was a great victory—the neatest and cleanest battle I was ever in—and Grant deserves the credit of it all." In his memoirs, misrepresenting the battle plan, Sherman declared the objective was to pressure the Rebel flank "so that Thomas's army could break through [the enemy's] center"; he then concluded that "the whole plan succeeded admirably . . . ."[4]

The nuances of some of Grant's statements also support the legend. For example, writing to his friend Elihu Washburn a few days after the engagement, Grant told the congressman that Chattanooga was the first battlefield he had "ever seen where a plan could be followed, and from one place the whole field be within one view." Seemingly not satisfied with implications, Grant forthrightly alleged in his widely read memoirs that the battle had been fought according to his orders.[5]

Sherman's most prominent biographer, Basil H. Liddell-Hart, an astute British military historian, was not misled. "Chattanooga brought fresh fame to both Grant and Sherman," he wrote, "yet like Shiloh, the controversy over it has raged almost more fierce than the battle. Both generals, loyal to each other, indulged too ingenuously in the 'general' habit of talking as if all had gone according to plan." But Bruce Catton, a staunch and talented literary booster of Grant and popular historian of the war, became a bit carried away. "Sherman was right," declared Catton, "in his remarks that Grant's 'combinations' had been extremely effective. . . . The hard smash at Missionary Ridge had been in the cards all along, and . . . [Grant] dominated the battlefield from beginning to end."[6]

Probably a biographer must have sympathy for his subject if he hopes to write well, and certainly Catton wrote well. His and Sherman's embellished praises of Grant at Chattanooga, however, are both inaccurate and unjust to the officers—regimental, brigade, and divisional—and the men in the ranks who actually played the decisive role at the crisis of battle.

The first thing to note is that the main source for Catton's interpretation of Grant's role in supposedly engineering an assault on the Rebel center is the Union commander's instruction to General Thomas on the evening of November 24, the night before the attack. Telling Thomas that his assault was to be in cooperation with Sherman, Grant stated: "Your command will either carry the rifle-pits and ridge directly in front of them or move to the left, as the presence of the enemy may require."[7]

The context of Grant's order, disregarded by Catton, is all-important. The instruction was postulated on the belief that Sherman was then atop Tunnel Hill—which, of course, he was not. Grant began by telling Thomas: "General Sherman carried Missionary Ridge as far as the tunnel . . . . His right now rests at the tunnel and on top of the hill . . . ." If Sherman had been already astride the keypoint of the battle area, the northern flank of Missionary Ridge, the whole Confederate position would have been in imminent danger. Sherman would advance at daylight, said Grant, and Thomas's movement would "be in cooperation." An assault on the ridge by Thomas was envisioned only after Sherman's attack broke the Rebels, bringing the collapse of the entire line, and was not even mentioned in Grant's order to Sherman on the same evening. To Sherman, Grant said that Thomas would "carry the rifle-pits in his immediate front, or move to the left to your support, as circumstances may determine best." At the most, an assault on the center of the ridge was considered in Grant's battle plan as a contingency; clearly, on the afternoon of the assault, Grant gave limited orders, to carry the breastworks at the foot of the ridge.[8]

Actually, Grant's reputation is better served when the gilding is eliminated. Given the situation as the Union commanders perceived it, and not as later students know it, if Grant had ordered an assault up the ridge against the center of the Confederate line he would have appeared reckless indeed—a general gambling contrary to sensible calculations.

Grant performed well at Chattanooga. His plan for the deployment of his army was sound. With a two-to-one manpower advantage—over 60,000 against about 32,000 to 35,000—Grant had seized and kept the initiative, using his full power to apply pressure against the enemy from three directions at the same time. By November 25, the Confederate command had been pinned down and had lost freedom of action. But the final attack, as it developed, was unplanned and unauthorized by Grant. He was still considering Sherman's Army of the Tennessee as the main attack force and seeking a way for that general to renew his assault against the Rebel right flank.

In fact, then, Grant's order to assault the Confederate rifle-pits resulted from the indecisiveness of his flanking plans and from faulty intelligence. Not only had Sherman failed to gain the northern end of the ridge where Grant anticipated that conclusive fighting would take place, but equally disappointing was news about the other end of the line. Stalled in the valley between Lookout Mountain and Missionary Ridge while trying to bridge a stream, General Hooker's soldiers had not gotten into position for an attack on the Confederate's southern flank. And Sherman was calling for help, saying that Rebels from the center of the ridge were being sent to defend against his attacks. Grant believed this was true. He himself, as well as other Union officers, thought he saw Confederate reinforcements moving northward along the crest of the ridge to strengthen the Rebel flank.

No such thing was happening. True enough, Rebel troops were being shifted during the morning and early afternoon of November 25. All of Carter Stevenson's division and part of B. Franklin Cheatham's and William Bate's divisions were involved in rearrangements. These movements, however, did not represent detachments from the center; but, of course, Grant acted on what he supposed was occurring, and the strange fortunes of war then worked in his favor.

Not only was Grant's order based on a mistaken concept, and issued because the battle plan had not developed as anticipated (a fact virtually always true of battles), but also, ironically, the assault he launched to aid Sherman resulted in placing the center of his army in an untenable position—a situation from which erupted a desperate charge that won the campaign. When the blue-clad troops took the rifle-pits they found little protection against Rebel fire from atop the ridge. General Grant apparently had not foreseen the dire circumstances in which the charge to the rifle-pits would leave the Union soldiers. Soon it became obvious, at least to the Federals under fire, that Confederates shooting from the side and top of the ridge would turn the area into, as Colonel Frederick Knefler, leader of the combined Seventy-ninth and Eighty-sixth Indiana, later wrote, "a hideous slaughter pen." "Something" had to be done, "and . . . quickly," recalled the colonel, who was in the very midst of the action.[9]

Thus the Federals, suddenly trapped in a terrible situation, found themselves attempting what had seemed impossible, the very thing which, a little earlier, they had dreaded the most: an assault straight up the heart of the ridge into the supposed strength of the gray-clad line. Palatable alternatives simply did not exist. The soldiers could retreat to their jumping-off point, disgraced before the troops of Sherman and Hooker, as well as taking more casualties while retracing their steps, or stay where they were, easy targets for the enemy above. Most of the Yankees were quickly steeled to the realization that forward and victory, or wounding or death, were their only acceptable choices.

From the beginning some soldiers expected, or suspected, it would be this way. And the order to advance and take the rifle-pits was not always clearly conveyed to officers who would direct the charge. Charles T. Clark of the One Hundred and Twenty-fifth Ohio, located in Charles Harker's brigade of Sheridan's division, explained that "the men in the ranks, and in many instances regimental commanders, did not know the precise wording of the order, the directions to regimental commanders being in most cases merely an order to advance at the given speed. . . . Having witnessed Sherman's efforts to carry the heights on the left," Clark thought, "there was no reason for supposing any less effort was expected at the center." Clark's

evaluation can be applied even more broadly, for one brigade commander testified to receiving only a general order to advance, and
even a division commander thought the intention was to assault the
ridge.[10]

Brigadier General August Willich, in his After Action Report,
stated that he understood the order was simply "to advance"—presumably, as he interpreted it, to take the ridge. A member of the
Fifteenth Ohio regiment, a unit in Willich's brigade, later claimed
that when the general was informed that an assault would be made
against the ridge, he laconically replied in his German-accented En-
glish, "Vell, I makes my vill." Brigadier General Absalom Baird,
commanding a division, reported that a staff officer from Thomas
instructed him that the capture of the rifle-pits "was intended as
preparatory to a general assault on the mountain" and that he would
be following Grant's wishes if he pushed "on to the summit."[11]

Major James Connelly, an aide to General Baird, was appalled by
what he heard. In a letter to his wife, Connelly wrote: "This, I confess,
staggered me; I couldn't understand it; it looked as though we were
going to assault the ridge, and try to carry it by storm, lined and ribbed
as it was with rifle pits, and its topmost verge crowded with Rebel
lines, and at least forty cannon in our immediate front . . . ." The
commander of the Tenth Kentucky, Lieutenant Colonel Gabriel C.
Wharton, wrote that an advance "would be to a harvest of death . . . ."
Located, like Wharton, in the left brigade of Baird's division, Lieutenant Colonel Myron Baker, Seventy-fourth Indiana, later described the
"discouraging appearance" of the "desperate enterprise." Colonel
Wallace W. Barrett of the Forty-fourth Illinois said that Colonel
Francis Sherman, his brigade commander, directed him, from the
jump-off point, "to go as far as I could."[12]

Some Indiana troops, who had been employed digging graves, they
knew not for whom, thought they now understood, reflecting on the
macabre idea that perhaps they had dug their own. "Recalling the
charges at Fredericksburg and Gettysburg," candidly remarked L.M.
Jewett, "it did not seem possible that a frontal assault could be
successfully made upon the heights and fortifications of Missionary
Ridge . . . ."[13]

Of course, many Yankee officers, probably most, understood that
their objective was the rifle pits at the base of the ridge—that and no
more. Major General Philip Sheridan clearly reported that his orders
were "to carry the enemy's rifle-pits at the base of Mission Ridge."

Likewise, General Wood said that he was ordered to advance and "carry the enemy's intrenchments at the base of Mission Ridge and hold them." The commander of the brigade on the right side of Wood's division, Brigadier General William B. Hazen, stated in his After Action Report, "On commencing the advance, the thought of storming Missionary Ridge had not entered the mind of any one . . . ."[14]

If some had not thought of storming the ridge, others who had considered it certainly did not believe that an assault on so forbidding a height could possibly be a success. As the mad surge up the ridge began, Grant, Thomas, and Major General Gordan Granger watched in spellbound disbelief from atop Orchard Knob. Then Grant, seemingly convinced that he was seeing a bad situation develop into a full-fledged disaster, became angry. Turning to General Thomas, he sharply inquired who had ordered the troops to climb the ridge. Thomas, who had been slow to order the men forward (perhaps because he was skeptical of advancing even to the first line of trenches), replied that he did not know, but certainly he had not ordered the assault. General Granger likewise disavowed any responsibility for giving the order. Anticipating a failure, Grant muttered something to the effect that somebody was going to pay for the debacle.

And then, as the rays of late afternoon sunlight, in kaleidoscopic panorama, penetrated between patches of gunsmoke and played upon glistening bayonets, swords, and rifle barrels all along the side of the ridge, Grant and the other generals watched the seemingly impossible unfold. The Yankee assault carried the very center of the supposedly impregnable Confederate position. From atop the ridge, and apparently all at once, the Stars and Stripes, along with Federal regimental flags, was waving in the cold, gentle breeze. General Thomas believed the hill was carried simultaneously at six different points.[15] It was so unexpected, and had seemed so unlikely, that afterward Union soldiers thought the charge up Missionary Ridge constituted one of the most dramatic and grand pageants of the war.

"The most brilliant feat ever performed by American Arms," Colonel Morton C. Hunter, commanding the Eighty-second Indiana, called the victory. A soldier in another Indiana regiment, even more expansive, wrote that the achievement was "the most brilliant victory in the annals of war." The spectacular success ranked among "the greatest miracles in military history," said Charles A. Dana, who declared that it was "as awful as a visible interposition of God."

Capturing the enthusiasm of the actual moment in the more earthy language of the soldier, General Gordan Granger triumphantly exclaimed to Grant, "When these men get going, all hell can't stop them!"[16]

Indeed, it was a magnificent charge. Colorful, courageous, and glorious, the victory also has long appeared inexplicable, some interpretations of Yankee success even bordering on the mystical and providential. In Union legend the charge came to seem almost invincible. The telling and retelling of the story magnified Federal boldness in the minds of veterans and contributed, in part, to obscuring what actually happened. Perhaps some forgot that courage and the quest for glory are never a match for the sickening thwack of a well-placed bullet as it smashes into flesh and bone.

The After Action Reports of the Union and Confederate armies (particularly the Confederate) leave no doubt about what happened and why. Prophets of Yankee doom should have been right. The Confederate Army, if manpower had been deployed efficiently and wise use made of the natural terrain, probably would have thrown back the Union assault on their center at the crisis of the battle. Detailed analysis, which now follows, unravels a fascinating story.

The time was near three o'clock on that Wednesday afternoon, as tense Yankees, 23,000 strong, anxiously formed in battle lines west of the ridge. Organized in four divisions, Brigadier General Absalom Baird was on the far left, and to his right along the line were, in order, the divisions of Thomas J. Wood, Philip H. Sheridan, and Richard W. Johnson. The signal for attack would be six guns fired from Orchard Knob in quick succession.[17]

Straight ahead, a mile or more to the east, loomed the ragged ridge, rising 500 or so feet above the plain. Both because of the ridge's rugged undulation and because of the difference in starting points, the distance charged to reach the rifle pits would vary from regiment to regiment. For some it would be more than a mile; for all it was well over a half mile. Debouching from a timbered area, the last part of the Union assault would be across open fields—the distance 500 to 700 yards—a level area where enemy fire was expected to be intense.[18]

A little before four o'clock,[19] the first of six signal guns was fired from the parapet on Orchard Knob, peppery Major General Gordan Granger personally directing and shouting the commands to "Fire!" Before the last gun had sounded, some of the leading elements were off, tramping excitedly toward the ridge. The men plunged forward, a solid mass over two miles in width, more troops than in Pickett's disastrous charge at Gettysburg or Hood's ill-fated assault a year later at Franklin.

Over on the Federal left, Baird's division, which had spent most of the day marching—first to reinforce Sherman, only then to be immediately counter-marched, struggling through marshes, streams, and thickets, to join up on the left of Wood's division—barely positioned itself in time for the assault. In fact, the six shots signalling the advance could not be distinguished by Baird from other firing, and consequently his brigades moved out unevenly. The initial surge of his right brigade, under Brigadier General John B. Turchin, was further complicated by thick underbrush and Citico Creek, so that when the unit had passed through the woods to the clearing, other brigades on the right and left were already crossing the open field.[20]

Turchin's brigade was not the only one to experience such problems. On the far right of the entire attack formation, where Brigadier General William P. Carlin's brigade constituted the Federal flank, the commander of the Tenth Ohio, Colonel Anson G. McCook, whose regiment was on the right of the brigade, reported "numerous obstacles, including a deep creek," all of which had thrown his unit into some confusion when it emerged from the edge of the timbered area.[21]

In spite of difficulties, however, most of the battle lines moved into the open plain in very good order. Flags were flying, bugles sounded, bands played, and the ranks were carefully dressed. General Thomas had long been noted as a stickler for infantry drill, and now that training clearly showed. Yankee skirmishers were out in front, preceding a long, blue, double line of infantry (in some cases three deep), who marched in quick time unflinchingly toward the ridge, many of the soldiers shouting and cheering. Where gaps had developed, caused by the wooded, difficult terrain, reserve regimental commanders hurried their troops forward into the first and second assault lines.[22]

The moment was exhilarating. "A scene never to be forgotten," according to Edwin W. Payne, who marched in the ranks of the Thirty-fourth Illinois Infantry—"a panorama to stir the blood into a wild tumult." Captain John W. Tuttle of the Third Kentucky described the assault as "one of the grandest spectacles ever seen," while Sylvanus Cadwallader said the experience was "never to be encountered twice in one lifetime." Another soldier recalled that,

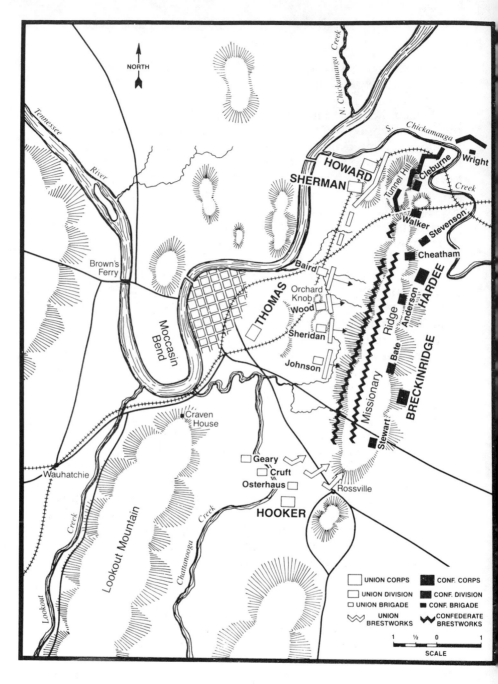

NORTH

Tennessee
River

N. Chickamauga Creek

S. Chickamauga

Wright

HOWARD
SHERMAN

Cleburne

Tunnel Hill
Creek

Walker

Stevenson

Cheatham

Baird

Brown's
Ferry

Orchard
Knob

Anderson

Moccasin
Bend

THOMAS

Wood

HARDEE

Sheridan

Bate

BRECKINRIDGE

Johnson

Missionary Ridge

Stewart

Craven
House

Geary

Cruft

Osterhaus

Rossville

Wauhatchie

HOOKER

Lookout
Creek

Lookout Mountain

Chattanooga Creek

UNION CORPS	CONF. CORPS
UNION DIVISION	CONF. DIVISION
UNION BRIGADE	CONF. BRIGADE
UNION BRESTWORKS	CONFEDERATE BRESTWORKS

1   ½   0   1

SCALE

Map 6. Missionary Ridge: Assault on the Confederate Center, Afternoon, November 25, 1863. *Map by J.L. Moon, Jr.*

although the sight was "appalling," yet "it was grandly sublime." And Major James Connelly, who served three years with the Army of the Cumberland, simply declared, without any qualification, "Our advance to the base of the ridge was the grandest sight I ever saw."[23]

At first, the only reaction of the Confederates was a scattering of shots from their pickets, who fell back quickly, seeking the cover of the trenches behind them. Then the Rebel artillerists opened fire. There were more than one hundred guns in the Confederate army, and over half of them were trained on the ranks of the advancing Federals. The ridge itself seemed to come alive, blazing and roaring, as the gray-clad soldiers unleashed a fierce cannonade, striking across hundreds of yards and into the Yankee lines.[24]

"Not less than fifty guns opened at once," estimated Gordan Granger, "throwing a terrible shower of shot and shell." The Rebel salvos from high on the ridge were unusually intriguing because, due to some atmospheric peculiarity, each round fired could be seen from the moment that it left the cannon's muzzle. Solid shots plowed into the Federal ranks; shells screamed overhead, sometimes bursting too high above the men to cause casualties, but always a source of fear, even when failing to explode, as some did. Horses became frantic and unmanageable. Some soldiers were terrified, supposing the danger to be far worse than it was. Actually, the shelling inflicted very few casualties, and most of the soldiers, though unquestionably filled with a sense of urgency to cross the open ground, maintained their composure, moving ahead in good order.[25]

From Orchard Knob and various positions in the Chattanooga trenches, Yankee artillery was firing in support of the charging infantry. General Granger was so excited that he seemed to forget his position as the commander of an army corps and went down into the gun pits to help the cannoneers, an act that apparently irritated General Grant. A duel between the battery on Orchard Knob and a Confederate battery on the ridge may have been rather discomfiting to Grant and General Thomas, but, with apparent indifference to danger, they ignored the fire, neither man seeking cover.[26]

Shells from the Union cannon exploded into the side of Missionary Ridge. Thundering reverberations of the guns of both sides sounded along the ridge, and even from distant Lookout Mountain. As the air became filled with acrid patches of dirty-white smoke, many soldiers in each army were impressed by the intense level of noise. John E. Gold, a Confederate soldier in the Twenty-fourth Tennessee Infantry, was located high up on the ridge. "There were a number of cannon in our rear that shot over our heads," he later wrote. "These guns were on top of the ridge, and we being in front and only a short distance from them, the report . . . was terrible to endure."[27]

The barrage of artillery fire sounded terrible, looked ugly, but hurt relatively few on either side. Of course, when a cannon shot did find a mark it left a hideous mess. On the crest of the ridge, a short distance north of General Bragg's headquarters, Robert D. Jamison of the Forty-fifth Tennessee had been watching the Federal lines move toward the ridge. Suddenly, one of the shells fired by the Yankee artillery smashed into Jamison's company, decapitating a soldier named Will Clark and also ripping away one of the shoulders of his brother, Newt Clark. Men standing nearby were stunned as they witnessed the ghastly scene, momentarily ignoring the grand pageant of the Union ranks steadily advancing across the plain below.[28]

Halfway to the rifle pits—and the ground began to be dotted with dead and wounded Federals. Stretcher bearers were already at work. From that point on the effect of Rebel infantry fire became more deadly.[29] But the Yankee assault continued to surge forward, gaining speed rapidly, spurred onward by the increasingly heavy and more effective enemy volleys.

Grant and his companions could see the army spread out before them from the command post on Orchard Knob, an unbroken view of the whole field. Bragg and other Confederate generals on Missionary Ridge saw, too, and from either position it was a fabulous spectacle. No great battle of the war surpassed this charge for a theatrical setting; perhaps none equalled it. "Probably none in history," later reflected a Federal officer, "was so well fitted for a display of soldierly courage and daring as the amphitheater of Chattanooga." Rebels on the high ground, with rifled-muskets and bayonets held in readiness, watched admiringly as the Yankees marched against them. "I think," recalled a Confederate officer, "that I noticed some nervousness among my men as they beheld this grand military spectacle, and I heard remarks which showed that . . . they magnified the host in their view to at least double their number."[30]

"The very air smelt of battle," thought W.J. Worsham of the Nineteenth Tennessee regiment. "It was indeed a grand spectacle," wrote Ralph J. Neal of the Twentieth Tennessee, and he speculated that "in modern times an entire army had not witnessed such a scene." Another Confederate soldier, James L. Cooper, echoed Neal's sentiment. "Every movement in the plains below was visible to us, and a sublime scene was presented . . . when the massive columns

21. Assaulting Missionary Ridge. *Harper's Weekly Magazine.*

began their . . . march." The battle of Missionary Ridge was the first time Confederate John C. Seaman had been under fire. Not surprisingly, the vision from the summit of the ridge made a deep impression. "At our feet, as it were, three distinct lines of bluecoats were in battle array," Seaman wrote, "presenting the most . . . awe-inspiring spectacle . . . that it was ever my . . . fortune to behold."[31]

Confederates defending the ridge were organized in two corps, Breckinridge on the left and Hardee on the right. Beginning at Rossville Gap, Breckinridge's divisions were aligned, from left to right, in the following order: first two brigades of Brigadier General Alexander P. Stewart's division; next William Bate's division; and, finally, the division of Brigadier General J. Patton Anderson. Then came Hardee's corps, the division of Brigadier General B. Franklin Cheatham located on Anderson's right flank, and, aligned from south to north, Brigadier William H.T. Walker on Cheatham's right, with part of Carter Stevenson's division next (part of Stevenson's division was in reserve), with, of course, Major General Patrick R. Cleburne on the northern flank. Hardee's corps numbered almost 18,000, while Breckinridge's corps, defending most of the section against which the Union now advanced, had only about 14,000 at hand, probably a little less.

Rebel artillery was placed every one hundred to two hundred yards along the crest, situated so that both direct fire and cross-fire could be delivered either against the open ground in front of the Confederate trenches at the base of the ridge or along the slopes of the ridge. The positions usually included two or three guns, though sometimes there was a full battery of either four or six guns, such as Captain Robert Cobb's Kentucky Battery, just south of the Crutchfield Road at Bragg's headquarters, or Captain C.H. Slocumb's Louisiana Battery on the right flank of Bate's division. Altogether, the Confederates had about fifty cannon defending Breckinridge's sector of the ridge but none in the trenches at the base, because they could not have been withdrawn up the ridge in the face of a Union assault.

On came the Federals. Quick time became double-quick, and finally many soldiers broke into a run. They were within three hundred yards or less of the rifle pits when cracking reports of Rebel volleys sounded from some points up and down the Confederate trenches. Charging soldiers saw countless little clouds of smoke appearing from scores of weapons. Here and there a storm of bullets tore into the Union ranks, and men went down, but the volleys, in many cases, did not come close to stopping even the first wave of skirmishers. Seeing the Rebel defenders begin to waver, some retreating up the ridge, the attackers pressed in as rapidly as possible, confident now that they were going to take the works at the base of the ridge.[32]

The Yankees had more than sufficient manpower. Not stopping to fire even one volley at the Confederates, the blue line swept into the rifle pits. It was an irrestible force, some shouting, as if in retribution, "Chickamauga! Chickamauga!" In a brief hand-to-hand fight Federals shot and bayonetted their opponents. At some points the Union first line was checked, but the on-coming second and third lines surged in with vastly superior numbers. The most determined resistance was met in front of Sheridan's right flank and in front of Johnson's sector, where Rebels from Bate's division put up a stiff fight. But courage was not enough. Overwhelmed and demoralized, surviving Confederates surrendered or fled.[33]

Many gray-clad soldiers already had left the base position—some, perhaps, because they sensed the rifle pits could not be held; some because they had been ordered to retire up the ridge if an enemy assault developed. And, in a tragic example of confusion, still others, either not receiving or not hearing instructions to fall back, held their ground, courageously obeying orders as they understood them. These men were killed, wounded, or captured, while some companies panicked and went to pieces when they supposed that other units were fleeing. Then, too, there were Confederates who preferred falling into the hands of the enemy to risking death from the firing that swept the face of the ridge. These surrendered.[34]

General Manigault described what was, from the Rebel viewpoint, a tragic affair. "The order had been issued to retire, but many did not hear it," he said, because of "the reports of their own pieces and the deafening roar of artillery." Other soldiers "supposed their comrades flying and refused to do likewise," and some "feared to retire up the hill, exposed to heavy fire in their rear . . . ." Manigault concluded: "All order was lost, and each striving to save himself took the shortest direction for the summit."[35]

Elated by their triumph, Yankees yelled and screamed, fired into the ranks of the Rebels retreating up the side of the ridge, or, filled with "enthusiasm and impetuosity," as General Wood described the emotions of his men, charged up the ridge in pursuit of the Rebels. Others simply milled about trying to catch their breath after the exhausting charge, and some were so blown that they fell upon the ground to rest. Rebel dead and wounded, tangible evidence of apparent Union victory, lay all about.[36]

But, suddenly, everything seemed to go wrong for the triumphant Federal troops. Confederates in the line midway up the slope, or crouched near the crest, were shooting as fast as they could load and fire. It was a murderous, plunging barrage. Artillery also began to zero in on the position. Federals scrambled for some semblance of cover. The trenches just won quickly became a death trap as Rebel infantry and artillery blazed away with devastating results. "Terrible was the effect of this fire on the dense lines of the enemy," recalled Brigadier General Alexander W. Reynolds, who, depressing his guns and opening on the Yankees below with canister, witnessed the havoc from atop the ridge.[37]

Now confusion plagued the Federals. Right before the assault, General Sheridan had examined the trenches with field glasses and, suspecting that they would prove untenable, thought maybe he had misunderstood his orders. He at once dispatched a staff officer, Captain J.S. Ransom, to check with General Granger whether it was the first line or the ridge that was to be carried by the charge. Before Ransom could return, the signal for advance had sounded, and the trenches were taken. Then Ransom galloped up on the left of the division and, first spotting Brigadier General George Wagner before checking with Sheridan, told Wagner that orders were only to take the rifle pits. Many men of Wagner's brigade had raced on to the ridge, started climbing it, and were already a good distance up the side. But Wagner, complying with Ransom's instructions, at once ordered his men back to the base of the ridge.[38]

One of Wagner's regimental commanders charging up the steep with his men was Lieutenant Colonel Elias Neff of the Fortieth Indiana. He later described how his regiment was restrained, only with difficulty, from a farther advance. "With the greatest reluctance, almost amounting to a refusal at first," Neff reported, the recall order was obeyed, as the troops "fell back suffering severely." Five other regimental commanders in Wagner's brigade also reported falling back by order, two of them, like Neff, stating that the order was reluctantly obeyed and resulted in unnecessary casualties. Having passed safely through the hail of fire sweeping the trenches, Federals who reached the relatively sheltered area on the side of the ridge naturally were reluctant to give ground, all the more if they thought, as some now did, that they would soon be ordered to assault the ridge anyway. Some Yankees, either failing to understand the order in all the noise and confusion or perhaps thinking it a stupid order, did not fall back. Lieutenant Colonel William H. Young, commanding the Twenty-sixth Ohio, estimated one-fifth of his regiment held their position in spite of the withdrawal order.[39]

Of the eleven brigades in the attacking force, Wagner's suffered far more than any other, taking 22 percent of all the casualties. Wagner later attributed his unusually high loss to "a concentrated fire of artillery from the front and flanks" as well as "a most deadly fire from small arms" inflicted while his regiments struggled up the ridge. Undoubtedly, although Wagner did not mention the fact, the unfortunate withdrawal order also contributed to the heavy casualties in his brigade, as his men were destined to charge up the ridge a second time into perhaps the most effective defensive fire anywhere on the Confederate line.[40]

On Wagner's right flank, since Wagner's brigade had been designated as the division's guide brigade, some soldiers from Brigadier General Charles Harker's demi-brigade were also climbing the ridge. General Harker thought his men were about one-third of the way up when Wagner's troops started falling back to the rifle pits. His left flank thus exposed to a continuous harassing fire, Harker instructed Colonel Emerson Opdycke to pull back his regiment, the One Hundred and Twenty-fifth Ohio, to the base of the ridge and re-form his ranks. Intending to recall his entire brigade—and some besides Opdycke did receive a recall order—Harker suddenly was stopped by General Sheridan.[41]

The division commander stated that he had not ordered anyone to fall back and, in fact, now planned to order an assault as soon as the troops were given a short breathing spell. Meanwhile, many of Opdycke's men, whom Opdycke estimated already had struggled halfway from the foot of the ridge to the summit, refused, just like some of Wagner's troops, to fall back. Their regimental historian later estimated that more than forty men remained. Having found natural defenses, they were firing at the Rebels from behind fallen trees, stumps, and rocks or from depressions in the ground, whatever offered a little protection.[42]

In all the excitement, Sheridan's division, predictably, was not the only one experiencing distressing blunders. Over in the ranks of the Eighty-seventh Indiana of Absalom Baird's division, Colonel Newell

Gleason watched as a staff officer, whom Gleason identified as coming from Wood's division, galloped up in the rear of the Eighty-seventh, yelling for the men to "Charge!" Many of the regiment responded at once, jumping up from the rifle pits and surging toward the ridge. Exasperated, Colonel Gleason raced to the staff officer, curtly informing the man that Ferdinand Van Derveer commanded the brigade and could be found farther along the line to the left. Gleason then rushed forward to stop the charge of his regiment, ordering the men to fall back and re-form.[43]

More blundering plagued the division—this time General Baird himself unwittingly contributing to it because of a garbled assault order. Thinking from the first that the goal was the crest of the ridge, Baird had instructed Brigadier General John Turchin, leader of his right-flank brigade, not to halt at the rifle pits but go for "the summit of the mountain." Turchin's brigade swept across the entrenchments, where some wavered for a moment, perhaps from fatigue, perhaps from fear, and then, officers urging them forward, began the long struggle up the ridge at a point that General Baird described as particularly steep and difficult to climb. The assault, however, had begun before Baird could give similar orders to his other brigade commanders; consequently, they were not supporting Turchin. And most troops on Turchin's right, in Samuel Beatty's brigade of Wood's division, had also halted near the foot of the ridge.[44]

Soon Turchin was well on his way up the ridge, but he had no support on either flank. Baird was starting to send forward his other brigades when he received orders not to permit his troops to go any farther. Perplexed, and unwilling to order Turchin back, Baird simply watched his troops on the side of the ridge, and waited.

Over on Baird's right, in the center of Wood's division, large numbers of Yankees had also bounded over the trenches and started up the ridge, brigade commander August Willich failing to understand that the troops were supposed to stop at the rifle pits. Since Willich's brigade occupied the middle position in the division, some men in the brigades to both right and left, seeing Willich's men sweep onward, were influenced to follow them up the ridge.[45]

When thus examined regiment by regiment, and brigade by brigade, it is clear that many accounts of the Federal assault on Missionary Ridge have been marred by over-simplification and generalization, a fondness for romanticizing, and a failure to recognize the tragic mistakes and widespread chaos inevitable in war. The popular, legendary concept, originally expressed in some Federal After Action Reports, that the vast mass of soldiers, "without waiting for an order," spontaneously and gallantly rushed forward in a patriotic "race for glory," contains only a particle of truth. The same may be said of the legend's corollary, that all behaved with "conspicuous courage," not an officer or man "manifesting fear or hesitation."[46]

The first Yankee advance to take the rifle pits was smoothly executed and achieved overwhelming success; what followed was anything but systematic. Muddled orders, disheartening blunders, spontaneous actions, and fear combined to create a mass of confusion, momentarily threatening to destroy what had just been gained.

Unquestionably, some Federals, impulsively and heroically, helped initiate a charge up the ridge. In many cases, however, soldiers swept on because their general officers had given them no explicit orders to stop at the rifle pits. Indeed, as previously noted, some had specific orders to go for the crest. And, certainly, many officers at the base of the ridge, as their reports confirm, ordered their units up the ridge.[47] General Sheridan said that Captain William Avery of Granger's staff came up, confirming the original order to carry the rifle pits but indicating that, if Sheridan thought the ridge itself could be taken, he should do so. At once Sheridan gave the order for his division to storm the ridge. Numerous After Action Reports establish that officers of various regiments and brigades in all four divisions now issued orders to assault the ridge.[48]

General Hazen reported: "Giving the men five minutes to breathe, and receiving no orders, I gave the word forward, which was eagerly obeyed."[49] Immediately many officers at all levels saw that their men could not stay long, enduring the intense fire from the ridge, without sustaining heavy casualties plus a loss of morale that would destroy any hope of a later advance. So they ordered the men forward, the orders sometimes issued by officers at a low level of command. And the soldiers were greatly encouraged by their officers during the charge, some competing with the men to be first up the ridge.

Equally clear is the fact that many soldiers quickly and enthusiastically responded to the forward command because, as Major S. F. Gray said, "Our only hope was to charge the hill." The men "raced to the protection of the mountain side," reported another officer, and

General Hazen, considering the terrific enemy fire, thought the "necessity" of storming the ridge "was apparent to every soldier of the command."[50]

If the Federals hoped to escape from the awful mess in which they were entangled, they would have to seize the ridge. This was the reality, cold and brutal. They must kill the Rebels before the Rebels killed them. If they were going to die anyway, then they wanted to die fighting. Thus the charge came—born of desperation, anger, and the instinct of war-wise combat veterans.

There were some Yankees who were not so brave, even in desperation. Colonel Jason Marsh, commanding the Seventy-fourth Illinois, reported that he found it "very difficult" to move the men forward from the rifle pits. It was not strange, Marsh thought, considering "the long, steep ascent . . . well calculated to appall the stoutest hearts," that men required "much urging to induce them to brave the danger." Years later, when he was general-in-chief of the U.S. Army, Sheridan acknowledged that he actually rode his horse into the trenches to force out the skulkers who were trying to shelter themselves there after the troops had started up the hill. And Major Benjamin G. Bennet, recently appointed to command the Eleventh Michigan regiment, apparently found the responsibility too heavy. In the heat of the action, he requested Captain Patrick H. Keegan to take command. To his credit thereafter, Major Bennet did serve as Keegan's second-in-command until he was killed while ascending the ridge.[51]

Thus a long, irregular, and crooked semblance of a Union line began struggling up the side of the ridge. The uncoordinated assault, many regiments intermingled, was far from irresistible. Carrying nine-pound rifles, eighty rounds of ammunition, plus accoutrements, and many wearing heavy overcoats, the Yankee soldiers, already having charged for a mile, found the going very tough at many points of the 500-foot ascent. But the blue-clad warriors were shouting and cheering one another onward. Ahead they could see Rebels clambering up the ridge, scrambling for safety; some Federals began to experience a growing confidence that the ridge could be taken. And the determination of the stronger men, pressing forward, leading the way, soon became contagious. Many of the Yankees, however unlikely it might have seemed to them at the start, were sensing victory.

12

We Will Carry the Line!

$\mathbf{A}$top the ridge in the Rebel lines Brigadier General J. Patton Anderson rode within a few yards of the breastworks, observing that "the utmost coolness and composure appeared to pervade the ranks." Anderson said "expressions of confidence" were heard from the men "as they loaded and fired with the greatest deliberation."[1] Perhaps Anderson's report is indicative of one Confederate problem: overconfidence on the part of some Rebels, nurtured by the natural strength of the terrain they defended.

Indeed the position could have been formidable, if the Confederate high command had recognized that, along with its strengths, the ridge also presented major difficulties. These disadvantages were not insurmountable, but apparently Bragg, Breckinridge, and the engineers who surveyed the defensive lines did not take them into consideration. Thinking the Yankees would never dare test such a seemingly strong position, one that could be reached only by a rigorous climb, they probably did not feel the necessity of carefully studying the ground and properly developing it for defense. Then, too, they had never waged a major defensive struggle, always having attacked—at Shiloh, Perryville, Stones River, and Chickamauga. Short on experience in fortifying a position from which to receive an assault, and never doubting the natural strength of the center, their overriding concern was with the flanks. The northern flank had been open to attack from the beginning of the siege, and now, Lookout Mountain having fallen to the Federals, the Rebel southern flank was also in peril.

Apprehension for the flanks so dominated the thinking of the Confederate high command that Bragg had considered withdrawing from the ridge when Lookout was lost, a move favored by General Hardee, who advised establishing a new line east of Chickamauga Creek. The deep stream wound northward across the rear of the entire Rebel position on Missionary Ridge, separating the army from its depot of supplies at Chickamauga Station. Bragg and Breckinridge, however, feared that a withdrawal might be detected, thus giving the Federals a chance to catch the Confederates at a disadvantage and deliver a decisive blow. Since all three generals agreed that the position on Missionary Ridge was a good one—Breckinridge saying that if the army could not make a sucessful stand on such favorable ground it could not do so anywhere—Bragg decided to remain.[2]

The defense of the ragged ridge was difficult because the ridge is so narrow at the top that, viewed from a distance, it seems hardly to crest on the west side before starting to decline on the east. Actually, the crest ranges in width from about seventy-five feet to almost six hundred feet. Defense was further complicated by varying elevations. As one walks the crest from north to south, the land rises gradually at points for fifty or more feet, only to descend, sometimes steeply, and then rise once more. Marred at places by deep ravines, and lazily winding in a manner reminiscent of a snake's trail in the dust, it is at times more like a series of hills than a ridge. It is not easily traversable ground, thus denying the Confederate army the ability to quickly and comfortably send reinforcements to any threatened point. In the event of a Yankee assault, the nature of the terrain dictated several clusters of reserve troops at strategic places. There is no evidence to indicate that this problem was considered.

In fact, no provision had been made in Breckinridge's corps for any reserve force to plug a gap in the event of a Yankee breakthrough. Part of Carter Stevenson's division, comprising the reserve in the rear of Hardee's corps on the Confederate right flank, was the only reinforcement unit available anywhere along Missionary Ridge. It was far too distant to render assistance to Breckinridge's sector, which stretched about three miles to the south of Hardee's position. Even assaults that ultimately fail, like those on both the second and third days at Gettysburg, or at Franklin, or at Fort Stedman, usually succeed in making some penetration of the enemy line, and the defense must be prepared to counter-attack. Generally speaking, Rebel reserve forces, considering both the narrowness of the crest and the congestion of the main defensive line, would have had to be deployed straight to their front, or not more than a few hundred yards to the right or left. Any extensive lateral movement would have been impossible, unless connecting trenches had been constructed under cover of the eastern slope of the ridge.

Equally distressing, the Confederate works along the top of the ridge, begun only a few days before the Federal attack, were badly planned and poorly constructed. A work detail started construction on November 23, but the number of men was insufficient, and they were also short on entrenching tools. Not until the night of November 24–25 were enough soldiers on the ridge to complete the task; but by then it was too late. Placed along the physical crest rather than what is termed the "military" crest—that is, along the top-most geographic line rather than along the highest line from which the enemy could be seen and fired on—these works severely handicapped the defenders. The least of the problems was the difficulty, in most places the impossibility, of depressing cannon sufficiently to fire effectively against an enemy coming up the ridge. Far worse, this line placed the Rebel infantry at a great disadvantage.

It was not simply that many soldiers could not fire proficiently at the enemy coming up the ridge directly in their front, which was bad enough. Also, there were several places within a few yards of the crest where the Federals, preparatory to a surge over the top, could catch their breath and marshal troops without receiving any enemy fire. Or they might unleash an enfilading fire on a Confederate strong-point, distracting the Rebel defenders from assailants coming straight at them. A properly developed Confederate line along a lower "military" crest would either have denied altogether such vantage points to the Yankees or, at the least, have subjected them to a murderous flanking fire. Brigadier General Arthur M. Manigault, for example, did lay out his own line below the natural crest, despite the engineer, a man who complained, said Manigault, of being overworked. Manigault's brigade experienced very little difficulty in stopping the enemy's advance toward its position.[3]

The Confederates were still further hampered because, if driven from the initial position, they had no place to the rear of the narrow ridge where they could try to form again and hold. All they could do was plunge down the eastern slope, which was almost as steep as the western. If a "military" crest had been developed, then the natural crest, in some places, would have provided a possible second line along which to rally in the event of a breakthrough. Having the line along the geographic crest also interfered with any deployment of reinforcements, a movement likely, as previously noted, to present a problem even under the best of circumstances. It should also be noted that some places existed along the uneven ridge where no single line would have been satisfactory, two or more positions being necessary to give adequate fields of fire to the flanks as well as straight ahead.

But possibly the worst Confederate blunder was the decision to place a substantial portion of the troops at the base of the ridge. Altogether, Bragg's army on Missionary Ridge had three defensive positions. The first, at the foot, was a generally strong line of rifle pits, located about two hundred yards in front of the ridge's base. Here the Rebels had constructed breastworks of logs and soil, taking advantage of the gently undulating ground, where rises in the terrain provided good observation and clear fields of fire. From one end of the Confederate line to the other the trees to the front had been felled and the Rebels looked west across six hundred to seven hundred yards of unbroken openness, a potential slaughter ground for their enemy. The second position, halfway up the ridge and designed to give protection for those who might be forced from the base, was much weaker than the first. In fact, it only existed—and that in unfinished fashion—along a portion of the front assaulted by Sheridan's and Johnson's divisions. The third and final position at the crest was, as just discussed, poorly conceived and only partially developed. Confederate dispositions ordered by General Breckinridge, and evidently General Bragg as well (certainly Bragg's was the overall responsibility), placed all of Brigadier General Alexander W. Reynold's brigade, three regiments from Brigadier General William B. Bate's brigade, and half of the men from each brigade in J. Patton Anderson's division in the rifle pits at the base of the ridge. Thus the Rebel line at the summit was unwisely thinned.

Accounts have come down in Confederate legend of soldiers spaced three or four feet apart, and in some places seven or eight feet; of men so far apart that two adjacent soldiers could swing their rifles without hitting each other or their rifles.[4] Possibly this was true in some places; but, applied to the line as a whole, it clearly is an exaggeration. Still, to recognize the exaggeration is not necessarily to destroy the point: the Rebel line certainly was thinner than necessary, and obviously thinner than if the troops at the base had been on the crest.

Federal troops assaulted on a front well over two miles wide. The Confederate rifle pits at the foot of the ridge ran for two and a half or two and three-quarter miles, and Breckinridge's line at the summit—theoretically stretching for more than four miles—actually had virtually all the manpower located right in the path of the Yankee march, the Confederates slightly overlapping the flanks of the Federal assault. Figuring that 10,500 Rebels were on the crest, there would have been a defender every one and a half feet, calculating on the basis of a straight line three miles long. The machinations of the ridge would change the figure somewhat, but even if one were figuring on a five-mile-long Rebel line, there would have been a defender every two and a half feet.

If all the Rebels in Breckinridge's corps had been massed on the crest along the two-and-a-half mile front that the Yankees assaulted, there would have been approximately one defender for every 1.6 attackers, calculating Federal strength at 23,000 and Confederate at 14,000. These are favorable odds for the defense, all other things being equal. An attacker usually needs at least a two-to-one advantage in the number of assaulting men, with reserves poised to immediately follow up an initial break in the defensive line. And the attackers' problem at Chattanooga was further complicated by having to first climb the ridge.

But, of course, Breckinridge's corps did not have all its strength on the ridge and, from the first, there was confusion about what would be expected from those men at the base in the event of an attack. In part, this mix-up probably stemmed from the Confederate engineers' initial indecision as to whether the ridge should be defended at the base or the crest. Anderson originally told Brigadier General Zachariah C. Deas, commanding his troops at the base of the ridge, to hold the position "to the last." Upon examining the ground, Deas became very disturbed, convinced that with the troops at hand he could not throw back an all-out Federal assault. Capture or annihilation would be the alternatives. Deas reported that he went to General Anderson "and begged that he would order the troops . . . to the crest of the ridge, where I was satisfied a much better fight could be made."[5]

Undoubtedly, the brigadier was right. And as Anderson reflected on the matter he agreed with Deas and requested permission from

Breckinridge to withdraw the troops from the base of the ridge. Breckinridge denied the request, but his orders did modify Anderson's original instructions, directing that in case of a general enemy assault Deas's troops "should not make stubborn resistance," but, according to Anderson's report, should "retire skirmishing to the top of the ridge and take position in line . . . on the crest." The new orders were of little comfort to Deas, who confided to Anderson that his men "were discouraged at the prospect of having to retire up so long and steep an aclivity under the enemy's fire." The consequences, he feared, would be disastrous.[6]

Others were also worried about the Confederate disposition of troops. General Bate, who earlier had instructed his men to hold the trenches "at all hazards," had changed his mind. In the early afternoon of November 25, General Bate began withdrawing his regiments from the rifle pits at the base of the ridge, intending to strengthen his line at the crest where, like Deas and Anderson, he felt that the best fight could be made. But General Breckinridge countermanded the order, and the troops, who were trudging upward, reversed and went back down the hill. Thus, when the Federal assault rolled forward, the Rebels had approximately thirty-five hundred men, about one-fourth of their strength in the general attack sector, positioned at the base of the ridge, contrary to the judgment of several Confederate brigadiers.[7]

It *was* a bad plan; and it is not surprising that Anderson, Deas, and the other brigade commanders in Anderson's division later laid the primary blame for defeat on Breckinridge and Bragg. But worse yet developed: the orders, be they good or bad, that no stubborn resistance should be made, with the troops falling back and climbing the ridge, were not always clear, either to the officers and men at the base of the ridge or to the soldiers at the summit.

As the heavy lines of Yankee infantry neared the rifle-pits, widespread confusion plagued the Rebels. Reynolds's entire brigade, positioned between the troops of Deas and Bate, had abandoned the ditches soon after the Union advance began, even before Federal skirmishers were close to the rifle pits.[8] The withdrawal occurred in obedience to orders intended to fill a gap at the crest of the ridge between Bate's and Anderson's troops. But the withdrawal was puzzling and disturbing to some men in the trenches. Also, some of Reynolds's men came up through Colonel Jesse J. Finley's brigade, throwing it into confusion as the battle began.

But, far worse, Reynolds's men were several hundred yards south of the gap in the Confederate line—a gap approximately one hundred and fifty yards wide—which they were supposed to fill. Only Captain James Garrity's Alabama battery, unsupported by infantry, was emplaced in the gap. The regiments of Reynolds's brigade, reorganized by Major James T. Weaver of the Sixtieth North Carolina regiment, were formed across the Crutchfield road in the left rear of Bate's division—more than a quarter of a mile away from the gap between Bate's right flank and Anderson's left; thus the opening remained unplugged.

Rapidly the situation worsened at the foot of the ridge. Some Rebels, according to the plan, delivered their rifle fire at the charging enemy and quickly retreated out of the works, endeavoring to join their comrades on the crest. Struggling from the base to the top, they had to brave both artillery and musketry fire. Many tried to cover the ground too fast, and a few even threw away their arms, accoutrements, and knapsacks. "Many failed to reach the summit at all, but fell exhausted," reported General Manigault; "some were killed or wounded and those who at last gained the crest reached it in a broken down and demoralized condition."[9]

Robert Watson of the Seventh Florida had been in the rifle pits at the base of the ridge when the Union advance began. "We mowed them down until they were within 30 yards of us," Watson wrote in his diary. Retreating up the ridge to the second line, the Floridian quickly saw that that position, too, was untenable. "Then came the worst part of the fight," he thought, "for the hill was dreadful steep and the enemy kept up a continual fire. . . . Many a poor fellow fell exhausted and was taken prisoner."

Besides carrying a rifled-musket, Watson had on a heavy knapsack, three days' rations in his haversack, and a canteen full of water. "I stopped several times and took a shot at the damned Yankees and at the same time it rested me," he wrote. Thinking that he would not be able to reach the crest with all the weight he carried, Watson said he tried to throw away the knapsack but could not get it off. This proved to be lucky, he reflected, "for a bullet struck my knapsack at the right shoulder and came out at the left, making 23 holes in my blanket." When Watson finally reached the top of the ridge he was "so much exhausted" that he "fell down and lay there for several minutes to recover breath," before seeking cover behind a log and preparing to fire again.[10]

Joseph E. Riley, Thirty-third Tennessee, never reached the summit of the ridge. As he toiled upward ahead of the Federals, a sudden pain struck him on the left side. A piece of shell, which Riley believed came from a Confederate cannon rather than a Union, ripped through his body and exited just below the right shoulder blade. Stunned, and breathing only with difficulty, as several ribs were broken, Riley first thought, he said, that he was dying. Then he remembered the enemy. "I arose and looking back saw the Yankees about 100 yards from me," he later remembered. "I tried to run, but my legs would not carry me up the slope. They overtook me and I never fired another shot at the Yankees."[11]

Another Confederate scrambling up the ridge said his company was hardly scratched while in the rifle pits but suffered terribly in falling back and climbing the steep hill. "It seemed," continued N.C. Howard, "that every Yankee within a mile was shooting at us." John Ward in the Eleventh Tennessee, like a number of his comrades, had no shoes, scraping, cutting, and bruising his bare feet as he struggled up the ridge.[12]

Rebel Brigadier General Alfred Vaughan thought his unit left the works at the base of the ridge last. "Skirmishing as it retreated," Vaughan said that his command scrambled to the top and formed on the right of Deas's brigade, "as rapidly as the exhausted condition of my men would permit." Years later, when serving in the U.S. Senate, Confederate General William Bate said that efforts of resistance by the Confederates retreating up the ridge were limited, at best. "Any check to the ascending forward movement was temporary. At some places . . . the resistance was vigorous and determined; . . . at other points there was . . . but little resistance."[13]

Sooner or later most Rebels did retreat up the hill, but, as Manigault, Colonel Tucker, and Vaughan all reported, they usually did so in such haste that, upon reaching the crest, they were too exhausted to fall into line and fight. Some were sick and faint from the exertion, a few even hemorrhaging. In some instances, only after considerable effort by their officers could the retreat of the men from the lower line be stopped at the crest and the soldiers rallied. Probably ten or fifteen minutes passed before these soldiers again were ready to fight.

Making the situation still worse, as should have been anticipated, soldiers atop the ridge, who had not known the lower entrenchments were to be abandoned, were perplexed and sometimes demoralized as they watched the men from the breastworks desperately climbing the hill. Also, they were hesitant to fire at the Yankees for fear of hitting their own men. On the other hand, the sight of the Confederates fleeing up the side of the ridge energized the charging Federals, doubtless helping to stimulate an impulse on the part of some to start up the hill after the Rebels.

On came the Yankees. Conspicuous in dress uniform was General Sheridan. Drinking from a silver flask just before ordering his division to charge up the ridge, the general had airily roared at Confederate artillerymen whose salvo spattered dirt upon his uniform: "That was ungenerous and I'll take those guns for that!" Now animated by the danger and the challenge, Sheridan waved his hat in one hand and his sword in the other, yelling at the top of his voice: "Forward, boys, forward! Give 'em hell! We will carry the line!" His horse shot from under him, the general went up the ridge on foot behind the men.[14]

Over in Richard Johnson's division on the right of the Union line, Brigadier General Carlin was shouting to his men: "Boys, I don't want you to stop until we reach the top of that hill!" And the colonel of the One Hundred and Fourth Illinois, one of Carlin's regiments, challenged his soldiers to be the first to go over the top. All up and down the line it was the same as regiment competed with regiment, and the men competed with each other, even, in some instances, a soldier to the rear grabbing and dragging backward a man in front in order to forge ahead. In Wood's division, General Willich was shouting encouragement to his men who, he thought, would have stormed the ridge "even without any command"; and on the far left, division commander Absalom Baird, apprehensive when Turchin's brigade had first charged up the ridge without support, now watched as his other two brigades, shouting and cheering, struggled up the ridge. One of Baird's regimental commanders, Major Robert M. Kelly, growled at his men not to allow any regiment to beat them to the top of the hill.[15]

The charge soon lost any semblance of order, men seeking the least difficult path of ascent and drawn to rocks, trees, and ravines, something that promised a little protection. Ravines, however, could easily become a trap, sometimes giving the Rebels a chance to line both sides near the crest, shooting as fast as they could load and fire. There were many losses, of course, in every Yankee unit.

William H. Friend of the One Hundred and Twenty-fifth Ohio, in the center of Sheridan's division, had a leg shattered as he climbed the ridge, and he died the next day shortly after the limb was amputated. Sergeant Henry Willour of the same regiment, struck in the left elbow

22. General Phillip Sheridan. *G.M.L. Johnson Papers. Tennessee State Library and Archives.*

by a minié ball as he ascended the ridge, would die in early January following an amputation. Farther to the left, in Wood's division, Jefferson McClelland of the Eighty-sixth Indiana fell near the crest, killed by a bullet through the chest. From the foot of the ridge, he had been in the forefront of the assault. Colonel E.H. Phelps was up in front, too, leading his Third Brigade on the left of Baird's division, when shot and killed halfway or more up the ridge.[16]

Color-bearers were falling right and left, some regiments losing a half-dozen by the time they reached the top. A colonel of the Eleventh Ohio described how Color Sergeant James B. Bell, wounded in five places, finally gave up and turned over the colors to someone else.[17]

As always, a few men were lucky. Captain Josiah Bruff, entrusted by a number of men with their money, had a wad of bills in a pocketbook he carried in his inside vest pocket. Soon after starting up the ridge a bullet struck, but, passing through all the money, which arrested much of its force, it inflicted only a minor wound instead of entering Bruff's chest. Literally, it seemed true that money had saved his life.[18]

Yankee progress toward the summit was very uneven, Johnson's division on the right experiencing considerable difficulty from determined Rebel resistance, as well as from confusion. The Confederates overlapped Johnson's right flank, and, advancing a few yards down from the crest, they opened up with both a heavy cross-fire and a strong frontal fire. The Federal advance was quickly brought to a halt as at least three regiments were thrown into confusion. An irritated Ohio captain reported that someone on his left yelled "fall back!" and the captain's regiment, the Thirty-third Ohio, started falling back to the rifle-pits at the base of the ridge. Colonel Anson G. McCook, Second Ohio, explained that he first tried to stop the retreat but, when only partially successful, finally ordered all his command to fall back and regroup.[19]

Whatever the reason, and undoubtedly gray-clad resistance had much to do with the episode, many troops in Brigadier General Carlin's brigade headed back down the slope. Quickly officers worked to reassure the men. Soon, about twenty minutes later according to one regimental commander, the advance resumed, the men again ordered to go to the top. Now the left of the brigade pushed toward the crest ahead of the right, seeking to avoid the worst of the enemy's flanking fire.[20]

John E. Gold, Twenty-fourth Tennessee, in General Strahl's bri-

23. General R.W. Johnson. *G.M.L. Johnson Papers. Tennessee State Library and Archives.*

gade, was one of the Rebels located some thirty or forty yards down the slope, firing at the Yankess in this sector. "Our squad kept shooting," he later wrote, "fully confident that we could hold the position for some time . . . unconscious that the Southern line was giving away on our right and that the Yankees were sweeping down the ridge in our rear. In fact," Gold concluded, "we did not know that our regiment had left the ridge." Finally surrounded late in the afternoon, Gold's little squad of about twenty men, which fought so stubbornly, would ultimately surrender.[21]

Meanwhile, as Johnson's division struggled, a mile and a half or two miles to the north, the Yankee left flank, Baird's division, confronted the steepest and roughest portion of the ridge. Lieutenant Colonel Myron Baker, leading the Seventy-fourth Indiana, said the ridge was "so steep that at some places it required all the strength we could put forth, together with what assistance might be derived from holding on to bushes and pulling one's self up by them, to make the ascent." The men "tugged up the hill as best they might, many of them at times, from exhaustion or the abrupt rise of the ground . . . compelled to drag themselves along on their hands and feet."[22]

From personal experience the author can attest that indeed the ridge is steeper and harder to climb in Baird's sector than a mile or so farther to the south. But, in many places, the very steepness of the ground protected the assaulting infantry from an effective enemy fire, unless, as in the case of part of Turchin's brigade, the soldiers found themselves moving up a ravine. The top of the ravine, reported Captain Edward Grosvenor, Ninety-second Ohio, "was crowned on either side by the enemy's rifle pits, which . . . enfiladed our position from right and left." Colonel Douglas Putnam, Jr., leading the Ninety-second, seemed scornful of death as he neared the summit. Boldly advancing within pistol range of the gray line, and cheering his men to come on, the colonel went down, severely wounded. Turchin's brigade would suffer more casualties than Baird's other two brigades combined.[23]

Farther to the right, over in Wood's division, General Hazen's brigade also faced a ravine-like, concave portion of the ridge. "Musketry fire from the ridge was very bad," Hazen reported, his command facing enfilading fire from both flanks. Too, Confederate artillery batteries positioned on the outside flanks of the concavity raked the slope with a terrible cross-fire. Although the ridge was easier to climb at this point than in Baird's sector, perhaps casualties might have been less if the ground had been steeper. The steeper the ground, the more likely were the Rebels to overshoot, even if they had a clear field of fire. Hazen's brigade suffered casualties second only to Wagner's brigade, which advanced on Hazen's right flank and also contended with the concavity of the ridge in that sector. In fact, Hazen's and Wagner's two units took nearly 40 percent of all the casualties endured by the eleven brigades that climbed the ridge.[24]

Long after the last gun of the war had been fired, Union veterans argued about which regiment first went, to use an expression from a later war, "over the top" at Missionary Ridge. General Wood marshalled an impressive array of eye-witness testimony, some from other than his own command, that troops of his division led the way. And it might be noted that General Baird's After Action Report, dated only a few days following the battle, credited some of Wood's troops as having "possibly reached the crest first. . . ." Reports of Lieutenant Colonel Gabriel C. Wharton, a regimental commander in Baird's division, and General Sheridan also lend support.[25]

Wood was probably right, despite the fact that Henry M. Cist, diligent historian of the Army of the Cumberland, gave the honor to Sheridan's division, a point of view perhaps favored by General Grant. Cist did concede, however, as General Thomas said, that the crest was won almost simultaneously at half a dozen different places. But the case for Wood's troops being first is made all the more likely from a study of the Confederate reports, evidence neglected by many earlier writers because several of these documents did not appear in the United States government's publication of the officers' official reports.

Initially, the Rebel line was breached at the position of J. Patton Anderson's old brigade, commanded at Missionary Ridge by Colonel William F. Tucker. After Action Reports by Anderson, Manigault, Deas, and Reynolds, and even Tucker's brief account, all locate the Union breakthrough in Tucker's line. And Tucker's line lay right in the center of the sector that Wood's division assaulted.[26]

Scrambling up the ridge on the far right of Wood's division was the First Ohio regiment of Hazen's brigade, commanded by Lieutenant Colonel Bassett Langdon. As he neared the crest, Langdon saw that the peculiar conformation of the ridge, forming a rough spur, gave protective cover until within a few yards of the top. Massing his men near the summit, Langdon gave the order to fix bayonets; then a Rebel bullet struck him (in the face, according to the report of Langdon's brigade commander). The lieutenant colonel slumped to the ground, lying prostrate from the wound, but his mind still functioned. Close at hand was Lieutenant Colonel James C. Foy, leading the Twenty-third Kentucky, which began the charge on the left of the First Ohio, although now the two regiments were intermingled.[27]

Obviously apprehensive, Foy questioned Langdon if they should go on. Langdon instructed him to pick out five or six good men, sight along a log that rested only twelve or fifteen steps away, and shoot the Rebels as they rose up from behind the embrasure to fire. Possibly it was one of the enemy behind the log who had shot Langdon. At any rate, Langdon knew they were there. The Federals soon had a deadly fire focused on the spot, either killing the Confederates or forcing them to scurry away. Then Langdon gave the order to charge, rising again, according to one report, moving forward, and cheering his soldiers onward before collapsing for a second time. Foy later praised Langdon, calling him "as brave and as prudent an officer as there is in the Army of the Cumberland," while General Hazen recommended that he be promoted to the rank of brigadier general.[28]

Langdon's troops, together with others from different commands, broke over the top, quickly killing or capturing the Rebels who had not fled. Hazen thought these men were the spearhead, the first on the crest. At once they fanned out both right and left, officers gathering whatever troops they could and selecting an objective. "Hastily collecting about twenty men from my own regiment . . . and a few from other regiments, I moved to the right on the crest and at double-quick," reported Major Joab A. Stafford of the First Ohio. The major intended to silence the Confederate cannon which had been sweeping the ridge with deadly effect. He drove the enemy away and captured two guns, only to find that four guns farther to the right, with a line of infantry support, were now opening on his little band. "Forward!" shouted Major Stafford, and again his men charged the Rebels. "It seemed incredible, nevertheless it is true," the major reflected, "that . . . the enemy broke and retreated in every direction, leaving their four guns and a great number of provisions in our hands." Interestingly, relative to who first reached the top, Stafford also stated that the "last battery was captured immediately in front of General Sheridan's left regiment, they being about one-half the way up the ridge."[29]

All along the line, fearless and heroic events were unfolding in the midst of the wild, confused fight. Also in Wood's division, Lieutenant Colonel William P. Chandler, Thirty-fifth Illinois regiment of Willich's brigade, had struggled to within a short distance of the enemy works on the crest when, he reported, "the men, being completely exhausted. . . , were compelled to halt at that critical point." Fearing that the assault would fail, the colonel moved quickly to the front, just in time to grasp the regimental colors as Corporal Adam Preston, the sixth color-bearer to fall, was killed. Yelling to his men to follow, Chandler carried the flag, riddled by more than thirty bullet holes, into the Rebel works, preceded, he said, "by a gallant soldier of the Sixty-eighth [Indiana], who was shot dead the moment he passed over their parapet."[30]

Chandler's leadership was important. One of the first officers on the summit, he promptly organized the troops in the immediate sector and, clearing his front of Rebel infantry, swept to the left, joining with still other Federals to rout a Confederate battery that had been raking the Yankees' ranks as they approached the crest.[31]

The Union soldiers were coming en masse, but many were falling as they went over the top. One Federal officer in the center of General Wood's division, Erastus Young, commanding Company A, Eighty-ninth Illinois, shouted "Forward and Victory!" as he reached the summit, only to be immediately struck and killed. Another Federal voice, carrying above the din and roar of battle, urging his men onward, was also silenced. Lieutenant John Reese, Company C, Sixty-eighth Indiana, took a bullet through his body just before going over the top and died within a few hours. And yet another lieutenant, named Wyman, would be found by a friend, his body resting on the side of the ridge "with his sword still grasped in his dead hand."[32]

And there were instances of quick thinking and daring as the blue-clad warriors arrived at the summit. Corporal Henry J. Angelbeck, Forty-first Ohio, saw a burning caisson, filled with ammunition and with two wounded horses attached. Cutting loose the horses, the corporal ran the burning carriage down the east side of the ridge after the fleeing Rebels where it exploded.[33]

Nearing the crest on the left side of Wood's division, Colonel Frederick Knefler, commanding the combined Seventy-ninth and Eighty-sixth Indiana regiments of Beatty's brigade, had halted his troops upon realizing the advance had isolated his regiments from any support on either flank. Under fire from artillery and small arms, Knefler's men clung to the ridge while the Confederates also rolled down lighted shells and hurled rocks at them. "We remained in our position, our flags and the enemy's almost touching," reported the

Hungarian-born Indianan, who once had fought with Louis Kossuth against the Hapsburgs, "keeping up a heavy fire until support came. . . ."[34]

Given orders to fix bayonets and charge, Knefler's men rose and struggled upward, but the effort failed as the Rebels threw them back. Again they charged, and that time the Yankees had mustered sufficient will—and manpower. Up and over the top of the ridge they came with a rush and a roar of triumph. "The enemy's works," said Colonel Knefler, "were covered with dead and wounded. . . ." The fighting here was severe, although it was over in a few minutes.[35]

Then Knefler's men, joining forces with Lieutenant Colonel Chandler's troops and others coming from their right, went running out along the ridge to the left, the whole contingent sweeping northward, "pouring a deadly fire on the enemy's flank whenever he attempted to make a stand," in the words of Chandler. "Thus was [the enemy] driven from his rifle-pits for one and a half miles," reported the lieutenant colonel, "our numbers constantly increasing by other commands coming up in our rear. . . ." Sometimes the Yankees turned captured artillery pieces on the fleeing Confederates, occasionally even forcing captured Rebel gunners to fire on their own men; and sometimes they stopped the Confederates from carrying off their batteries by killing the horses that pulled them.[36]

Soon Knefler's and Chandler's Federals were well into the sector of the ridge assaulted by Baird's division. Apparently it was Turchin's brigade of Baird's division that first reached the crest here, pouring into the enemy's works at the point of a steep and prominent knob crowned by Rebel artillery. "Stubbornly did the enemy contest the works," reported Lieutenant Colonel Hiram F. Devol, Thirty-sixth Ohio Infantry. "A terrible—almost hand-to-hand—fight ensued," Devol continued, but the Confederates were driven back, the survivors making "a second stand on the crest from four to six rods beyond, but they were . . . killed, captured, or routed."[37]

Quickly troops of Turchin's brigade were in communication with the Yankees from Wood's division, linking up and continuing the leftward sweep along the summit of the ridge. And then, coming over the top at the next spur to the left of the one taken by Turchin, were soldiers from Ferdinand Van Derveer's brigade. Major Joseph L. Budd now commanded the Thirty-fifth Ohio regiment, Henry V.N. Boynton having been wounded. Just as Bassett Langdon, so Major Budd found that the spur of a ridge provided shelter from which to fire at the

Rebels while marshalling men for the final surge into their parapet. That surge was not long in coming, and Van Derveer described it: "As my men sprang over the works, the enemy's cannoneers were caught in the act of loading and were bayoneted or driven off before they could fire their pieces." Five guns were here captured, claimed Van Derveer, three by the Thirty-fifth Ohio and two by the Second Minnesota.[38]

There was no time to savor the triumph, the gray-clads quickly launching a counter-attack against the disorganized Federals. Regimental and even company organizations were "completely merged in a crowd of gallant and enthusiastic men," said Lieutenant Colonel Judson W. Bishop, and the Confederate attack was "promptly met by a charge *en masse* by the crowd, which, after a few minutes of desperate hand-to-hand fighting, cleared the ridge, leaving the place in our undisputed possession, with some 200 or 300 prisoners."[39]

Lieutenant Axel H. Reed had charged into the Rebel works here, with the Second Minnesota. Later Reed recorded in his diary: "I reached the top of the ridge and fired two shots into the retreating and confused Rebels, and then in company with many disorganized troops, followed them up, every man for himself." Suddenly Reed saw a Confederate flag straight ahead, its red bars flapping in the breeze, the enemy rallying about it to make a stand. "I fired at a Rebel that had just mounted a horse," he remembered, "and before I got loaded again a minié ball struck my right arm, shattering the bone for eight inches below the ebow." Tearing the strap from his haversack and, with the assistance of a wounded comrade, tying the arm to stop the flow of blood, Reed tramped down the ridge unaided, seeking the regimental surgeon. After his arm had been cut off and laid on a table, Reed is said to have remarked to those around him, "I had rather have that, that way, than to have been whipped by the rebels up there."[40]

Clearly the Yankees were whipping the Rebels, many of Wood's troops, and virtually all of Baird's, sweeping leftward as they reached the top of the ridge. It could hardly have worked better if it had been planned. Ater Action Reports indicate that following the initial Yankee breakthrough by Wood's troops, a general northward sweep took place, providing an extremely effective flanking movement against the Rebel positions. Faced both by a frontal assault and by a thrust to their left flank, the Confederate positions, partly in Wood's sector, and especially in Baird's sector, seem to have collapsed somewhat like a string of dominoes falling northward. While substantial numbers of Confederates who had escaped being killed or captured as Yankees came over the top were gaining some strength as they retreated northward, the Federals pursuing them were building strength much more rapidly.

For instance, Colonel Newell Gleason of the Eighty-seventh Indiana and a host of officers in Van Derveer's brigade quickly formed the troops of the Thirty-fifth Ohio, Second Minnesota, One hundred and First Indiana, and the Eighty-seventh Indiana and then led a charge, in Gleason's words, "along the ridge to the left, gained the next point, and dashed farther on to the left, nearly along the whole front of the Third Brigade," which was Phelps's. Brigadier General Van Derveer reported that the Rebels were driven for "near half a mile," making "a very determined resistance" that lasted for about thirty minutes, finally ending with the retreat of the Confederates as darkness enshrouded the battle area.[41]

Over in Sheridan's sector, the Rebel line had been penetrated soon after Wood's soldiers to their left had first reached the crest. And there, too, many daring and heroic acts unfolded. A Union bugler, his leg severed by an artillery shot, sat on a rock outcropping, blowing the call to charge until he collapsed.[42] Private Benedict Waldvogel, Company A, Forty-fourth Illinois, killed a Confederate captain and captured the captain's entire company. Lieutenant Colonel Elias Neff, who had experienced difficulty persuading his Fortieth Indiana to climb the ridge, set a conspicuous example as he neared the top, taking the regimental colors after several color-bearers had fallen and planting them on the Rebel works near the headquarters of General Bragg, which today is just south of where Interstates 75 and 24 cross the ridge.[43]

Also in Sheridan's division, in Francis Sherman's brigade, the Twenty-fourth Wisconsin's first color-bearer was shot, the next bayoneted, and the next decapitated; then eighteen-year-old first lieutenant and adjutant of the regiment Arthur MacArthur, Jr., grasped the flagstaff, labored up the ridge shouting, "On Wisconsin!," and planted the standard on the enemy works, waving it so the whole regiment could see.[44] This action also occurred near Bragg's headquarters.

In his report, MacArthur's regimental commander said of him: "I think it is no disparagement of others to declare that he was the most distinguished on a field where many of the regiment displayed conspicuous gallantry. . . ." A century later, MacArthur's son, General

Douglas MacArthur, would tell the story that Phil Sheridan, arriving on the scene, wrapped his arms around the muddy eighteen-year-old and instructed the young man's comrades to "Take care of him. He has just won the Medal of Honor." Twenty-seven years after Missionary Ridge, after seemingly interminable red tape, Arthur MacArthur, Jr., did receive the Medal of Honor.[45]

Probably such an honor was the last thing on MacArthur's mind as he stood atop the ridge waving the regimental banner of the Twenty-fourth Wisconsin. Sheridan's troops were soon establishing footholds at several places, and enfilade fire from these penetrations subjected Confederate strong points to destructive pressure. Some of Sheridan's men worked their way along the ridge, both to the right and to left, taking Rebel positions from the flank and rear and forcing them to retreat or surrender. In this sector, however, there apparently was not as much of a mass Yankee buildup and sweep along the ridge by troops from various regiments—"the crowd," as Lieutenant Colonel Judson W. Bishop dubbed them—as ocurred on part of Wood's front and much of Baird's sector. In Sheridan's area, the Rebels generally did not retreat along the crest, either north or south, in large numbers, many simply going down the back side of the ridge when confronted with Union breakthroughs.[46]

Confederate Division Commander J. Patton Anderson certainly had known there were vulnerable points in his sector, but, ironically, he had not been particularly concerned about his old brigade, now led by Colonel William Tucker. Observing the conformation of the ridge, Anderson noted, "several spurs projected along my front, affording cover to the attacking forces, and protecting them from any but a direct fire and in places even from that. . . ." As the fighting swirled nearer the crest, Anderson thought the most threatening point was in front of Zachariah Deas's brigade, on the spur known as "Polk's Headquarters."[47]

Hastening north to that location, Anderson passed Colonel Tucker who, in Anderson's words, seemed "entirely confident of his ability to hold his position against all odds, and so expressed himself on parting with me." Yet, before Anderson even reached Deas's brigade, having first to ride past Manigault's line, the division commander was hailed by a staff officer, who claimed a Yankee flag could be seen flying from the Rebel works along Tucker's front. "I could not believe it," reported Anderson, "and told him it could not be so, for only a few moments before I had left Colonel Tucker at that point, and it was then in no danger." But, turning to look in the direction indicated by Captain Cornelius I. Walker, Anderson realized at once that the officer spoke the truth.[48]

Indeed, the center of Tucker's brigade had given way, and a section of Captain S.H. Dent's battery soon fell into the hands of Federal troops, Rebel cannoneers fighting with their swab sticks, only to be quickly overpowered and killed or captured as the number of Yankees on the ridge mounted.[49] According to Tucker, the Union infantry came over the top right at the center of his brigade, having massed a large force behind "a high projecting point" of the ridge. "When they suddenly appeared in front of our men at this unexpected point," said Tucker in his candid After Action Report, the result was "a panic," and the Rebels "gave way before them, and in spite of the efforts of their officers, continued to break on each side of the point where the enemy entered our lines, until the whole brigade fell back in disorder." Immediately General Anderson had moved to stop the breakthrough, ordering a regiment from Manigault's brigade to change front and throw back the Federals in Tucker's line. But before the men could be formed and a counter-attack launched, the Yankees also breached the Rebel line where Manigault's line joined Deas's brigade.[50]

South of Tucker's position, General Bate had spotted scattered troops a few hundred yards to his right making their way to the top of the ridge, apparently without resistance. "Believing them to be Confederates falling back from the trenches," Bate reported, he ordered his right flank troops not to fire upon them. But the general sent forward a staff officer to determine for sure if the soldiers scaling the ridge were Confederates. In a few minutes the answer came back that the troops were Yankees. Bate ordered his men to open fire, which drove the climbers to their left, although not checking their determined ascent of the ridge. Almost certainly these were the Federals who broke through the center of Tucker's brigade and into the gap between Bate's and Anderson's divisions, for Bate said, "In a few minutes I saw a [Yankee] flag waving at the point in the line of General Anderson's division, beyond the depression in the ridge, where a section of [Captain S.H.] Dent's [Alabama] battery had been firing and was then located." Bate's report complements Anderson's.[51]

Like Anderson, Bate tried to send reinforcements for a counterattack in the penetrated sector. Turning to James Weaver, Bate

ordered the major to take the men of Reynolds's brigade and counter-
attack immediately. Across five hundred yards they moved to the
north on a dead run, reaching a point on Bate's right flank. But too
much time had elapsed. They soon confronted a determined, elated
force of Federals who, far from waiting to be attacked, at once launched an assault against the Confederates. Weaver's troops broke and
retreated in disorder; also, reported Bate, "Union troops turned our
guns upon us and opened a fire of musketry from our right and rear.
This . . . caused my right to give back." Suddenly Bate realized he had
all the problems he could handle in his own sector. Federals had
gained the summit of the ridge on his left and were "rapidly enveloping the division. . . ."[52]

In fact, the entire Rebel position along the ridge was quickly
crumbling now, Yankee columns penetrating at several points, massing strength, and flanking and enveloping Confederate positions
right and left. There was nothing to do but retreat. Here and there
efforts were made to reestablish lines and retake the crest, but these
were limited and soon smashed by the victorious, confident Federals.

A Yankee in the Sixth Indiana remembered a Rebel officer calling
to his men to rally around him, shouting encouragement as he did,
and vowing "We can drive them back!" C.C. Briant described how a
soldier named Tom Jackson, of the Sixth, then "set his gun against a
cannon, unbuckled his cartridge box, which dropped at his feet, and
not uttering a word, crouched like a cat, and started on a quick run
toward his victim. . . . But fortunately for either Tom or the rebel
officer," said Briant, "the fellow, . . . when Tom was within ten feet of
him, with one desperate bound cleared the top of the ridge and
disappeared down . . . the bluff. Tom did not venture any further, but
called out: 'My God! come and see them run!' " Briant added that
when he later asked Jackson what had "made him act so strangely" in
his attempted attack on the Confederate officer, Jackson said that he
"wanted to bring the fellow in alive!"[53]

One of the Confederates leaving the top of the ridge was W.J.
Worsham of the Nineteenth Tennessee Infantry. The Rebels went
down the slope "under a most galling fire," he wrote, and Worsham
vividly recalled the actions of Tom Kennedy, an Irishman of Company C. "As we descended the ridge," Worsham said, Kennedy "did
not stop to load his gun, but would turn around every now and then,
take off his hat and shake it at the enemy, while the minnie balls were
hissing all around him." Kennedy survived Missionary Ridge, only to
fall later in the fighting around Atlanta.[54]

24. Missionary Ridge about the turn of the century. *Chickamauga-Chattanooga National Military Park.*

25. Missionary Ridge about the turn of the century. *Chickamauga-Chattanooga National Military Park.*

Far from hurling figurative defiance at the Federals, James L. Cooper of the Twentieth Tennessee was simply trying to get away safely from the top of the ridge. But then a sudden pain hit. "I knew that I had been shot," he said. The sensation, as Cooper described it, was "as if some one had struck me with a board."[55]

From the viewpoint of a sixteen-year-old Rebel, Smith Powell of the Thirty-sixth Alabama regiment, the Confederate retreat was a matter of "every man for himself in a helter-skelter race down Missionary Ridge. Everything I had," said Powell, "was shot off of me—canteen, haversack, cartridge box. This stopped my shooting at my friends in blue. . . . Breaking my old Springfield against a tree, I trusted to my feet and came out unhurt."[56]

But for the Nineteenth Tennessee's Lieutenant Colonel B.F. Moore, who had a strong premonition of death before the battle, there was not another day to live. Earlier, about noon, Colonel Moore's father, who farmed nearby, had come up to the regiment, and the despondent colonel had given him everything of value, his money, watch, and knife, convinced he would not survive the engagement. It was a premonition realized within hours, Moore being shot and killed very near his father's farm during the last stages of the fight on Missionary Ridge. Moore's brother became a prisoner.[57]

Some Rebel units, driven from the crest, began to rally and fire at the pursuing enemy. Colonel William Shy, who would die a year later in the Battle of Nashville, spotted a field band from the Twentieth Tennessee and ordered them to play "Dixie." This, said Ralph J. Neal of E Company, "seemed to do more toward rallying the men than all else." Neal also remembered seeing General Bragg "sitting on his horse with a large flag, appealing to the men to stand." But some Confederates hooted at Bragg as they passed by.[58]

There were Confederates who still, as earlier in the war many did, had blacks along with them as personal body servants. One man who fought at Missionary Ridge later recalled an impressive occurrence he witnessed involving a young Rebel and his slave named Alf. When A.B. Ellis, Thirteenth Tennessee Infantry, stationed in the center of Missionary Ridge, was shot down, his leg partially crushed, Alf, according to Thomas J. Firth, rushed to his master, picked him up, and carried him on his back for several miles to the rear, very possibly saving Ellis's life.[59]

For Confederates who had fought valiantly and successfully, the defeat and retreat from the ridge were indeed bitter. Writing to friends a few days afterward, Joel T. Haley, Thirty-seventh Georgia Infantry, said: "Let it suffice that Bate's brigade, and least of all the Thirty-seventh Georgia regiment, was in no way responsible for the disaster which occurred." Continuing in an agonized vein, Haley wrote that he "never felt more confidence in the anticipation of victory, nor did more to achieve it. We expended nearly sixty rounds of cartridges and . . . reformed and fought resolutely till an hour after dark . . . then withdrawing sadly, silently, to the rear." Despondently closing his letter in a manner appearing frequently following Missionary Ridge, Haley sought aid from Divine Providence. "The situation at present I do not profess to comprehend," he stated; "I trust that *He* who doeth all things well, will deliver us in due time if we do our whole duty. . . ."[60]

The Confederate disaster on Missionary Ridge clearly was preventable. Obviously, President Davis made one of his greatest blunders when he weakened the besieging Rebel army by sending Longstreet's corps to Knoxville. And General Bragg compounded the error, both by acquiescence and later by dispatching reinforcements to Longstreet, *after* he knew the Federals in Chattanooga were being strengthened by Hooker and Sherman. But, aside from that mistake, the After Action Reports establish that Rebel defensive planning and execution were equally bad. In retrospect, the chances of making so many mistakes, particularly when fighting on the defensive, are unlikely, and yet it all happened: the Confederate works along the top of the ridge were both inadequately conceived and inadequately constructed for repelling an attack; no provision was made for reserve forces to counter-attack a Union penetration of the defensive line; the Rebel force was divided, many troops placed at the base of the ridge, leaving those on the crest spread thinner than necessary; confusion reigned as the front line on the plain at most points was ordered to withdraw if attacked, but many of the soldiers either did not hear or did not follow the order; discomfiture also plagued the Confederates on the summit, because many never knew that the men at the base were to retire up the ridge as the enemy approached, and they were disconcerted to see their comrades scrambling up the hill, supposing them to have panicked; and, of course, those Rebels on the crest were fearful of hitting their own men if they fired at the Yankees coming behind them. All in all, the Confederate defense of the center of Missionary Ridge was thoroughly muddled. And the Rebel reports certainly indicate that much of the blame must rest on Breckinridge and Bragg.

13

The Whole Army Is in Retreat

The sun was sinking as the ringing cheers of victory were raised by General Cleburne's men and then taken up and re-echoed by the entire Confederate right wing. Satisfied that his right flank was secure, General Hardee rode south along the ridge only to learn that the left-center of the Rebel position had been carried by assault. A formidable Yankee infantry force moved steadily northward along the crest of the ridge toward his left flank. Obviously, the hard-fought triumph against superior numbers on the Confederate right wing would be of no consequence now. Hardee, Cleburne, and other officers must act fast just to extricate the right-flank regiments before they too would be consumed in the wake of the disaster at the center of the line. In the midst of the rejoicing of his men, this appalling information was conveyed to Cleburne by General Hardee, who ordered him to take command of Walker's and Stevenson's divisions in addition to his own and form a line across the ridge to stop the Federal advance. Also, he must take whatever measures were required to quickly and safely withdraw all the soldiers of the army's right wing.[1]

Colonel James C. Nisbet later described the immediate situation as he received the news of defeat. "When darkness came on, and everything was quiet about the tunnel, except an occasional shot on the picket line . . . my men wanted to get supper as they had eaten nothing during the day." The colonel said he was waiting for orders from General Gist, "supposing everything had gone well all along the line as it had with us, and expecting to renew the battle the next morning." Thus Nisbet gave his consent for the men to build fires and prepare supper. "Soon the captured coffee was boiling in the camp kettles, and the meat frying in the pans," he wrote. Riding up to Lieutenant R.T. Beauregard's battery and beginning to talk with the artillery officer, Nisbet said, they spotted some horsemen coming, one of them calling out: "Is Colonel Nisbet there?"

It was General Cleburne, approaching with the astonishing news that the Federals were on the ridge, and if the line formed to halt them gave way they would be in position to cut off the line of retreat across the Chickamauga Creek. "Have you no orders? Where's General Gist?" Cleburne blurted. When Nisbet responded that he had no orders and did not know where General Gist might be, Cleburne then said: "The whole army is in retreat. I give you orders to withdraw your brigade and battery to Chickamauga Station, Western and Atlantic Railroad; there you will find rations in the depot."[2]

When Cleburne located General Gist, commanding Walker's division, he directed him to form a line across the ridge. Brigadier General Lucius Polk was ordered to station a force at the Shallow Ford Bridge, over the Chickamauga, and hold it "at all hazards," and Govan's brigade was instructed to contest any enemy advance on the road leading to the bridge. All vehicles that could be spared were sent across the Chickamauga. Cleburne's hastily formed line across the ridge remained unchallenged, however.[3]

Earlier, when Hardee had arrived on the left of his corps and learned the dismaying fact of the Union breakthrough, he had found that division commander B. Franklin Cheatham was already facing his men southward to blunt the Federal advance. Despite Bragg's fervent criticisms and obvious animosity toward the forty-three-year-old, powerfully built, and colorful Nashvillian, Cheatham's dispositions were sound and an important factor enabling the Confederate right wing to make an orderly retreat. When the Yankee breakthrough meanced his flank, Cheatham had responded at once, throwing back Brigadier General John K. Jackson's brigade so that its front was facing south astride the path of the enemy advance. At the same time, Cheatham gave John C. Moore's brigade instructions to support Jackson. "General Cheatham ordered me to march my brigade by the flank in rear of and to the left of Jackson's, so as to cover the base of the ridge and support that brigade," stated Moore in his

After Action Report. During this movement, just as Moore's lead men passed the left flank of Jackson's brigade, the latter's men gave way in the face of Yankee pressure and rushed back through the ranks of Moore's brigade. "After stopping them and restoring some order," continued Moore in his report, "the two brigades fought as one, both officers and men, though we had at first great difficulty in holding them in line."[4]

Just possibly, Moore may have experienced some satisfaction in having to restore order in Jackson's unit. Clearly, after his criticisms of Jackson's role on Lookout Mountain the previous day, Moore was taking advantage, in his report, of another opportunity to mention anything that might be derogatory about the general. "I did not see General Jackson or any of his staff whom I recognized, except Captain Moreno, during the engagement," wrote Moore. "The enemy made great efforts to drive us from the position, but failed." Jackson responded in kind, charging in his report that Moore "goes out of his way" to be critical, and sarcastically stating: "I did not think it necessary for me to show myself to him," when "he was not under my command . . . ." If Moore wanted to see him, Jackson said, "he could have found me at all times during the engagement near the right of my line, which was on the top of the ridge, while the left was down the hill. If General Moore means to reflect upon the conduct of my brigade," concluded Jackson, "I am glad to say that there are other witnesses who bear different testimony."[5]

Meanwhile, Cheatham had Brigadier General Edward C. Walthall's brigade changing front also, to meet the Federal advance if the penetration should reach that far north. Precisely which Confederate unit, or units, then stopped the Union advance is a bit difficult to determine, and E.T. Sykes, in his history of Walthall's brigade, later credited Walthall with displaying "a mastery in the art of military tactics," as he made "the Napoleonic move that saved a portion of Hardee's corps from capture . . . ." Probably Sykes gave Walthall too much praise. The combined efforts of Moore's and Jackson's brigades apparently were sufficient to check the main attack of the Yankees. Not only Moore said that the enemy failed to drive him from his position; even Walthall reported that the Federals never got closer to his own position "than 200 yards, and not in very large force."[6]

Sykes seems to have been correct about one point, however. Bragg's praise of Hardee for "a prompt and judicious movement," in throwing "a portion of Cheatham's division across the ridge facing the enemy," was misleading. Hardee evidently had nothing to do with the change of position, either Cheatham or Walthall recognizing the necessity for action and beginning the movement. Hardee simply approved the obvious. Later, in a letter to his friend, the Reverend John W. Beckwith, Hardee admitted that he had "received more credit than I deserve." He knew that Cheatham and Walthall deserved the accolades for throwing up a defense across the ridge after the Yankee breakthrough. Also, he recognized that the credit for handling the troops on the right belonged to Cleburne. But General Bragg, because of his prejudice against Cheatham, could hardly have been expected to give that officer any credit. Significantly, Bragg did praise Cleburne, "whose command defeated the enemy in every assault on the 25th, and who eventually charged and routed him on that day, . . . and who afterward brought up our rear with great success. . . ." Bragg, in fact, commended Cleburne "to the special notice of the Government."[7] About Cheatham he was silent.

After night fell, about 7:45 P.M., Hardee began pulling out his units, starting on the left. Cheatham withdrew, followed by Walker's division commanded by Gist, then by Stevenson's. Cleburne waited until last, charged by General Hardee with the duty of covering the retreat to Chickamauga Station. It took a sharp attack by Lowrey's brigade to drive back the Yankee skirmishers in his front and thus free the Confederates from contact with the enemy. "In the gloom of nightfall," wrote Hardee a few years later, "Cleburne's division, the last to retire, sadly withdrew from the ground it had held so gallantly, and brought up the rear of the retiring army."[8]

The late November night turned bitter cold. Colonel Nisbet testified that a sleety rain fell as the men slogged through a muddy branch. While the profanity of drivers, trying to move their teams hauling the guns, carried clearly across the cold air, the time dragged on. By nine o'clock everything was safely across the Chickamauga, except the pickets and, as Cleburne expressed it, "the dead and a few stragglers lingering here and there under the shadow of the trees for the purpose of being captured, faint-hearted patriots succumbing to the hardships of the war and the imagined hopelessness of the hour." The pickets were eventually withdrawn without the loss of a man, according to Captain Buck's record, and later the Chickamauga bridge was fired.[9]

"The scene of disorder at Chickamauga Station beggars description," wrote Buck, and "can only be appreciated by one who has seen a freshly beaten army." Another soldier said that at Chickamauga

26. General Benjamin Franklin Cheatham. *Dahlgren Collection. Tennessee State Library and Archives.*

Station the men found "everything in confusion—stragglers in-numerable hunting their commands. Cleburne's division alone seems to maintain any order. Ah the bitter humiliation of this disastrous day." And Colonel Nisbet said that his brigade marched into the station "in good order, was halted, came to a front and stacked arms. But we found most of Bragg's army already there, a howling mob. They had set fire to an empty wooden storehouse whose lurid flames illuminated the country for miles around. . . . This was my first experience of the demoralization of defeat."[10]

Some of the soldiers remembered General Bragg. One man related that the general tried to rally the soldiers after the breakthrough, stationing himself in the midst of the fleeing mass, shouting, "Here is your commander!" But the men only responded, if they bothered to reply at all, with a favorite line, "Here's your mule!" This was a standing joke with many Confederates, said to have originated early in the war when a peddler, charging that the soldiers had stolen his mule, was invited to search the camp and see if he could find it. As he searched, cries of "Here's your mule" came from all sides, the soldiers enjoying their sport immensely at the expense of the hapless peddler. And there were also Confederates who reportedly jeered when they saw Bragg, crying, "Bully for Bragg, he's hell on retreat." Years later, a Tennessee soldier wrote that he best remembered Bragg "sitting upon his horse at the ford of Chickamauga Creek watching the infantry wade through the cold water on our retreat. . . . Some of us, knowing the bad effect on our feet of marching in wet shoes, sat down and removed both shoes and socks, taking time also to replace them on the other side. . . ." Continuing, Marquis Lafayette Morrison said, "We halfway expected General Bragg to rebuke us, but he did not."[11]

Perhaps Bragg was overcome with despondency at the time that Morrison recalled. In his report Bragg said: "A panic which I had never before witnessed seemed to have seized upon officers and men, and each appeared to be struggling for his personal safety, regardless of his duty and his character. . . ."[12] Unquestionably, much of the Confederate center and left had collapsed and fled from the ridge in a rout. Besides the Yankee forces, which had succeeded in carrying the Confederate line at a half dozen or more points, General Hooker's command was also rolling up the Rebels' left flank. After the long delay in crossing Chattanooga Creek, Hooker's three divisions had pushed on to Rossville Gap and turned north against the Confederate position on the ridge. Cruft's division marched along the crest, while

Osterhaus's division moved on a parallel route along the east side of Missionary Ridge and Geary's division advanced on the west side.

Because the ridge was so narrow, Cruft halted to reorganize, forming his division into four short lines. The time required to put his lead division into a columnar formation permitted Hooker's other two divisions to come abreast of Cruft's unit. All three then advanced at an aggressive pace, making it difficult if not impossible for the Confederates, many of whom were taken aback by this threat to their flank, to prepare a determined resistance. If the Rebels attempted to defend a position against Cruft's advance along the ridge's crest, they were subjected to a flanking fire from the two Yankee supporting divisions. If they continued to resist, the enemy would soon overlap their flanks and be in their rear. If they descended the ridge there was a good chance of being shot or captured by the Federal flank divisions. And Confederates who withdrew northward along the ridge were subject to being surrounded and captured by Johnson's division from Thomas's Army of the Cumberland.[13]

Within approximately an hour after the charge began, the Army of the Cumberland had overrun the center of the Confederate line, while Hooker's divisions had smashed feeble resistance on the Confederate left and established contact with General Thomas's right flank. Bragg's army, except for the right flank and a portion of Bate's division, had broken into headlong flight toward its base at Chickamauga Station—"entirely routed and . . . nearly all the artillery having been shamefully abandoned by its infantry support," according to Bragg's own words.[14]

In the midst of the Confederate disaster was General Manigault. "I have on several occasions been repulsed and driven back when taking part in an attack," he recalled, "but never before or since have I been one of a routed army, where panic seemed to seize upon all, and all order, obedience, and discipline, were for the time forgotten and disregarded." Manigault confirmed Bragg's description, earlier quoted, of panic seizing many officers. "To stop the men in their mad flight, even after leaving the enemy hundreds of yards in their rear, was almost impossible," continued Manigault. "The officers generally seemed to lose their presence of mind. Threats and entreaties alike proved unavailing, and I only succeeded by telling them to reach the brow of a hill still further to the rear, and there to throw themselves upon the ground behind the crest, assuring them that in this way only could they be saved." The general also said that he collected the more resolute men and authorized them to "shoot down all who went beyond that point. . . ." In this manner, he "at last succeeded in forming the nucleus of a line . . . and in a reasonably short time matters again assumed a respectable appearance." Yet, Manigault added, "it was a long time before they got over the mortification of defeat. . . ."[15]

Caught in the midst of the tumultuous retreat were, of course, the wounded and the dying. W.M. Pollard of Tennessee had been shot in the chest and feared that his life was ebbing away. "I was left all alone," he recorded in his diary, "but two of our soldiers, strangers to me, raised me up, putting their arms around me and my arms around each of them. . . ." In this fashion they carried him along, dragging his feet, to a field hospital. "An ambulance was within a few feet of me," Pollard continued, saying that he called to one of the men in his company who happened to pass by, grabbing the soldier's hand and telling him, "I would never let him go till I was put in the ambulance. The surgeon brought me a glass of whiskey, had me put in the ambulance and I was carried to Dalton."[16]

Another wounded Tennessean, Tom Webb, was not so fortunate, even though he had friends rather than strangers trying to help him. Lying on the battlefield, shot in the head, Webb's "blood and brains" smeared his face and clothes, said Sam Watkins, "and he still alive. . . . We did not wish to leave the poor fellow in that condition," continued Watkins, "and A.S. Horsley, John T. Tucker, Tennessee Thompson and myself got a litter and carried him on our shoulders through that . . . night back to Chickamauga Station." Despite their efforts, the next morning Dr. J.E. Dixon examined Webb and told the men that it was "utterly impossible" for him ever to recover. There was nothing to do except leave him. "We took hold of his hand, bent over him and pressed our lips to his—all four of us," Watkins recorded. "We kissed him good-bye and left him to . . . the advancing foe, in whose hands he would be in a few moments."[17]

And there were the wounded who could never be moved from the spot where they had fallen; whose exact fate would never be known. Such was the loss of Lieutenant Colonel Julius Porcher of the Tenth South Carolina Infantry. "He was wounded a few moments before the line broke," recalled General Manigault. "Unfortunately no litter was nearby at the time on which to remove him. During the confusion which soon after took place he was lost sight of, and fell into the hands of the enemy. Nothing more was ever heard of him or of his fate." Manigault said that inquiries by flag of truce failed to turn up any information about Porcher. General Manigault concluded by stating, "I do not doubt that his wound was mortal, and that he died within an hour after receiving it." The one certainty is that all traces of the Confederate officer were lost to his family and friends.[18]

As the Confederate debacle unfolded on that late November evening, General Sheridan looked eastward from a vantage point atop the ridge. He said that the enemy's "disorganized troops, a large wagon train, and several pieces of artillery could be distinctly seen fleeing through the valley below within a distance of half a mile."[19] Sheridan decided on pursuit. Without waiting for orders, he pushed his division down the eastern face of the ridge on the heels of the enemy. He sent Harker and Wagner forward against the Rebel rear guard, with Francis Sherman's brigade in reserve. Wagner's brigade was deployed on the left side of the Crutchfield Road, along which the Confederates were fleeing toward Chickamauga Station, while Harker's men deployed on the right of the road.

Soon Wagner captured nine pieces of Confederate artillery and a host of enemy stragglers. While Wagner sent two regiments to silence a battery firing from a knoll to the left of his line of advance, Harker's brigade divided at a fork in the road, part of his men tramping off to the southeast as the others continued along the main route with the rest of Wagner's troops. About a mile from Missionary Ridge, these Yankees ran into strong resistance. "The road ran on a high, formidable ridge," said Sheridan, "on which the enemy had posted eight pieces of artillery, supported by a heavy force" of infantry.[20]

The exultant, hard-charging Federals had run into the delaying position held by Bate's division, the only division along the Confederate center that had maintained its formation and made an orderly withdrawal. Instructed by General Bragg to hold the position "as long as tenable," thus covering the chaotic retreat of Breckinridge's corps, Bate had hastily established two delaying lines, the first of which the Yankees now encountered. In command of this main front line was Brigadier General Jesse J. Finley, with orders from Bate to hold as long as possible, only falling back upon the second line when severely pressed.

The Confederate position was semi-circular, forming a concavity into which the Federals marched as they followed the Crutchfield road, with artillery fire from the flanks along the ridge suddenly raking the advancing troops. It was nearly dark, but Sheridan determined to drive ahead, even though he had no artillery support. An initial attack up the face of the ridge being turned back, Sheridan brought up Wagner's two regiments, the Twenty-sixth Ohio and the Fifteenth Indiana, the same that were earlier detached to silence enemy artillery firing from a hill to the north. Placing Wagner in command of the attack, Sheridan ordered the fight renewed. In virtual darkness Wagner advanced across rough terrain, his men reaching a point on the left of the ridge from which they swept the Rebels with rifled-musketry.

In describing the action for his report, Sheridan became uncharacteristically colorful: "When the head of the column reached the summit of the hill, the moon rose from behind, and a medallion view of the column was disclosed as it crossed the moon's disk and attacked the enemy, who outflanked on the left and right, fled, leaving two pieces of artillery and many wagons. This was a gallant little fight."[21]

Bate's report gives a rather different impression of the "gallant little fight." The Confederate wrote: "This fight was made by a retreating force against an advancing and victorious one. It lasted for nearly an hour after night, and staid the onward movement which was pressing us back to the bridge" over the Chickamauga. After this engagement, "Not pursued by the enemy, I leisurely moved the command to the pontoon bridge. . . . My command being in good order, I moved it to the east bank of the Chickamauga and bivouacked. . . ."[22] Perhaps Sheridan's pursuit was not quite as formidable and his success not as solid as his After Action Report might lead one to think.

While Sheridan pursued, other Federals scoured the battle area in search of better weapons, prepared food, or tried to assist the wounded. John Ely of the Thirty-sixth Illinois said that when the Rebels had been driven from Missionary Ridge, the regiment re-formed its lines, stacked arms, and made details of men to care for the wounded. Searching the ground for abandoned weapons, Ely reported, "we all exchanged our muskets for rifles, either Enfield or Springfield." Ely wrote that he found one "all smeared with some good reb's blood." After preparing and eating "a scanty supper," Ely recorded, he "took a walk by moon light down the hill." The night was "cold and frosty," and most of the wounded had been gathered together, with fires built up nearby them. The dead, of course, still remained on the field.[23]

Among the living, but wounded, there were some who seemed to have miraculously cheated death. Major William M. Clark, surgeon of the Fifteenth Ohio, related that a young boy came back with one arm hanging limp at his side, cheering and swinging his cap with the other, apparently "inspired with a noble rage, which spurned death and any obstacle however great." The surgeon examined the soldier and found that "the limp arm was literally shot off, that the shot had knocked him down and that in falling, his coat sleeve had been twisted so as to stop the flow of blood, and in this condition he had started back down the ridge, cheering and waving his cap."[24]

The time was about 9:00 P.M. when Lieutenant Axel Reed, badly wounded atop the ridge, having tramped down the hill and ridden three miles in a wagon, had his right arm amputated in Chattanooga at the Fourteenth Army Corps hospital. Later, Reed wrote that it was impossible to relate "the scenes of horror that fell under my eyes" at the time. Of the twenty-one wounded men in his ward, Reed reported, twelve did not recover.[25]

Also on the night of November 25, a worker for the Christian Commission, visiting a field hospital, questioned a wounded Yankee about where he had been shot. The soldier strangely replied, "Almost up." The worker explained that he was asking, "In what part of the body are you wounded?" But the soldier, deliriously enthralled by the memory of the inspiring charge up the ridge, answered, "Almost up to the top." Then the Commission man pulled back the injured Federal's blanket, viewing a nasty, mortal wound. The Union soldier, glancing at his body, then said: "Yes, that's what did it. I was almost up. But for that I would have reached the top." Then the soldier repeated faintly, "Almost up," and died.[26]

After visiting several of the hospitals in Chattanooga, General Richard Johnson wrote to his wife, crying out: "Oh the horrible wounds—In all parts of the body, some with legs off, others with arms off, while others were wounded through the chest. . . . *Duty* only could call me to such a place."[27] Thus misery and death dogged the Federals, despite their triumph, and equally oppressed the defeated Confederates. The gods of war, as usual, had dispensed suffering and horror to both armies without discrimination.

A hungry Confederate, Marcus B. Toney, First Tennessee, remembered tramping into Chickamauga Station on the retreat, spying a large pile of bacon about to be burned, and running his bayonet through a side of it as he envisioned a good supper. Suddenly, enemy guns opened fire, a wounded comrade was pleading for help, and Toney lost his bacon while he and three others set out carrying

Samuel Seay to safety. Through the night they toiled, getting wet in the cold water as they crossed the Chickamauga, while their human burden got heavier and heavier. But their efforts saved Seay.[28]

Another Rebel "good Samaritan" was not so fortunate during the retreat. Joseph Hoover of the Forty-fifth Tennessee Infantry said his lieutenant sent him and another soldier named Jack Woods back to help Isaac Eaton, "a little fellow," who was wounded in the thigh. "We were helping him along as best we could," recalled Hoover, when "the Blamed Yankees" took all "three of us prisoners. They kept us on the ridge all night." Hoover watched as the Federals collected their own dead, spreading coverings over their faces, but, alleged Hoover, leaving the dead Confederates uncovered.[29]

J.H. Warner was also captured by the Federals. The Tennessean, a member of the Nineteenth Tennessee Infantry, said he spent a miserable night in the railroad depot, without any fire, suffering from the cold and feeling very lonesome as he anticipated the confines of a Northern prison. Perhaps Warner would have been willing to change places, if such had been possible, with James L. Cooper of the Twentieth Tennessee. Although wounded as he retreated from Missionary Ridge, Cooper did manage to escape capture. Struggling on through the night, the following day, and the next night, he finally arrived at Dalton, Georgia. "I was completely broken down, and my wounds were quite painful," he related. "I got on the [railroad] cars and started, on top in a cold rain, for Marietta, where I went to the hospital. . . ."[30]

Captain Samuel T. Foster of the Twenty-fourth Texas (who wrote of the Yankees attacking Tunnel Hill, "still they advance, and still we shoot them down—and still they come. Oh this is fun to lie here and shoot them down. . . .") was also among the wounded. "At first I could not realize that I was shot," said Foster. "It felt like someone had struck my leg with the side of a ramrod, or a stick and benumbed it somewhat." Later, after he had been carried to a field hospital, Foster's wound was examined by a surgeon who "run his fingers in and out" of the wound, "until he said there was no foreign substance left in there to hinder it from healing up." Like James Cooper, Foster soon found himself on a train to a hospital in Marietta, where he remained for several months unable to walk.[31] Much suffering was yet to be endured, but at least Cooper and Foster were both free and safe. Many Confederates would have envied them.

J.W. Simmons of the Twenty-seventh Mississippi had pulled duty as sergeant of the guard and been ordered "to look well to the prisoners." In his keeping was a young man sentenced to death for having forged a furlough pass to visit his wife. Otherwise, the soldier had a good military record, and had been wounded in an earlier action. "I have often wondered why this prisoner, knowing his fate, did not make a break for liberty during that night's march," wrote Simmons. While it would have been the duty of Simmons and the other guards, under such a circumstance, to have shot at the prisoner, Simmons said: "I have never thought any of us would have aimed with much accuracy, knowing all the circumstances and his reputation as a fighter." But the prisoner did not attempt to escape and was later executed by a firing squad. "Of the many thousand solemn scenes it was my misfortune to witness or perform during the war," Simmons would later write, "this was the saddest."[32]

A Pennsylvania Federal, Frank Wolfe, wrote on November 26: "I have seen enough of fighting to last me a lifetime. . . ." Wolfe and a friend named Tom had ridden over the battlefield together. He recounted watching a burial detail laying a father and his son, a Union captain and a Union private, respectively, side by side in a grave. Also, Wolfe remarked on the horror of two houses, with wounded men inside, which had been burned. The charred remains assaulted his sensitivities. "I saw death in almost every conceivable form that could revolt humanity," he wrote. "Just as we reached the extreme right of Mission Ridge, . . . we came upon a party of five badly cut up." These wounded soldiers were Confederates from Alabama. Wolfe and his companion had lunched on some bread, meat, and half a bottle of wine—"prime maderia"—the remainder of which they now shared with the stricken Confederates. "Tom and myself gave them the balance of the bread and meat, poured the half bottle of wine down their throats, rekindled their fires [which others had set earlier], and wrapped them as comfortably as possible. I found their wounds still undressed. One was shot in the lungs and evidently dying. . . . They bade God bless us! as we left them."[33]

These and many more were the disturbing scenes of carnage; the indescribable and inevitable aftermath of a great battle, everywhere evident in the environs of Chattanooga on the night before Thanksgiving 1863 and for days thereafter. During the fight for Missionary Ridge it had occurred to General Thomas that Orchard Knob would make a beautiful burying ground for Union soldiers slain in the engagement. Soon after the battle, he ordered a military cemetery laid out on the little hill. The chaplain who would be in charge of burial services came to Thomas and asked if the dead should be buried by states—Ohioans here, Pennsylvanians there, and so on. Thomas pondered the question and then shook his head. "No—no, mix 'em up," he said. "I'm tired of states' rights."[34]

The Union had won a very important victory at Chattanooga. Bruce Catton even stated that "the Confederacy had passed the last of the great might-have-beens of the war. Its supreme attempt to restore the lost balance had failed."[35] Certainly the Confederacy had made a great effort to achieve victory in the west, transferring men from Virginia and Lee's army to reinforce Bragg. The Federal army might have been destroyed at Chickamauga, or starved into surrender at Chattanooga, or flanked out of Chattanooga and forced either to retreat or to fight under undesirable circumstances. But none of these possibilities had materialized. "It had been highly important for the Union army to take and hold Chattanooga before the November elections," wrote historian Allan Nevins, as he evaluated considerations of a nonmilitary character. "Had it lost its grip upon the city and been forced back toward Nashville, a heavy depression would have settled upon the Northwest. Now a sense of elation pervaded the great area from Ohio to Kansas."[36] And now it was the Confederates who faced the worst, as the whole army retreated.

14

I Fear We Both Erred

Still, as the Rebel army fell back into North Georgia, the fighting of the Chattanooga campaign was not over; not totally. On the morning of November 26, General Hooker requested of General Thomas permission to follow the retiring enemy. Thomas assented and added John Palmer's corps to the pursuing column. The march was delayed, however, because of the destruction of a bridge over the west bank of the Chickamauga; but by nightfall Palmer had reached Graysville, and Hooker's own infantry force had advanced to within five miles of Ringgold, poised to resume the pursuit at daybreak of the twenty-seventh.[1]

Bragg was worried, and with good cause. Privately he expressed a fear that the wagon trains and artillery would probably be lost. In the crisis he called upon General Cleburne. About midnight, an officer from General Bragg reached Cleburne, conveying a verbal order that he place his command in a defensive position at a pass through the hills a short distance below Ringgold and hold it at all costs up to a stated hour of the next day. Cleburne's strength was about 4,000 men. Anticipating that the pursuing Federals would be much more numerous (Hooker did have about 16,000 troops), and knowing that he would be totally without support, Cleburne stated these facts to Bragg's staff officer. Also, he added that he was accustomed to obeying orders, but, fearing this action would result in the destruction of his division, Cleburne requested that the messenger put the order in writing as a protection to himself in case of disaster. This was done.[2]

Cleburne then roused his 4,000 men from sleep, waded them through the icy waters of the creek, and sent Captain Buck to Bragg with a full report of what had been set in motion, while he himself rode ahead to examine in the darkness, as best he could, the narrow gorge he had been assigned to defend. Buck was also told to ask for more specific instructions. Arriving at army headquarters about four in the morning, Buck said, he found that "a single candle only intensified the darkness of the room beyond the reach of its feeble rays." Buck received a warm greeting from Colonel Brent and then "a voice from the gloom inquired who it was. 'Captain Buck of General Cleburne's staff,' replied Brent. Anyone at all acquainted with General Bragg will remember that he was far from emotional, and not at all 'gushing' in his nature," Buck later wrote. At Colonel Brent's answer, however, Buck said, "footsteps were heard advancing, and to my surprise, I may say embarrassment, he extended his hands, and grasping my right one in both of his gave the order. . . ." Buck was to "Tell General Cleburne to hold his position at all hazards, and keep back the enemy, until the artillery and transportation of the army is secure, the salvation of which depends upon him." Buck thought that Bragg "exhibited more excitement than I supposed possible for him. He had evidently not rested during the night."[3]

Meanwhile, General Cleburne formed his plan for a defensive fight at Taylor's Ridge, quickly perceiving that his men would be caught in a dangerous position if the enemy should succeed in turning either flank. Taylor's Ridge, similar in appearance to Missionary Ridge except for a heavier covering of timber, rose abruptly just east of the town of Ringgold, about twenty miles southeast of Chattanooga. The ridge ran nearly due north and south, and was intersected, opposite the town, by a narrow gorge barely wide enough for the passage of the Western and Atlantic Railroad, a wagon road, and a large branch of the East Chickamauga Creek. As the wagon road continued southeast from the gap toward Dalton, the winding creek was bridged at three points within a short distance. Thus, if either Confederate flank was turned, the retreat route could be easily blocked by capturing or destroying these bridges.[4]

The gap through the ridge extended about a half mile. Its western mouth, into which the Federals would be approaching, broadened out toward the north. Looking from the Rebel position toward the advancing Yankees, the ridge on the right, or north of the gap's western mouth, rose gradually, while on the left or south side the ascent was abrupt. Cleburne placed his lines to extend both right and left from the mouth of the gap. "On the precipitous hill to the left of the gap and creek I placed the Sixteenth Alabama," reported Cleburne, "with instructions to conceal itself and guard well the left flank." Along the side of this hill he deployed three companies, while for the defense of the gap itself the general established four short lines across its narrow opening, with skirmishers thrown forward to occupy a patch of woods in front of these lines. For a reserve force, three regiments were placed in the center of the gap. Cleburne ordered his remaining units to take position "near the rear mouth of the gap with directions to observe my right flank and prevent the enemy from turning me in that quarter."[5]

These dispositions were barely completed when Hooker's skirmishers, about eight o'clock in the morning, were seen advancing toward the gap, driving the Confederate cavalry back into the gorge. "Close in rear of the ridge our immense train was still in full view," Cleburne testified, "struggling through the fords of the creek and the deeply cut up roads leading to Dalton, and my division, silent, but cool and ready, was the only barrier between it and the flushed and eager advance of the pursuing Federal army."[6] On came a solid column of Yankee infantry, a brigade of Peter J. Osterhaus's division, marching by fours down the railroad track.[7] In front of the mouth of the gap stood Cleburne, on foot, at the spot where he had placed two Napoleon guns under the command of Lieutenant Richard W. Goldthwaite. "I had screens of withered branches built up in front of these," wrote Cleburne, "so as to effectually conceal them from view, and made the artillerymen shelter themselves in the ravine close by."[8]

The approaching Union column was allowed to come within short range. A private in the Thirteenth Arkansas Infantry, supporting Goldthwaite's Napoleons and thus standing near Cleburne, said that, when the nearest line of Federal troops was about fifty yards away, the general, watching them through field glasses, almost sprang into the air, clapped his knee, and shouted in a strong Irish accent, "NOW, Lieutenant, give it to 'em, NOW!" The first blast into the column was followed by volley after volley as both artillery and massed infantry fire tore into the enemy ranks. When the smoke cleared, there were "patches of men scattered all over the field" and the rest were running for cover "as fast as their legs could carry them."[9]

The Federals recoiled, seeking shelter under the railroad embankment. Although the Union troops were momentarily stunned by the severe fire, the confusion in their ranks was brief. While the soldiers who went to ground along the railroad began to engage the Rebels in front of the gorge in a brisk firefight, other Union infantry advanced against Cleburne's right flank. From Osterhaus's division, four regiments under command of James A. Williamson were deployed to ascend the ridge on the Federal left. And John Geary ordered four of his regiments, under command of William R. Creighton, still farther to the left with the same objective of turning the enemy's right flank.[10]

The first flanking attack under Williamson's command went in against Confederate troops led by Major W.A. Taylor. Steadily the Federals clawed their way up the side of the ridge in spite of a heavy fire directed at them, continuing to advance until Colonel Hiram Granbury sent two companies to reinforce Taylor, giving him sufficient strength to charge down the hill upon the force assaulting him. Cleburne reported that Taylor's charge routed the attackers, "capturing between 60 and 100 prisoners and the colors of the Twenty-ninth Missouri Regiment."[11]

Meanwhile, the second Federal flanking force had moved into position farther toward the Confederate right flank. General Geary described the action: "Under an accurate and galling fire poured down upon them from the heights 500 feet above with effect that began to tell upon his ranks, Creighton steadily ascended the steep side of the hill. . . . Our fire was withheld until half way up and within close range. . . ." Then, said Geary, "Volley after volley was poured into the opposing hosts above, and a murderous fire swept back into our own lines."[12]

General Cleburne had spotted this force ,moving to his right, and he notified General Polk, in rear of the gap, to meet and check it. "Luckily General Polk had already heard of this movement," reported Cleburne, "and anticipating my order, sent the First Arkansas up the hill and met the enemy's skirmishers within a few yards of the top." With the help of the Seventh Texas Infantry, and after an obstinate fight, the Yankees were driven down the hill. They did not retire permanently, however, soon regrouping for another assault. In fact, both Federal flanking columns made several vigorous assaults, only to be forced back each time. Finally, Creighton fell mortally wounded, and General Geary decided to pull his men back to the base of the ridge. By this time still more Yankees had begun to assault yet another point of the Rebel right flank. These too were repulsed by regiments under the command of General Mark P. Lowrey and Polk, the latter throwing up some slight defensive works along the ridge in anticipation of another attack.[13]

Meanwhile, the Federals had deployed a force to attack Cleburne's other flank. The enemy "sent what appeared to be a brigade of three regiments to the creek upon my left, and crossed over some companies of skirmishers," Cleburne said. "These were promptly met and stopped by a detachment from the Sixteenth Alabama, posted on the left-hand hill, and the main body was for some time held in check by [James M.] Dulin's skirmishers on the face of the left-hand hill, and the other skirmishers of [Daniel C.] Govan's brigade, on the creek bank and in the patch of woods to the left of the railroad."[14]

During all this time Govan's men, positioned at the mouth of the gorge, had been subjected to a heavy fire. And Cleburne remained near the front line, with Govan, where he had a panoramic view as he watched every movement of the enemy. Much to his displeasure, Cleburne saw the Federals charge and gain a lodgment in some houses near his line, from which sharpshooters could mount an effective fire against the Confederate cannoneers. Osterhaus had ordered the charge. "The Thirteenth Illinois Infantry executed the order in magnificent style," Osterhaus reported. "They charged through a hailstorm of balls, and gained the position assigned to them and held it, although the rebels poured a murderous fire into those brave men from the gorge in front and the hill on the right."[15]

After a few minutes the Federals concentrated a force under cover of the buildings and charged Govan's position, only to be repulsed by a withering infantry fire, and canister from Goldthwaite's Napoleon guns. Goldthwaite then shelled the houses with such destructive effect that the "annoyance" (Cleburne's word) from that position was at last relieved.[16]

For nearly five hours, until past noon, Cleburne's division battled to hold the gorge. The hard-pressed Confederates, as on Missionary Ridge, again resorted to hurling stones upon their opponents, or clubbing them with rocks in close, hand-to-hand fighting—if pistols were empty or failed to fire, or muskets seemed too cumbersome to be swung as clubs in such tight quarters. After the struggle, Cleburne was amused when one of the prisoners, an Irishman, saw Christopher

Cleburne, the general's teen-age brother, and declared, "Ah, you are the little devil who smashed me jaw with a rock!"[17]

At last came a dispatch from General Hardee, saying that the train had now reached a safe distance, and Cleburne could withdraw when, in his judgment, such was advisable. The division soon fell back beyond Taylor's Ridge and formed in line, ready to fight again if necessary. But the Federal pursuit had ended, General Grant riding up and telling Hooker to discontinue the movement. Hooker turned back to Chattanooga.

The engagement at Ringgold was a small-scale affair in comparison with Missionary Ridge, but it secured the line of Confederate retreat and thus, obviously, was invaluable to the army. Cleburne's service would be officially recognized by a joint resolution of thanks from the Confederate Congress, which credited him with saving the wagon train and artillery. The Union had won Chattanooga, but the total destruction of the Rebel army, despite the debacle in the center of Missionary Ridge, had not been accomplished, and an immediate march southeast into Georgia would not follow. Now the wrecked Army of Tennessee would recuperate in the northern part of Georgia.

Bragg at last would step down from command of the army. Back on October 30, Stoddard Johnson had noted in his journal that President Davis had telegraphed Bragg stating that he thoroughly sustained him in the face of all opposition to his retention of the army command. "General Bragg will regret that he has not insisted on being relieved," Johnson predicted.[18] He was right.

In a telegram to General Samuel Cooper on the night of November 28, Bragg closed with a simple statement: "I deem it due to the cause and to myself to ask relief from command and an investigation into the causes of the defeat." Bragg blamed the soldiers in his report of November 30, stating, "no satisfactory excuse can possibly be given for the shameful conduct of our troops on the left in allowing their line to be penetrated. The position was one which ought to have been held by a line of skirmishers against any assaulting column. . . ." On December 1, he wrote to Jefferson Davis, speaking of "my shameful discomfiture" in the Chattanooga operations, which were "justly disparaging to me as a commander." But he still blamed others for the failure. Rather than the men in the ranks, the commander now lashed out once more against his generals. "The warfare against me has been carried on successfully, and the fruits are bitter." He said that Breck-inridge "was totally unfit for any duty from . . . drunkenness" and that "Cheatham is equally dangerous." In the midst of such recriminations, however, Bragg penned one very accurate statement: "I fear we both erred in the conclusion for me to retain command here after the clamor raised against me."[19]

Indeed, both Bragg and Davis had "erred" during the Chattanooga campaign, and not merely in the decision to retain Bragg in command when many of the chief officers, as well as men in the ranks, wished to have him replaced. When Davis suggested that Bragg might send Longstreet with two divisions against Burnside at Knoxville, the Confederate president was apparently unaware of either strategic or tactical reality. Even if Burnside was defeated, which by no means could be assumed, Grant would not have been forced to retreat from Chattanooga as long as his communication line back to Nashville was intact. Also, Davis had seemed oblivious to the Federal concentration of forces at Chattanooga, which left Bragg, with Longstreet gone, badly outnumbered—approximately two to one. Bragg appears to have been equally blind to the gathering storm. So anxious was he to be rid of Longstreet that he accepted Davis's plan without any qualms. Bragg's influence with Davis was such that if Bragg had disliked the Longstreet move, and told the president so, it would not have been carried out. But like Davis, Bragg, too, had failed to see the seriousness of the Union concentration at Chattanooga and eventually ordered two more divisions to reinforce Longstreet in the hope that Grant would detach part of his Chattanooga force to aid Burnside. This Bragg was doing, as previously discussed, almost on the eve of the battle for Chattanooga.

These were not Bragg's worst mistakes, however. After seizing the initiative with the bloody victory at Chickamauga, the Confederate commander failed to take advantage of the disorganized Union army when its soldiers were despondent in defeat. Instead of attacking and maintaining momentum, Bragg elected to pursue a siege operation in which his enemy's supplies were never completely cut off. Still, Bragg well might have been successful in starving the Yankees in Chattanooga except for the colossal blundering at Brown's Ferry that allowed them to open a good supply line into the town. Bragg simply had not deployed adequate strength in Lookout Valley to hold that strategic terrain. Yet his siege operation depended on controlling the ground between Lookout and Raccoon Mountain. Then the ensuing Confederate counterattack, resulting in the fight at Wauhatchie, was both poorly conceived and numerically inadequate. After Brown's

Ferry and Wauhatchie, Bragg's attempt to besiege the Federals was clearly thwarted. Thomas R. Hay wrote that "Bragg was deeply chagrined at the collapse of his hopes of starving the Federal army shut up in Chattanooga. He should have held the crossing at Brown's Ferry at all costs. Once lost, a vigorous effort might have been made to regain possession." The Union movement, Hay rightly concluded, "was the beginning of the end," for the Confederates at Chattanooga.[20]

The momentum of the struggle no longer lay with the Rebels, and to detach troops to Knoxville following these actions was foolhardy. After mid-November, when Sherman's four divisions arrived to strengthen Grant, the initiative had fully passed to the Federal commander. There was nothing then for Bragg to do except retreat to a better defensive position or strengthen his present lines, awaiting an attack by a much stronger Union force. In actuality, he neither retreated nor did anything to make his defensive position more formidable.

Although facing a superior foe, the Confederate army should have made a better stand. Judging from the battle on the northern flank of Missionary Ridge, where deployment of troops, concept of defensive tactics, and leadership were sound, it is clear that the Confederates along the center of the ridge could have made a tougher fight. There were many reasons they did not wage a strong battle.

First, Bragg did not expect that the center of his line would be attacked, anticipating that the northern flank would bear the brunt of the Union effort. This, indeed, was precisely the movement Grant intended. To meet it, Bragg sent the divisions of Cheatham and Stevenson to reinforce his right flank after Lookout Mountain was lost on the night of November 24. Thus, he did make adequate disposition of his forces to repel Grant's main assault against his northern flank. But he not only did not expect a major attack against his center; Bragg also overestimated the natural strength of Missionary Ridge. As previously detailed, the ridge's terrain presents problems which, if not recognized and provided for, make the position a potential trap for the defenders.

Most Confederate regimental lines were positioned along the geographical crest of the ridge, compelling the defenders either to allow the enemy to reach the ridge's top unmolested or else to leave their cover and advance to the edge of the ridge to fire effectively. Too, the ridge was so narrow that the deployment of reserve forces in the event of an enemy breakthrough would have been difficult. There were no reserve forces available for the Confederate center anyway. Also, nothing had been done to cope with geographical features that promised to aid an attacking enemy, such as protrusions of the ridge, beneath which Federals might marshall their strength in relative security, prior to overwhelming a segment of the Rebel line. And a gap had been left in the Confederate line between Bate's and Anderson's divisions, intended for Reynold's brigade but never filled.

Even with all these problems, Bragg's forces along the center of the ridge still enjoyed favorable odds for defensive warfare, about 14,000 men against some 23,000 Federals. But—and perhaps this constituted the worst Confederate mistake—approximately one-fourth to one-third of the total force was deployed at the base of the ridge, rather than everyone being united at the crest. Exactly what purpose this lower line was intended to serve is difficult to understand. If meant to give early warning of an attack, it was too heavily manned, and unnecessary anyway, for the height of Missionary Ridge provided an excellent observation point. If the line were intended to harm an attacking force by firing one volley and retreating up the ridge, then fuzzy command thinking plagued the Rebels. Obviously, much more damage could be done from the top of the ridge against an enemy slowly struggling up its side.

With the purpose of this deployment being so murky, the confusion that abounded is not surprising. Some were not sure whether to stand and fight or retreat up the face of the ridge. Confederates at the top of the ridge, sometimes equally confused as to the mission of those at the base, thought the bottom line had panicked, and they also found that their comrades were in the line of fire. In any case, when the Rebels on the lower line at last scrambled to the crest, many were physically exhausted, incapable of standing up to make a determined fight. And, when the attackers reached the top of Missionary Ridge, they encountered far fewer effective Rebel warriors than they would have if the Confederate defense had been better planned. Having never fought a major defensive engagement, obviously lacking experience in defensive combat, the Rebel effort was poorly conceived, poorly engineered, and poorly coordinated. Over on Lookout Mountain the Confederates had not been well organized and had been poorly led, but their conduct of the defense of Missionary Ridge, except for the north flank, was still worse.

Bragg had failed in another way also. He had not kept the soldiers busy. While he himself sat idly by during much of the siege, he did not keep the men employed either. Neither in improving their defensive position nor in harassing the Federals did Bragg make any meaningful demands on his army. Almost certainly, combat efficiency had deteriorated significantly in the two months since the battle of Chickamauga.

Meanwhile, the morale of the Union army had been correspondingly improving. Time eased the pain of the Chickamauga defeat. Then, with plenty of food, significant reinforcements, and a new commander, the combat efficiency of the Federals at Chattanooga almost certainly exceeded that of the Confederates by later November. Having seized the initiative, Grant developed a plan to maintain it, using his superior numbers to "pin down" Bragg so that he finally had no freedom of action, forcing him to fight a totally defensive engagement. Grant's attack was intended to apply his power, actual or potential, against the Rebels from three directions at once. Sherman would make the main attack on the Rebel right. The menace of Thomas's and Hooker's forces would prevent Bragg from detaching any substantial reinforcements to strengthen his northern flank. (Indeed, if the Confederate center had held against Thomas's Army of the Cumberland, it might still have collapsed from the advance of Hooker's army on the southern flank.)

As the battle developed, Grant and his staff officers thought, incorrectly, that Bragg was reinforcing the troops opposing Sherman. Deeming Sherman's situation critical, Grant ordered Thomas to attack the lower line of trenches at the base of the ridge, as a diversion to stop reinforcements supposedly going to the Confederate right flank. Grant still considered Sherman's troops his main assaulting force and sought to enable "Old Cump" to renew his advance.

Then came the climax of the battle, as Thomas's soldiers not only took the rifle-pits but also charged to the crest of Missionary Ridge and broke the center of the Confederate line. The charge did not begin as the result of some sudden expression of revenge for Chickamauga or as an outpouring of patriotic fervor. Neither was it ordered by Grant, although he had conducted well the operation at Chattanooga up to that point. And not all Federal troops enthusiastically made the charge, some having to be forcefully driven from behind cover to join the attack. Basically, the charge to the crest resulted from sound decisions of experienced combat leaders (officers of regimental, brigade, and divisional level), along with many leading enlisted men, whose immediate goal was to escape from the trap in which the advance to the rifle-pits had placed them. They did what they sensed had to be done, and, coupled with the numerous Confederate blunders, the effort resulted in a decisive Union triumph. Afterward, it was easy to forget the danger and the desperate situation. Few bothered to study the Confederate defensive position and its problems. Adventure, pageantry, and heroes dominated the thinking of Union veterans as they recalled the magnificent victory.

When the campaigns of the Civil War are analyzed, the struggle for Chattanooga stands out as a decisive engagement. The victorious emergence of the Union forces, in one dramatic hour, from a situation in which they had been trapped and besieged, resulted in reversing the course of the action, placing the Federals in a position to carry the fight into the deep South. The triumphant Union forces would soon undertake the final stages of destroying the Confederacy.

That the victors would have remembered the charge as some glorious, near-miraculous event is only to be expected. After all, most of mankind does not see or long remember the blunders, the chance factors, and the horrors of war. Not even the vanquished are inclined to do so—not for long anyway. It's something else that the common run of humanity finally remembers and partially creates: "The life of a soldier . . . was so exciting and agreeable," as Confederate General Liddell recalled, "that it often . . . made me think that war had too many natural charms for the peace of man."[21]

Notes

Chapter 1

1. Clarence C. Buell and Robert U. Johnson, eds., *Battles and Leaders of the Civil War*, 4 vols. (New York, 1887–88), III, 652. Glenn Tucker, *Chickamauga: Bloody Battle in the West* (rpt. Dayton, Ohio, 1972), 261, 415. John B. Turchin, *Chickamauga* (Chicago, 1888), 116.
2. Shelby Foote, *The Civil War: A Narrative*, 3 vols. (New York, 1958–75), II, 737.
3. *War of the Rebellion: A Compilation of the Official Records of the Union and Confederate Armies*, 129 vols. (Washington, D.C., 1880–1901), serial 1, vol. XXX, pt. 1, 635. Hereafter cited as *OR*. All references are to serial 1.
4. Glenn Tucker, "The Battle of Chickamauga," *Civil War Times Illustrated* (May 1969), 30. Foote, *Civil War*, II, 735.
5. Foote, *Civil War*, II, 736. Tucker, "Battle," 29.
6. Tucker, *Chickamauga*, 269, 279, 280.
7. Tucker, "Battle," 34.
8. Stanley F. Horn, ed., *Tennessee's War, 1861–1865, Described by Participants* (Nashville, 1965), 212.
9. Joseph B. Mitchell, *Decisive Battles of the Civil War* (New York, 1955), 165. Foote, *Civil War*, II, 711.
10. Information on the Snodgrass family and house was taken from files in the Chickamauga-Chattanooga National Military Park Library. Hereafter the park library will be cited as CCNMPL.
11. Bruce Catton, *This Hallowed Ground* (New York, 1956), 349.
12. Francis F. McKinney, *Education in Violence: The Life of George H. Thomas* (Detroit, 1961), 252.
13. Mark M. Boatner III, *The Civil War Dictionary* (New York, 1959), 152. Hereafter Boatner's work will be cited as *CWD*. Foote, *Civil War*, II, 750.
14. Foote, *Civil War*, II, 751, 752.

15. McKinney, *Education*, 250. Thomas B. Van Horn, *History of the Army of the Cumberland* (Cincinnati, 1873), 353.

16. James R. Sullivan, *Chickamauga and Chattanooga Battlefields*, National Park Service Historical Handbook. Series No. 25 (Washington, D.C., 1956), 23.

17. James Lee McDonough, *Stones River—Bloody Winter in Tennessee* (Knoxville, 1980), 177. Foote, *Civil War*, II, 753.

18. Tucker, *Chickamauga*, 357. Horn, *Tennessee's War*, 212. Boatner, *CWD*, 152. Foote, *Civil War*, II, 753, 754.

19. John Beatty, *Memoirs of a Volunteer, 1861–1863* (New York, 1946), 252, 253, 254.

20. Horn, *Tennessee's War*, 213.

21. Thomas L. Livermore, *Numbers and Losses in the Civil War in America, 1861–1865* (New York, 1969), 102–6.

22. Fairfax Downey, *Storming of the Gateway: Chattanooga, 1863* (New York, 1960), 117.

23. Livermore, *Numbers*, 105, 106. Tucker, *Chickamauga*, 388, 389.

24. Foote, *Civil War*, II, 756.

25. Samuel R. Watkins, *"Co. Aytch," Maury Grays, First Tennessee Regiment* (Jackson, Tenn., 1952), 98.

26. John A. Wyeth, *With Sabre and Scalpel* (New York, 1917), 254–56.

27. Story written by W.W. Gifford in the family Bible; copy in the CCNMPL.

28. James Alfred Sartain, *History of Walker County, Georgia* (Dalton, Ga., 1932), I, 101, 102, 108.

29. S.S. Canfield, *History of the Twenty-first Regiment Ohio Volunteer Infantry* (Toledo, 1893), 163. W.W. Lyle, *Lights and Shadows of Army Life* (Cincinnati, 1865), 373, 374.

30. J.B. Jones, *A Rebel War Clerk's Diary*, 2 vols. (Philadelphia, 1866), II, 50.

31. Ibid.

32. Emory M. Thomas, *The American War and Peace: 1860–1877* (Englewood Cliffs, N.J., 1973), 147, 148. Emory M. Thomas, *The Confederate Nation: 1861–1865* (New York, 1979), 186–89. McDonough, *Stones River*, 44, 45.

33. David M. Potter, *Division and the Stresses of Reunion: 1845–1876* (Glenview, Ill., 1973), 129, 130, 134, 135, 141.

Chapter 2

1. Robert S. Henry, *"First with the Most" Forrest* (Indianapolis, 1944), 191.

2. *OR*, XXX, pt. 4, 681.

3. James Longstreet, *From Manassas to Appomattox* (Philadelphia, 1896), 461.

4. Thomas L. Connelly, *Autumn of Glory: The Army of Tennessee, 1862–1865* (Baton Rouge, 1971), 231, 232. Foote, *Civil War*, II, 760.

5. Foote, *Civil War*, II, 758.

6. Isaac Henry Clay Royse, *History of the One Hundred and fifteenth Regiment Illinois Volunteer Infantry* (Terre Haute, Ind., 1900), 169.

7. Benjamin Mabry to wife, Sept. 24, 1863, CCNMPL. John Lewis to fiancée, Oct. 8, 1863, CCNMPL. Henry W. Howard to brother, Nov. 11, 1863, CCNMPL. Abraham Kipp to mother, Nov. 11, 1863, CCNMPL.

8. McDonough , *Stones River*, 26–34, 226–28.

9. G. Moxley Sorrel, *Recollections of a Confederate Staff Officer*, ed. Bell I. Wiley (Jackson, Tenn., 1958), 191.

10. *OR*, XXX, part 2, 138.

11. William M. Polk, *Leonidas Polk: Bishop and General*, 2 vols. (New York, 1915), II, 288. Thomas L. Connelly and Archer Jones, *The Politics of Command: Factions and Ideas in Confederate Strategy* (Baton Rouge, 1973), 69–70.

12. *OR*, XXX, pt. 4, 705, 708. Connelly and Jones, *Politics of Command*, 70.

13. *OR*, XXX, pt. 2, 67–68. Polk, *Leonidas Polk*, II, 283.

14. Polk, *Leonidas Polk*, II, 284. Connelly, *Autumn of Glory*, 237. Foote, *Civil War*, II, 762. Grady McWhiney, "Braxton Bragg," *Civil War Times Illustrated* (April 1972), 6. Also see McWhiney's *Braxton Bragg and Confederate Defeat: Field Command* (New York, 1969), 320, 326–30, for important background material on the Bragg-Polk relationship.

15. Connelly, *Autumn of Glory*, 238.

16. *OR*, XXX, pt. 2, 65–66. Connelly and Jones, *Politics of Command*, 70.

17. St. John Liddell Journal, in the Daniel C. Govan Papers, Southern Historical Collection, University of North Carolina, Chapel Hill. Hereafter cited SHC, UNC.

18. Ibid.

19. Henry, *Forrest*, 198.

20. Ibid., 199, 498.

21. Connelly, *Autumn of Glory*, 241.

22. Stanley F. Horn, *The Army of Tennessee: A Military History* (New York, 1941), 288.

23. Hal Bridges, *Lee's Maverick General: Daniel Harvey Hill* (New York, 1961), 238. Horn, *Army of Tennessee*, 288. Wilbur Thomas, *General James "Pete" Longstreet, Lee's "Old War Horse": Scapegoat for Gettysburg* (Parsons, W. Va., 1979), 190. Longstreet, *Manassas to Appomattox*, 465. Connelly and Jones, *Politics of Command*, 70–71.

24. Liddell's Journal, Govan Papers, SHC, UNC.

25. Connelly, *Autumn of Glory*, 247–48.

26. Davis to Bragg, Oct. 3, 1863, in the Jefferson Davis Papers, Louisiana Historical Association Collection, in the Howard-Tilton Memorial Library, Tulane University, New Orleans.

27. *OR*, XXX, pt. 2, 148.
28. Connelly, *Autumn of Glory*, 249, 250.
29. Stoddard Johnson Journal, in the William P. Palmer Collection of Braxton Bragg Papers, Western Reserve Historical Society, Cleveland, Ohio. Buckner's letter to Bragg with Bragg's inscription on it is in the Simon Bolivar Buckner Papers, at the Henry E. Huntington Library, San Marino, Calif.
30. *OR*, XXXI, pt. 3, 651. Also see Robert S. Henry, *The Story of the Confederacy* (New York, 1931), 314, 315.

Chapter 3

1. McDonough, *Stones River*, 38–42. Tucker, "Battle," 8, 9.
2. Tucker, "Battle," 9. Roy P. Basler, ed., *The Collected Works of Abraham Lincoln*, 8 vols. (New Brunswick, N.J., 1953), V, 295. Hereafter cited as *Lincoln Papers*.
3. *OR*, XXX, pt. 1, 142, 149.
4. *Lincoln Papers*, VI, 498. *OR*, XXX, pt. 1, 148, 161.
5. William M. Lamers, *The Edge of Glory: A Biography of General William S. Rosecrans, U.S.A.* (New York, 1961), 384, 385. Foote, *Civil War*, II, 767.
6. *Lincoln Papers*, VI, 510. *OR*, XXX, pt. 4, 306–7. Foote, *Civil War*, II, 768.
7. B.F. Scribner, *How Soldiers Were Made; or the War As I Saw It Under Buell, Rosecrans, Grant and Sherman* (New Albany, Ind., 1887), 46–47.
8. *OR*, XXXI, pt. 1, 216. William C. Oates, *The War Between the Union and the Confederacy, and Its Lost Opportunities, With a History of the Fifteenth Alabama Regiment and the Forty-eight Battles in Which It Was Engaged* (New York, 1905), 270, 273.
9. Cartter Patten, *Signal Mountain and Walden's Ridge* (Signal Mountain, Tenn., 1962), 24.
10. John K. Duke, *History of the Fifty-third Ohio Volunteer Infantry during the War of the Rebellion, 1861–1865* (Portsmouth, Ohio, 1900), 117–18.
11. Lamers, *Rosecrans*, 384–89. William S. McFeely, *Grant: A Biography* (New York, 1981), 143. Ulysses S. Grant, *Personal Memoirs of U.S. Grant*, 2 vols. (New York, 1885–86), II, 27. Foote, *Civil War*, II, 803.
12. McFeely, *Grant*, 20. McDonough, *Stones River*, 38. While McFeely gives Grant's height as 5'7", he was listed as being a little over five feet tall when he entered West Point.
13. McFeely, *Grant*, 14.
14. K. Jack Bauer, ed., *Soldiering: The Civil War Diary of Rice C. Bull, 123RD New York Volunteer Infantry* (San Rafael, Calif., 1977), 96.
15. McFeely, *Grant*, 16, 17, 18, 33, 37, 40.
16. Ibid., xii.

17. Ibid., 144.

18. Horace Porter, *Campaigning With Grant* (New York, 1897), 2, 5.

19. Edward G. Longacre, "A Perfect Ishmaelite: General 'Baldy' Smith," *Civil War Times Illustrated* (Dec. 1976), 10.

20. Foote, *Civil War*, II, 807, 808.

21. *Battles and Leaders*, III, 687–89, 714, 717, 718. *OR*, XXXI, pt. 2, 27–28. Longacre, "Smith," 14–15.

22. McFeely, *Grant*, 146. *Battles and Leaders*, III, 685.

23. Otto Eisenschiml and Ralph Newman, eds., *The Civil War: The American Iliad as Told by Those Who Lived It* (New York, 1956), 532.

24. C.C. Briant, *History of the Sixth Regiment Indiana Volunteer Infantry* (Indianapolis, 1891), 254–55.

25. Thomas J. Ford, *With the Rank and File* (Milwaukee, 1898), 25.

26. Canfield, *Twenty-first Ohio*, 160.

27. Ibid., 159.

28. Clyde C. Walton, ed., *Private Smith's Journal: Recollections of the Late War* (Chicago, 1963), 104.

29. Canfield, *Twenty-first Ohio*, 160.

30. Gilbert E. Govan and James W. Livingood, *The Chattanooga Country, 1540–1962: From Tomahawk to TVA* (Chapel Hill, N.C., 1952), 236.

31. Ford, *Rank and File*, 25, 26.

32. Foote, *Civil War*, II, 804.

33. In addition to sources already cited, consult the following: John Obreiter, *History of the Seventy-seventh Pennsylvania Volunteers* (Harrisburg, Pa., 1905), 137, who testified that food which was "mouldy and almost rotten from exposure in transit, which had been condemned as unsafe for use, was seized by the famishing men and greedily devoured." Also see Edwin W. Payne, *History of the Thirty-fourth Illinois Infantry* (Clinton, Iowa, n.d.), 77; E. Hannaford, *The Story of a Regiment: A History of the Camps and Associations in the Field of the Sixth Regiment of Ohio Volunteer Infantry* (Cincinnati, 1868), 486; *History of the Services of the Third Battery Wisconsin Light Artillery in the Civil War of the United States*, compiled principally from members themselves (Berlin, n.d.), 44–45; James A. Barnes et al., *The Eighty-sixth Regiment Indiana Volunteer Infantry* (Crawfordsville, Ind., 1895), 221; *History of Battery M, First Illinois, Light Artillery*, by members of the battery (Princeton, Ill., 1892), 99; Willis D. Maier to Annie F. Howells, Oct. 22, 1863, cited in Bell I. Wiley, *The Life of Billy Yank: The Common Soldier of the Union* (New York, 1971), 228; Royse, *Hundred and fifteenth Regiment Illinois*, 168–69; Robert G. Athearn, ed., *Soldier in the West: The Civil War Letters of Alfred Lacey Hough* (Philadelphia, 1957), 157, 159, 162; Henry Steele Commager, ed., *The Blue and the Gray: The Story of the Civil War as Told By Participants*, 2 vols. (Indianapolis and New York, 1950), II, 894–95.

34. Athearn, *Hough Letters*, 157.

Chapter 4

1. James W. Livingood, *Hamilton County* (Memphis, 1981), 45.
2. R. Lockwood Tower, ed., *A Carolinian Goes to War: The Civil War Narrative of Arthur Middleton Manigault, Brigadier General, C.S.A.* (Columbia, S.C., 1983), 128, 129.
3. W.J. Worsham, *The Old Nineteenth Tennessee Regiment, C.S.A.* (Knoxville, 1902), 95, 96.
4. Robert Watson diary, pt. 2, CCNMPL.
5. G.E. Goudelock to wife, Oct. 5, 1863, CCNMPL. W.E. Yeatman memoirs, Confederate Collection, Tennessee State Library and Archives, Nashville. Hereafter cited as TSLA. R.A. Jarman, from "The Aberdeen *Examiner*," Aberdeen, Miss. Jan. 31, 1890, in the CCNMPL. Watkins, *First Tennessee*, 121, 122.
6. J.W. Harris to mother, Nov. 19, 1863, Confederate Collection, TSLA. *Confederate Veteran*, 40 vols. (Nashville, 1893–1932), XXXIII, 138. Johnson Journal, Bragg Papers, Western Reserve.
7. J.W. Harris to George, Oct. 13, 1863, TSLA.
8. Thigpen to W.J. Melton, Nov. 15, 1863, CCNMPL. W.R. Montgomery to Aunt Frank, Oct. 16, 1863, CCNMPL. Wesley Thurman Leeper, *Rebels Valiant: Second Arkansas Mounted Rifles (Dismounted)* (Little Rock, 1964), 199. Frank E. Vandiver, ed., *The Civil War Diary of General Josiah Gorgas* (University, Ala., 1947), 69.
9. The Atlanta *Confederacy*, from the Louisiana State University newspaper files, Baton Rouge.
10. Watson diary, CCNMPL.
11. Carrol H. Clark diary, CCNMPL.
12. Joab Goodson to niece, Sept. 28, 1863, CCNMPL.
13. E.E. Betts to H.V. Boynton, Dec. 10, 1895, CCNMPL.
14. Jarman, Aberdeen *Examiner*, CCNMPL.
15. Catton, *This Hallowed Ground*, 358.
16. Athearn, *Hough Letters*, 156. See also Joseph K. Marshall, Confederate Veteran Questionnaire, TSLA.
17. Charles W. Bryan, Jr., "The Civil War in East Tennessee," (Ph.D. diss., Univ. of Tennessee, 1978), 134, 135. Minerva McKamy, "Recollections of the War between the States," TSLA.
18. Bryan, "Civil War," 136.
19. Quoted in Govan and Livingood, *The Chattanooga Country*, 236.
20. Bryan, "Civil War," 135.
21. *OR*, XXX, pt. 2, 722.
22. McDonough, *Stones River*, 72.
23. John P. Dyer, *From Shiloh to San Juan: The Life of "Fightin' Joe" Wheeler* (Baton Rouge, 1961), 98, 100. *OR*, XXX, pt. 2, 723.

24. Patten, *Signal Mountain*, 25, 26. Dyer, *Wheeler*, 102, 101. See also Jesse C. Burt, "Fighting With 'Little Joe' Wheeler," *Civil War Times Illustrated* (May 1960), 19.
25. E.S. Bruford to "Dear Atkison," Oct. 10, 1863, National Archives of the United States. Record Division—Rebel Archives—War Department.
26. *OR*, XXX, pt. 2, 723. W.C. Dodson, ed., *Campaigns of Wheeler and His Cavalry, 1862–1865* (Atlanta, 1899), 123.
27. Dyer, *Wheeler*, 103.
28. Henry Campbell diary, CCNMPL.
29. Connelly, *Autumn of Glory*, 269. Dyer, *Wheeler*, 105.
30. Bruford letter, Oct. 10, 1863, National Archives.
31. Johnson Journal, Bragg Papers, Western Reserve.
32. Tower, *Manigault Narrative*, 129–30.
33. Dyer, *Wheeler*, 106.
34. Govan and Livingood, *The Chattanooga Country*, 21.
35. Glenn Tucker, "The Battles for Chattanooga!" *Civil War Times Illustrated* (Aug. 1971), 6. James W. Livingood, "Chattanooga's Crutchfields and the Famous Crutchfield House," *Civil War Times Illustrated* (Nov. 1981), 20–25.

Chapter 5

1. *OR*, XXXI, pt. 1, 82.
2. Ibid., 77, 78.
3. Hannaford, *Sixth Ohio*, 488.
4. Ibid.
5. *OR*, XXXI, pt. 1, 86, 84.
6. Briant, *Sixth Indiana*, 258. *OR*, XXXI, pt. 1, 86.
7. Hannaford, *Sixth Ohio*, 489. Briant, *Sixth Indiana*, 259. *OR*, XXXI, pt. 1, 80, 86. Foote, *Civil War*, II, 809.
8. *OR*, XXXI, pt. 1, 80, 86.
9. Ibid., 224.
10. Oates, *Fifteenth Alabama*, 275, 276.
11. *OR*, XXXI, pt. 1, 85.
12. Oates, *Fifteenth Alabama*, 277.
13. *OR*, XXXI, pt. 1, 78.
14. Oates, *Fifteenth Alabama*, 279.
15. Liddell's Journal, Govan Papers, SHC, UNC.
16. Braxton Bragg to Longstreet, Oct. 28, 1863, Bragg Papers, Western Reserve.
17. James G. Longstreet to Brent, Oct. 27, 1863, Bragg Papers, Western Reserve.

18. Walter H. Hebert, *Fighting Joe Hooker* (New York, 1944), should be consulted for information about the general's appearance and character.
19. Longstreet, *Manassas to Appomattox*, 474.
20. Liddell's Journal, Govan Papers, SHC, UNC.
21. Brent to Longstreet, Oct. 28, 1863, Bragg Papers, Western Reserve. Longstreet, *Manassas to Appomattox*, 475–76. *OR*, XXXI, pt. 1, 218.
22. *OR*, XXXI, pt. 1, 218.
23. Connelly, *Autumn of Glory*, 260.
24. Mary de Forest Geary, *A Giant in Those Days* (Brunswick, Ga., 1980), should be consulted for general information on Geary.
25. *OR*, XXXI, pt. 1, 113, 114.
26. John Richards Boyle, *Soldiers True: The Story of the One Hundred and Eleventh Pennsylvania* (New York, 1903), 161, 165.
27. George K. Collins, *Memoirs of the One Hundred and forty-ninth Regiment New York Volunteer Infantry* (Syracuse, N.Y., 1891), 198.
28. *OR*, XXXI, pt. 1, 114. E.P. Alexander, *Military Memoirs of a Confederate: A Critical Narrative* (New York, 1907), 471.
29. *OR*, XXXI, pt. 1, 114, 115.
30. Ibid.
31. Ibid.
32. Tucker, "Chattanooga," 21.
33. Grant, *Memoirs*, II, 41. Tucker, "Chattanooga," 22. According to Bratton's After Action Report, Coker was a captain, not a major as Tucker said. See *OR*, XXXI, pt. 1, 233.
34. Downey, *Chattanooga*, 248–49.
35. *OR*, XXXI, pt. 1, 98.
36. Ibid., 98, 110, 227–228. Also see Connelly, *Autumn of Glory*, 261.
37. For a good discussion of the nature of the night see Tucker, "Chattanooga," 23–25, which concludes that there was light from the moon.
38. Johnson Journal, Bragg Papers, Western Reserve.
39. Geary, *Giant in Those Days*, 173.

Chapter 6

1. Liddell's Journal, Govan Papers, SHC, UNC.
2. Johnson Journal, Bragg Papers, Western Reserve.
3. Liddell's Journal, Govan Papers, SHC, UNC.
4. Tucker, "Chattanooga," 25.
5. Alfred T. Roman, *The Military Operations of General Beauregard*, 2 vols. (New York, 1884), II, 162.
6. Beauregard to Bragg, Oct. 7, 1863, National Archives of the United States. Record Division—Rebel Archives—War Department.

7. Ibid. Also see Connelly and Jones, *Politics of Command,* 139–40.
8. *OR,* XXX, pt. 4, 745.
9. Longstreet, *Manassas to Appomattox,* 468–69.
10. Ibid., 470.
11. *OR,* LII, pt. 2, 554.
12. Liddell's Journal, Govan Papers, SHC, UNC. Also, Bragg to Davis, Oct. 31, 1863, is quoted in Don C. Seitz, *Braxton Bragg: General of the Confederacy* (Columbia, S.C., 1924), 392.
13. Horn, *Army of Tennessee,* 294.
14. Liddell's Journal, Govan Papers, SHC, UNC.
15. Connelly, *Autumn of Glory,* 263.
16. Longstreet, *Manassas to Appomattox,* 474.
17. Hardee to Longstreet, April 8, 1864, in William J. Hardee Papers, Alabama State Department of Archives and History, Montgomery.
18. Longstreet to Bragg, Nov. 5, 1863; Bragg to Longstreet, Nov. 6, 1863; in Bragg Papers, Western Reserve.
19. Longstreet to Bragg, Nov. 5, 11, 1863; and Bragg to Longstreet, Nov. 11, 1863; in Bragg Papers, Western Reserve.
20. Bragg to Longstreet, Nov. 12, 1863, Bragg Papers, Western Reserve.
21. Horn, *Army of Tennessee,* 294.
22. William T. Sherman, *Memoirs of General William T. Sherman,* 2 vols. (New York, 1875), I, 357–58.
23. Foote, *Civil War,* II, 835.
24. Grant, *Memoirs,* II, 49, 58. J.F.C. Fuller, *Decisive Battles of the U.S.A.* (New York, 1942), 277.
25. Rawlins to M.E. Hurlbut, Nov. 16, 1863, Rawlins Papers, Chicago Historical Society, quoted in McFeely, *Grant,* 147.

Chapter 7

1. John Y. Simon, ed., *The Papers of Ulysses S. Grant,* 10 vols. (Carbondale, Ill., 1973–82), IX, 370–71.
2. *Battles and Leaders,* III, 716.
3. Ibid., 715.
4. Ibid., 716.
5. Ibid.
6. *OR,* XXXI, pt. 3, 216.
7. *Battles and Leaders,* III, 715.
8. Grant, *Memoirs,* II, 50. *Battles and Leaders,* III, 694.
9. *Battles and Leaders,* III, 694, 715, 716.
10. Boatner, *Civil War Dictionary,* 144.
11. *OR,* XXXI, pt. 2, 31. *Battles and Leaders,* III, 695.

12. *Battles and Leaders, III,* 717. *OR,* XXXI, pt. 2, 314.
13. *Battles and Leaders,* III, 698. *OR,* XXXI, pt. 2, 32.
14. McKinney, *Education in Violence,* 289.
15. Briant, *Sixth Indiana,* 269.
16. John Ely diary, CCNMPL.
17. Wolfe to Lloyd, Nov. 26, 1863, CCNMPL.
18. Tower, *Manigault Narrative,* 130, 131.
19. *OR,* XXXI, pt. 2, 94–95.
20. Ibid., 254, 255.
21. Wilbur Thomas, *General George H. Thomas: The Indomitable Warrior* (New York, 1964), 432.
22. Tower, *Manigault Narrative,* 132, 133.

Chapter 8

1. Sherman, *Memoirs,* I, 362, 363.
2. Basil H. Liddell-Hart, *Sherman, Soldier, Realist, American* (New York, 1929), 214. J.F.C. Fuller, *The Generalship of Ulysses S. Grant* (New York, 1929), 168.
3. *OR,* XXXI, pt. 2, 593. Because all references henceforth are to volume XXXI, part 2, the citation will simply be *OR* and the page numbers. Lloyd Lewis, *Sherman: Fighting Prophet* (New York, 1932), 319. Liddell-Hart, *Sherman,* 215.
4. Liddell-Hart, *Sherman,* 214. Lewis, *Sherman,* 317, 318. *Battles and Leaders,* III, 716.
5. Payne, *Thirty-fourth Illinois,* 82. Lewis, *Sherman,* 319.
6. *Battles and Leaders,* III, 712.
7. Ibid. *OR,* 654.
8. Battles and Leaders, III, 712.
9. Ibid.
10. Frank Wolfe to "My Dear Lloyd," Nov. 26, 1863, CCNMPL. *Battles and Leaders,* III, 712. Payne, *Thirty-fourth Illinois,* 82. *OR,* 646–47, 649, 651, 654.
11. Henry H. Wright, *A History of the Sixth Iowa Infantry* (Iowa City, Iowa, 1923), 234. *Battles and Leaders,* III, 712. *OR,* 573.
12. Wright, *Sixth Iowa,* 235. *OR,* 573.
13. *OR,* 747. Fuller, *Grant,* 171.
14. *OR,* 747.
15. *OR,* 573.
16. *OR,* 44.
17. *OR,* 745–46. Liddell-Hart, *Sherman,* 215.
18. *OR,* 746.

19. Irving Buck, "Cleburne and His Division at Missionary Ridge and Ring-gold Gap," *Southern Historical Society Papers*, 49 vols. (Richmond, 1876), VIII, 465. *OR*, 747.
20. *OR*, 748. Buck, "Cleburne," *SHSP*, VIII, 465–66.
21. *OR*, 748.
22. Buck, "Cleburne," *SHSP*, VIII, 466.
23. Ibid.
24. Ibid.
25. *OR*, 748.
26. *OR*, 749.
27. Payne, *Thirty-fourth Illinois*, 87.

Chapter 9

1. Tucker, "Chattanooga," 32.
2. Foote, *Civil War*, II, 847.
3. Tucker, "Chattanooga," 32.
4. Richard Eddy, *History of the Sixtieth Regiment New York State Volunteers* (Philadelphia, 1864), 305, 306.
5. Collins, *One Hundred and forty-ninth New York*, 207.
6. *OR*, 315.
7. *OR*, 154, 155, 315, 390–91.
8. Boatner, *Civil War Dictionary*, 145.
9. *OR*, 155.
10. *OR*, 390.
11. *OR*, 693.
12. Robert D. Jamison Letters and Recollections, 82, 165, CCNMPL.
13. *OR*, 719.
14. *OR*, 732.
15. *OR*, 695, 704–5, 731.
16. *OR*, 693, 704. Jarman, Aberdeen *Examiner*, CCNMPL.
17. *OR*, 704.
18. *OR*, 395, 693–95.
19. Collins, *One Hundred and forty-ninth New York*, 211. *OR*, 394, 694, 698, 699.
20. *OR*, 694, 699.
21. *OR*, 699, 394.
22. *OR*, 732, 705.
23. *OR*, 695, 731, 732.
24. *OR*, 732.
25. *OR*, 395, 393, 705.
26. *OR*, 705, 732.

27. *OR*,732.
28. *OR*,732, 695–96.
29. E.T. Sykes, *Walthall's Brigade* (Columbus, Miss., 1905), 539.
30. *OR*,156, 317.
31. John Geary to Mary, Dec. 4, 1863, Geary letters, CCNMPL.
32. Hebert, *Hooker*, 265.
33. *OR*,339, 340.

Chapter 10

1. *OR*, 749. Buck, "Cleburne," *SHSP*, VIII, 467. *Battles and Leaders*, III, 713. Liddell-Hart, *Sherman*, 216.
2. Buck, "Cleburne," *SHSP*, VIII, 467.
3. *OR*, 748–49.
4. *OR*, 749, 726, 735.
5. *OR*, 574. *Confederate Veteran*, XXVIII, 185.
6. Lewis, *Sherman*, 320.
7. *OR*, 574, 631, 633, 636. Wright, *Sixth Iowa*, 236. *Battles and Leaders*, III, 713.
8. Norman D. Brown, ed., *One of Cleburne's Command: The Civil War Reminiscences and Diary of Captain Samuel T. Foster, Granbury's Texas Brigade, CSA* (Austin, Tex., 1980), 59–62.
9. *OR*, 633, 636. Marcus B. Toney, *The Privations of a Private* (Nashville, 1905), 63.
10. *OR*, 636, 574.
11. *OR*, 749. Wright, *Sixth Iowa*, 236.
12. *OR*, 750, 636, 631, 575.
13. *OR*, 750. Irving A. Buck, *Cleburne and His Command* (Jackson, Tenn., 1959), 169. See also Howell and Elizabeth Purdue, *Pat Cleburne, Confederate General: A Definitive Biography* (Hillsboro, Tex., 1973), 246, 247.
14. *OR*, 748–49.
15. *OR*, 634. Brown, *One of Cleburne's Command*, 62.
16. *OR*, 750.
17. *OR*, 575, 633.
18. *OR*, 735.
19. *OR*, 632, 633, 735, 736.
20. *OR*, 633, 735, 736. Frank Wolfe to "My dear Lloyd," Nov. 26, 1863, CCNMPL.
21. *OR*, 360, 368–69, 370, 634.
22. *OR*, 634.

23. *OR*, 652, 653.
24. *OR*, 652, 636.
25. *OR*, 643–44, 647–48, 736, 748.
26. *OR*, 750.
27. *OR*, 749, 750. Buck, *Cleburne*, 169. *Confederate Veteran*, XXIX, 325.
28. Buck, *Cleburne*, 169. *OR*, 653, 751.
29. *OR*, 360–61, 369. Brown, *One of Cleburne's Command*, 62.
30. *OR*, 751, 737.
31. *OR*, 751, 737. Buck, *Cleburne*, 171.
32. *OR*, 737–38, 751. Toney, *Privations*, 63.
33. *OR*, 644, 648, 653, 369.
34. *OR*, 649, 634, 636–37.
35. *Confederate Veteran*, XXVIII, 185; XXI, 541.
36. *OR*, 634, 655.
37. *Battles and Leaders*, III, 713. Payne, *Thirty-fourth Illinois*, 88.
38. *OR*, 575; italics added.
39. *OR*, 575–76. Lewis, *Sherman*, 321.
40. *OR*, 752.
41. *OR*, 44.
42. *OR*, 115, 116.

Chapter 11

1. *OR*, 253.
2. *Battles and Leaders*, III, 716, 717, 720.
3. *OR*, 34, 96, 132, 133.
4. James M. Rusling, *Men and Things I Saw in Civil War Days* (New York, 1899), 147. Sherman, *Memoirs*, I, 364.
5. Grant to Washburn, Dec. 2, 1863, in the Illinois State Historical Library, Springfield. Grant, *Memoirs*, II, 88.
6. Liddell-Hart, *Sherman*, 218. Bruce Catton, *Grant Takes Command* (Boston, 1968), 91–93.
7. Catton, *Grant*, 76, 92. *OR*, 44.
8. *OR*, 44, 43.
9. J. Russell Young, *Around the World with General Grant*, 2 vols. (New York, 1879), II, 626–27. Tucker, "Chattanooga," 39.
10. Charles T. Clark, *Opdycke Tigers: One Hundred and Twenty-fifth Ohio Volunteer Infantry* (Columbus, Ohio 1895), 165–66. Also see *OR*, 213, 273.
11. *OR*, 264, 508, and see also Turchin's report, 512. Alexis Cope, *The Fifteenth Ohio Volunteers and Its Campaigns in the War of 1861–1865* (Columbus, Ohio 1916), 385.

12. Paul M. Angle, ed., *Three Years in the Army of the Cumberland: Letters and Diary of Major James A. Connolly* (Indianapolis, 1959), 156. *OR*, 547, 544, 199.

13. S.F. Horrall, *History of the Forty-second Indiana Volunteer Infantry* (Chicago, 1892), 204. Leonidas M. Jewett, "The Boys in Blue at Missionary Ridge," *Military Order of the Loyal Legion of the United States, Ohio Commandery* (Cincinnati, 1908), VI, 93.

14. *OR*, 189, 257, 258, 281.

15. *OR*, 96.

16. *OR*, 517, 69. Barnes, *Eighty-sixth Indiana*, 246.

17. *OR*, 189.

18. *OR*,192, Sheridan said the distance was at least one and one-eighth mile; 199, 200, 202, 203, 230, 238, 306, 517, 525, 534.

19. *OR*, 132, Granger said the time was 3:40; Richard Johnson reported 3:45, p. 459; William McIntire, 4:00, p. 470; and C.E. Briant, 4:00, p. 472. Benjamin P. Thomas, ed., *Three Years with Grant As Recalled By War Correspondent Sylvanus Cadwallader* (New York, 1955), 149, reported 4:10.

20. *OR*, 508, 512.

21. *OR*, 474.

22. *OR*, 242, 538. Barnes, *Eighty-sixth Indiana*, 246–47. Henry F. Perry, *History of the Thirty-eighth Regiment Indiana Volunteer Infantry* (Palo Alto, Calif., 1906), 114. Thomas, *Three Years with Grant*, 150.

23. Payne, *Thirty-fourth Illinois*, 89. Hambleton Tapp and James C. Klotter, eds., *The Union, The Civil War, and John W. Tuttle: A Kentucky Captain's Account* (Frankfort, Ky., 1980), 158. Thomas, *Three Years With Grant*, 150. Angle, *Letters and Diary of Connolly*, 150.

24. *OR*, 219, 281. *Third Wisconsin Light Artillery*, 49. *Battery M, First Illinois Light Artillery*, 115.

25. *OR*, 132, 544.

26. James H. Wilson, *Under the Old Flag*, 2 vols. (New York, 1912), I, 297.

27. John E. Gold reminiscences, Confederate Collection, TSLA.

28. Jamison Letters, CCNMPL.

29. Clark, *One Hundred and Twenty-fifth Ohio*, 165.

30. *Battles and Leaders*, III, 720. Alexander, *Military Memoirs*, 476.

31. Worsham, *Nineteenth Tennessee*, 100. W.J. McMurray, *History of the Twentieth Tennessee Regiment Volunteer Infantry, C.S.A.* (Nashville, 1904), 136. *Confederate Veteran*, XXXIII, 138; XXX, 458.

32. *OR*, 212, 221; Lieutenant Colonel Douglas Hapeman, One Hundred and fourth Illinois, Carlin's brigade, Johnson's division, reported that five men in his regiment were struck by the first volley. J.H. Haynie, *The Nineteenth Illinois* (Chicago, 1912), 271. Henry M. Cist, *The Army of the Cumberland* (New York, 1882), 254. Clark, *One Hundred and Twenty-fifth Ohio*, 168. Watson diary, CCNMPL.

33. *OR*, 485, 277, 309, 527, 190, 479. Axel H. Reed diary, CCNMPL. Barnes, *Eighty-sixth Indiana*, 248. John Ely diary, CCNMPL. Cist, *Army of the Cumberland*, 254. Clark, *One Hundred and Twenty-fifth Ohio*, 165. J. Patton Anderson report, April 25, 1864, William P. Palmer Collection, Western Reserve Historical Society, Cleveland.

34. Arthur M. Manigault report, Dec. 8, 1863, J. Patton Anderson papers, in the P.K. Yonge Library of Florida History, University of Florida, Gainesville. Alexander, *Military Memoirs*, 277–78.

35. Alexander, *Military Memoirs*, 477–78.

36. *OR*, 258, 309, 526, 543, 200, 202, 203, 206, 208, 478.

37. *OR*, 278, 301, 306, 464, 480, 517, 532, 541, 547. Reynolds report, Dec. 15, 1863, is in the Anderson papers, P.K. Yonge Library, Gainesville.

38. *OR*, 190, 207.

39. *OR*, 217, 212, 214, 220, 221, 225.

40. *OR*, 210.

41. Tapp and Klotter, *John W. Tuttle*, 158. *OR*, 230.

42. Clark, *One Hundred and Twenty-fifth Ohio*, 169, 170. *OR*, 230, 234.

43. *OR*, 532.

44. *OR*, 508, 509, 512, 513.

45. *OR*, 509, 258, 264, 282.

46. *OR*, 274, 310.

47. *OR*, 190, 195, 197, 202, 209, 223, 270, 278, 282, 286, 301, 305, 480, 509, 528, 532, 548.

48. *OR*, 190, 191.

49. *OR*, 282.

50. *OR*, 278, 305, 281, 209.

51. *OR*, 202. E.B. Parsons, "Missionary Ridge," *Military Order of the Loyal Legion of the United States, Wisconsin Commandery* (Milwaukee, 1891), I, 200.

Chapter 12

1. Anderson report, Palmer Collection, Western Reserve.

2. William C. Davis, *Breckinridge: Statesman, Soldier, Symbol* (Baton Rouge, 1974), 386.

3. Tower, *Manigault Narrative*, 134.

4. Kenneth Roy Flint, "The Battle of Missionary Ridge." M.A. Thesis, Univ. of Alabama, 1960, 128.

5. Anderson report, Palmer Collection, Western Reserve. Deas report, Anderson papers, P.K. Yonge Library, Gainesville.

6. Ibid.

7. *OR*, 740, 741.

8. *OR*, 741.
9. Manigault report, Anderson Papers, P.K. Yonge Library, Gainesville.
10. Watson diary, CCNMPL.
11. Confederate Veteran Questionnaire, TSLA.
12. *Confederate Veteran*, XXI, 283; XVI, 420.
13. Vaughan report, Anderson papers, P.K. Yonge Library, Gainesville. *Confederate Veteran*, III, 356.
14. Richard O'Connor, *Sheridan the Inevitable* (Indianapolis, 1953).
15. Catton, *This Hallowed Ground*, 367. OR, 264, 509, 546.
16. Clark, *One Hundred and Twenty-fifth Ohio*, 179, 178. Barnes, *Eighty-sixth Indiana*, 254. OR, 540, 544, 548.
17. *OR*, 519.
18. Clark, *One Hundred and Twenty-fifth Ohio*, 179.
19. *OR*, 464, 471, 474, 476.
20. *OR*, 464, 468, 471, 474, 477.
21. Gold reminiscences, TSLA.
22. *OR*, 544; see also 509, 521, 541, 546.
23. *OR*, 526.
24. *OR*, 281.
25. *OR*, 509, 548, 190.
26. See these reports in the Anderson papers, P.K. Yonge Library, Gainesville.
27. *OR*, 282.
28. *OR*, 290, 282, 286, 293.
29. *OR*, 282, 293.
30. *OR*, 268, 265, 261.
31. *OR*, 261, 268.
32. *OR*, 270, 272, 283. Clyde C. Walton, ed., *Private Smith's Journal: Recollections of the Late War* (Chicago, 1963), 123.
33. *OR*, 283.
34. *OR*, 305.
35. *OR*, 305.
36. *OR*, 305, 268, 271, 276, 299.
37. *OR*, 509, 513, 523.
38. *OR*, 509, 520, 523, 538, 528.
39. *OR*, 535.
40. Reed diary, CCNMPL.
41. *OR*, 532, 528, 537, 539.
42. William Manchester, *American Caesar: Douglas McArthur, 1880–1964* (Boston, 1978), 14.
43. *OR*, 200, 210.
44. Manchester, *McArthur*, 14, 15.
45. Douglas McArthur, *Reminiscences* (New York, 1964), 8, 9. Manchester, *McArthur*, 15.

46. McMurry, *Twentieth Tennessee*, 137. *OR*, 535.
47. Anderson report, Palmer Collection, Western Reserve.
48. Ibid.
49. McMurry, *Twentieth Tennessee*, 132.
50. Tucker report, Anderson papers, P.K. Yonge Library, Gainesville. Anderson report, Palmer Collection, Western Reserve.
51. *OR*, 741.
52. *OR*, 741–42.
53. Briant, *Sixth Indiana*, 276, 277.
54. Worsham, *Nineteenth Tennessee*, 101.
55. *Confederate Veteran*, XXXIII, 139.
56. *Confederate Veteran*, XXIX, 22.
57. Worsham, *Nineteenth Tennessee*, 99, 101.
58. McMurry, *Twentieth Tennessee*, 137.
59. *Confederate Veteran*, XXXV, 152.
60. Haley letters, Confederate Collection, TSLA.

Chapter 13

1. *OR*, 752.
2. Bell Irvin Wiley, ed., *Four Years on the Firing Line*, by James C. Nisbet (Jackson, Tenn., 1963), 160–61.
3. *OR*, 752. Buck, *Cleburne*, 171.
4. *OR*, 705–6.
5. *OR*, 706, 690–91.
6. *OR*, 540, 706, 697.
7. *OR*, 655, 697, 666. Sykes, *Walthall's Brigade*, 540–41. Nathaniel Cheairs Hughes, *General William J. Hardee: Old Reliable* (Baton Rouge, 1965), 177.
8. Buck, *Cleburne*, 173.
9. *OR*, 753. Buck, *Cleburne*, 172.
10. Buck, *Cleburne*, 172. Coleman diary, quoted in Hughes, *Hardee*, 176. Nisbet, *Four Years*, 163.
11. Watkins, *First Tennessee*, 126. M.L. Morrison, Confederate Questionnaire, TSLA.
12. *OR*, 665.
13. *OR*, 318–19.
14. *OR*, 665.
15. Tower, *Manigault Narrative*, 143.
16. Pollard diary, Confederate Collection, TSLA.
17. Watkins, *First Tennessee*, 126, 127.
18. Tower, *Manigault Narrative*, 144.

19. *OR*, 191.
20. *OR*, 191.
21. *OR*, 191.
22. *OR*, 743.
23. Ely diary, CCNMPL.
24. Cope, *Fifteenth Ohio*, 385.
25. Reed diary, CCNMPL.
26. General O.O. Howard, "Grant at Chattanooga," in *Personal Recollections of the War of the Rebellion*, I, 253, quoted in Catton, *Grant Takes Command*, 85.
27. Johnson to wife, Dec. 7, 1863, CCNMPL.
28. Toney, *Privations of a Private*, 64.
29. Joseph Hoover, Confederate Veteran Questionnaire, TSLA.
30. J.H. Warner, *Personal Glimpses of the Civil War: Nineteenth Tennessee* (Chattanooga, 1914), 13. *Confederate Veteran*, XXXIII, 139.
31. Brown, *One of Cleburne's Command*, 62–65.
32. *Confederate Veteran*, IX, 86.
33. Wolfe to "My Dear Lloyd," Nov. 26, 1863, CCNMPL.
34. Thomas B. Van Horn, *The Life of Major General George H. Thomas* (New York, 1882), 213.
35. Catton, *This Hallowed Ground*, 371.
36. Allan Nevins, *The War for the Union*, 4 vols. (New York, 1960), III, 211.

Chapter 14

1. Hebert, *Hooker*, 266.
2. Horn, *Army of Tennessee*, 302. Buck, *Cleburne*, 176.
3. Buck, *Cleburne*, 176.
4. *OR*, 754.
5. *OR*, 754–55.
6. *OR*, 755.
7. Hebert, *Hooker*, 266.
8. *OR*, 755.
9. P.D. Stephenson, "Reminiscences of the Last Campaign of the Army of Tennessee, from May, 1864, to January, 1865," *Southern Historical Society Papers*, XII (1884), 38–39.
10. *OR*, 321.
11. *OR*, 756.
12. *OR*, 403.
13. *OR*, 756, 321, 403–4, 604, 756.
14. *OR*, 756.
15. *OR*, 604.

16. *OR*, 757.
17. Buck, *Cleburne*, 185.
18. Johnson Journal, Palmer Collection, Western Reserve.
19. *OR*, 682, 666; LII, pt. 2, 745.
20. Thomas R. Hay, "The Battle of Chattanooga," *Georgia Historical Quarterly* (June 1924), 135. McWhiney, *Braxton Bragg*, helped the author to better understand the Confederate Commander. See especially pages 251, 252, 319–34, 365–67, 372–92.
21. Liddell Journal, Govan Papers, SHC, UNC.

ORGANIZATION OF THE

UNION ARMY

In the Chattanooga Campaign

REPRINTED FROM *War of the Rebellion: A Compilation of the Official Records of the Union and Confederate Armies*

Organization of the forces under command of Maj. Gen. Ulysses S. Grant, U.S. Army, engaged in the campaign.

ARMY OF THE CUMBERLAND
Maj. Gen. George H. Thomas

GENERAL HEADQUARTERS
1st Ohio Sharpshooters, Capt. Gershom M. Barber
10th Ohio Infantry, Lieut. Col. William M. Ward

FOURTH ARMY CORPS
Maj. Gen. Gordon Granger

FIRST DIVISION[a]
Brig. Gen. Charles Cruft

Escort
92d Illinois, Company E. Capt. Mathew Van Buskirk

---

[a]The First Brigade and Battery M, 4th U.S. Artillery, at Bridgeport, Ala.; the 115th Illinois and 84th Indiana, of the Second Brigade, and 5th Indiana Battery, at Shellmound, Tenn.; and the 30th Indiana and 77th Pennsylvania, of the Third Brigade, and Battery H, 4th U.S. Artillery, at Whiteside's, Tenn.

Second Brigade

Brig. Gen. Walter C. Whitaker

96th Illinois: Col. Thomas E. Champion
Maj. George Hicks
35th Indiana, Col. Bernard F. Mullen
8th Kentucky, Col. Sidney M. Barnes
40th Ohio, Col. Jacob E. Taylor
51st Ohio, Lieut. Col. Charles H. Wood
99th Ohio, Lieut. Col. John E. Cummins

Third Brigade
Col. William Grose

59th Illinois, Maj. Clayton Hale
75th Illinois, Col. John E. Bennett
84th Illinois, Col. Louis H. Waters
9th Indiana, Col. Isaac C.B. Suman
36th Indiana, Maj. Gilbert Trusler
24th Ohio, Capt. George M. Bacon

SECOND DIVISION
Maj. Gen. Philip H. Sheridan

First Brigade
Col. Francis T. Sherman

36th Illinois: Col. Silas Miller[a]
Lieut. Col. Porter C. Olson
44th Illinois, Col. Wallace W. Barrett
73d Illinois, Col. James F. Jacquess
74th Illinois, Col. Jason Marsh
88th Illinois, Lieut. Col. George W. Chandler
22d Indiana, Col. Michael Gooding
2d Missouri: Col. Bernard Laiboldt[a]
Lieut. Col. Arnold Beck
15th Missouri: Col. Joseph Conrad
Capt. Samuel Rexinger

[a]Temporarily in command of a demi-brigade.

24th Wisconsin, Maj. Carl von Baumbach

Second Brigade
Brig. Gen. George D. Wagner

100th Illinois, Maj. Charles M. Hammond
15th Indiana: Col. Gustavus A. Wood[a]
Maj. Frank White
Capt. Benjamin F. Hegler
40th Indiana, Lieut. Col. Elias Neff
51st Indiana,[b] Lieut. Col. John M. Comparet
57th Indiana, Lieut. Col. George W. Lennard
58th Indiana, Lieut. Col. Joseph Moore
26th Ohio, Lieut. Col. William H. Barnes
97th Ohio, Lieut. Col. Milton Young

Third Brigade
Col. Charles G. Harker

22d Illinois, Lieut. Col. Francis Swanwick
27th Illinois, Col. Jonathan R. Miles
42d Illinois: Col. Nathan H. Walworth[a]
Capt. Edgar D. Swain
51st Illinois: Maj. Charles W. Davis
Capt. Albert M. Tilton
79th Illinois, Col. Allen Buckner
3d Kentucky, Col. Henry C. Dunlap
64th Ohio, Col. Alexander McIlvain
65th Ohio, Lieut. Col. William A. Bullitt
125th Ohio: Col. Emerson Opdycke[a]
Capt. Edward P. Bates

Artillery
Capt. Warren P. Edgarton

1st Illinois Light, Battery M. Capt. George W. Spencer
10th Indiana Battery, Capt. William A. Naylor
1st Missouri Light, Battery G, Lieut. Gustavus Schueler

---

[b]Between Nashville and Chattanooga *en route* to join brigade.
[a]Temporarily in command of a demi-brigade.
[a]Temporarily attached from the Artillery Reserve.

1st Ohio Light, Battery I[b], Capt. Hubert Dilger
4th United States, Battery G[b], Lieut. Christopher F. Merkle
5th United States, Battery H[b], Capt. Francis L. Guenther

THIRD DIVISION
Brig. Gen. Thomas J. Wood

First Brigade
Brig. Gen. August Willich

25th Illinois, Col. Richard H. Nodine
35th Illinois, Lieut. Col. William P. Chandler
89th Illinois, Lieut. Col. William D. Williams
32d Indiana, Lieut. Col. Frank Erdelmeyer
68th Indiana: Lieut. Col. Harvey J. Espy
Capt. Richard L. Leeson
8th Kansas, Col. John A. Martin
15th Ohio, Lieut. Col. Frank Askew
49th Ohio, Maj. Samuel F. Gray
15th Wisconsin, Capt. John A. Gordon

Second Brigade
Brig. Gen. William B. Hazen

6th Indiana, Maj. Calvin D. Campbell
5th Kentucky: Col. William W. Berry
Lieut. Col. John L. Treanor
6th Kentucky, Maj. Richard T. Whitaker
23d Kentucky, Lieut. Col. James C. Foy
1st Ohio: Lieut. Col. Bassett Langdon
Maj. Joab A. Stafford
6th Ohio, Lieut. Col. Alexander C. Christopher
41st Ohio: Col. Aquila Wiley
Lieut. Col. Robert L. Kimberly
93d Ohio: Maj. William Birch
Capt. Daniel Bowman
Capt. Samuel B. Smith
124th Ohio, Lieut. Col. James Pickands

---

[b]Temporarily attached.

Third Brigade
Brig. Gen. Samuel Beatty

79th Indiana, Col. Frederick Knefler
86th Indiana, Col. George F. Dick
9th Kentucky, Col. George H. Cram
17th Kentucky, Col. Alexander M. Stout
13th Ohio, Col. Dwight Jarvis, Jr.
19th Ohio, Col. Charles F. Manderson
59th Ohio, Maj. Robert J. Vanosdol

Artillery
Capt. Cullen Bradley

Illinois Light, Bridges' Battery, Capt. Lyman Bridges
6th Ohio Battery, Lieut. Oliver H.P. Ayres
20th Ohio Battery[a], Capt. Edward Grosskopff
Pennsylvania Light, Battery B, Lieut Samuel M. McDowell

ELEVENTH ARMY CORPS[b]
Maj. Gen. Oliver O. Howard

GENERAL HEADQUARTERS
Independent Company, 8th New York Infantry, Capt. Anton Bruhn

SECOND DIVISION
Brig. Gen. Adolph von Steinwehr

First Brigade
Col. Adolphus Buschbeck

---

[a]Temporarily attached from the Artillery Reserve.
[b]Maj. Gen. Joseph Hooker, commanding Eleventh and Twelfth Army Corps, had under his immediate command the First Division, Fourth Corps, the Second Division, Twelfth Corps, portions of the Fourteenth Corps, and the First Division, Fifteenth Corps. Company K, 15th Illinois Cavalry, Capt. Samuel B. Sherer, served as escort to General Hooker.

33d New Jersey, Col. George W. Mindil
134th New York, Lieut. Col. Allan H. Jackson
154th New York, Col. Patrick H. Jones
27th Pennsylvania: Maj. Peter A. McAloon
        Capt. August Riedt
73d Pennsylvania: Lieut. Col. Joseph B. Taft
        Capt. Daniel F. Kelley
        Lieut. Samuel D. Miller

Second Brigade
Col. Orland Smith

33d Massachusetts, Lieut. Col. Godfrey Rider, Jr.
136th New York, Col. James Wood, Jr.
55th Ohio, Col. Charles B. Gambee
73d Ohio, Maj. Samuel H. Hurst

THIRD DIVISION
Maj. Gen. Carl Schurz

First Brigade
Brig. Gen. Hector Tyndale

101st Illinois, Col. Charles H. Fox
45th New York, Maj. Charles Koch
143d New York, Col. Horace Boughton
61st Ohio, Col. Stephen J. McGroarty
82d Ohio, Lieut. Col. David Thomson

Second Brigade
Col. Wladimir Krzyzanowski

58th New York, Capt. Michael Esembaux
119th New York, Col. John T. Lockman
141st New York, Col. William K. Logie
26th Wisconsin, Capt. Frederick C. Winkler

Third Brigade
Col. Frederick Hecker

80th Illinois, Capt. James Neville
82d Illinois, Lieut. Col. Edward S. Salomon

68th New York, Lieut. Col. Albert von Steinhausen
75th Pennsylvania, Maj. August Ledig

Artillery
Maj. Thomas W. Osborn

1st New York Light, Battery I, Capt. Michael Wiedrich
New York Light, 13th Battery, Capt. William Wheeler
1st Ohio Light, Battery I[a], Capt. Hubert Dilger
1st Ohio Light, Battery K, Lieut. Nicholas Sahm
4th United States, Battery G[a], Lieut Christopher F. Merkle

TWELFTH ARMY CORPS[b]

SECOND DIVISION
Brig. Gen. John W. Geary

First Brigade
Col. Charles Candy
Col. William R. Creighton
Col. Thomas J. Ahl

5th Ohio, Col. John H. Patrick
7th Ohio: Col. William R. Creighton
Lieut. Col. Orrin J. Crane
Capt. Ernst J. Krieger
29th Ohio, Col. William T. Fitch
66th Ohio: Lieut. Col. Eugene Powell
Capt. Thomas McConnell
28th Pennsylvania: Col. Thomas J. Ahl
Capt. John Flynn
147th Pennsylvania, Lieut. Col. Ario Pardee, Jr.

---

[a]Temporarily attached to Second Division, Fourth Army Corps.
[b]The First Division engaged in guarding the Nashville and Chattanooga Railroad from Wartrace Bridge, Tenn., to Bridgeport, Ala., etc. Maj. Gen. H.W. Slocum, the corps commander, had his headquarters at Tullahoma, Tenn.

Second Brigade
Col. George A. Cobham, Jr.

29th Pennsylvania, Col. William Rickards, Jr.
109th Pennsylvania, Capt. Frederick L. Gimber
111th Pennsylvania, Col. Thomas M. Walker

Third Brigade
Col. David Ireland

60th New York, Col. Abel Godard
78th New York, Lieut. Col. Herbert von Hammerstein
102d New York, Col. James C. Lane
137th New York, Capt. Milo B. Eldredge
149th New York: Col. Henry A. Barnum
Lieut. Col. Charles B. Randall

Artillery
Maj. John A. Reynolds

Pennsylvania Light, Battery E, Lieut. James D. McGill
5th United States, Battery K, Capt. Edmund C. Bainbridge

FOURTEENTH ARMY CORPS

MAJ. GEN. JOHN M. PALMER

Escort
1st Ohio Cavalry, Company L, Capt. John D. Barker

FIRST DIVISION
Brig. Gen. Richard W. Johnson

First Brigade
Brig. Gen. William P. Carlin

104th Illinois, Lieut. Col. Douglas Hapeman
38th Indiana, Lieut. Col. Daniel F. Griffin

42d Indiana, Lieut. Col. William T.B. McIntire
88th Indiana, Col. Cyrus E. Briant
2d Ohio, Col. Anson G. McCook
33d Ohio, Capt. James H.M. Montgomery
94th Ohio, Maj. Rue P. Hutchins
10th Wisconsin, Capt. Jacob W. Roby

SECOND BRIGADE
Col. Marshall F. Moore
Col. William L. Stoughton
19th Illinois, Lieut. Col. Alexander W. Raffen
11th Michigan, Capt. Patrick H. Keegan
69th Ohio, Maj. James J. Hanna
15th United States, 1st Battalion, Capt. Henry Keteltas
15th United States, 2d Battalion, Capt. William S. McManus
16th United States, 1st Battalion, Maj. Robert E.A. Crofton
18th United States, 1st Battalion, Capt. George W. Smith
18th United States, 2d Battalion, Capt. Henry Haymond
19th United States, 1st Battalion, Capt. Henry S. Welton

Third Brigade[a]
Brig. Gen. John C. Starkweather

24th Illinois, Col. Geza Mihalotzy
37th Indiana, Col. James S. Hull
21st Ohio, Capt. Charles H. Vantine
74th Ohio, Maj. Joseph Fisher
78th Pennsylvania, Maj. Augustus B. Bonnaffon
79th Pennsylvania, Maj. Michael H. Locher
1st Wisconsin, Lieut. Col. George B. Bingham
21st Wisconsin, Capt. Charles H. Walker

Artillery
1st Illinois Light, Battery C, Capt. Mark H. Prescott
1st Michigan Light, Battery A, Capt. Francis E. Hale
5th United States, Battery H[b], Capt. Francis L. Guenther

---

[a]During the engagements of the 23d, 24th, and 25th was in line of battle holding fort and breastworks at Chattanooga.
[b]Temporarily attached to Second Division, Fourth Army Corps.

SECOND DIVISION
Brig. Gen. Jefferson C. Davis

First Brigade
Brig. Gen. James D. Morgan

10th Illinois, Col. John Tillson
16th Illinois, Lieut. Col. James B. Cahill
60th Illinois, Col. William B. Anderson
21st Kentucky, Col. Samuel W. Price
10th Michigan, Lieut. Col. Christopher J. Dickerson
14th Michigan[c], Col. Henry R. Mizner

Second Brigade
Brig. Gen. John Beatty

34th Illinois, Lieut. Col. Oscar Van Tassell
78th Illinois, Lieut. Col. Carter Van Vleck
3d Ohio[d], Capt. Leroy S. Bell
98th Ohio, Maj. James M. Shane
108th Ohio, Lieut. Col. Carlo Piepho
113th Ohio, Maj. Lyne S. Sullivant
121st Ohio, Maj. John Yager

Third Brigade
Col. Daniel McCook

85th Illinois, Col. Caleb J. Dilworth
86th Illinois, Lieut. Col. David W. Magee
110th Illinois, Lieut. Col. E. Hibbard Topping
125th Illinois, Col. Oscar F. Harmon
52d Ohio, Maj. James T. Holmes

Artillery
Capt. William A. Hotchkiss

2d Illinois Light, Battery I, Lieut. Henry B. Plant
Minnesota Light, 2d Battery, Lieut. Richard L. Dawley
Wisconsin Light, 5th Battery, Capt. George Q. Gardner

---

[c]Detached at Columbia, Tenn.
[d]Detached at Kelley's Ferry, Tennessee River.

THIRD DIVISION
Brig. Gen. Absalom Baird

FIRST BRIGADE
Brig. Gen. John B. Turchin
82d Indiana, Col. Morton C. Hunter
11th Ohio, Lieut. Col. Ogden Street
17th Ohio: Maj. Benjamin F. Butterfield
Capt. Benjamin H. Showers
31st Ohio, Lieut. Col. Frederick W. Lister
36th Ohio, Lieut. Col. Hiram F. Devol
89th Ohio, Capt. John H. Jolly
92d Ohio: Lieut. Col. Douglas Putnam, Jr.
Capt. Edward Grosvenor

Second Brigade
Col. Ferdinand Van Derveer

75th Indiana, Col. Milton S. Robinson
87th Indiana, Col. Newell Gleason
101st Indiana, Lieut. Col. Thomas Doan
2d Minnesota, Lieut. Col. Judson W. Bishop
9th Ohio, Col. Gustave Kammerling
35th Ohio: Lieut. Col. Henry V.N. Boynton
Maj. Joseph L. Budd
105th Ohio, Lieut. Col. William R. Tolles

Third Brigade
Col. Edward H. Phelps
Col. William H. Hays

10th Indiana, Lieut. Col. Marsh B. Taylor
74th Indiana, Lieut. Col. Myron Baker
4th Kentucky, Maj. Robert M. Kelly
10th Kentucky: Col. William H. Hays
Lieut. Col. Gabriel C. Wharton
18th Kentucky,[a] Lieut. Col. Hubbard K. Milward
14th Ohio, Lieut. Col. Henry D. Kingsbury
38th Ohio, Maj. Charles Greenwood

---

[a]Detached at Brown's Ferry, Tenn.

Artillery
Capt. George R. Swallow

Indiana Light, 7th Battery, Lieut. Otho H. Morgan
Indiana Light, 19th Battery, Lieut. Robert G. Lackey
4th United States, Battery I, Lieut. Frank G. Smith

ENGINEER TROOPS
Brig. Gen. William F. Smith

Engineers
1st Michigan Engineers (detachment), Capt. Perrin V. Fox
18th Michigan Infantry, Maj. Willard G. Eaton
21st Michigan Infantry, Capt. Loomis K. Bishop
22d Michigan Infantry, Maj. Henry S. Dean
18th Ohio Infantry, Col. Timothy R. Stanley

Pioneer Brigade
Col. George P. Buell

1st Battalion, Capt. Charles J. Stewart
2d Battalion, Capt. Correll Smith
3d Battalion, Capt. William Clark

ARTILLERY RESERVE
Brig. Gen. John M. Brannan

FIRST DIVISION
Col. James Barnett

First Brigade
Maj. Charles S. Cotter

1st Ohio Light, Battery B, Lieut. Norman A. Baldwin
1st Ohio Light, Battery C, Capt. Marco B. Gary
1st Ohio Light, Battery E, Lieut. Albert G. Ransom
1st Ohio Light, Battery F, Lieut. Giles J. Cockerill

Second Brigade

1st Ohio Light, Battery G, Capt. Alexander Marshall
1st Ohio Light, Battery M, Capt. Frederick Schultz
Ohio Light, 18th Battery, Lieut. Joseph McCafferty
Ohio Light, 20th Battery[a], Capt. Edward Grosskopff

SECOND DIVISION

First Brigade
Capt. Josiah W. Church

1st Michigan Light, Battery D, Capt. Josiah W. Church
1st Tennessee Light, Battery A, Lieut. Albert F. Beach
Wisconsin Light, 3d Battery, Lieut. Hiram F. Hubbard
Wisconsin Light, 8th Battery, Lieut. Obadiah German
Wisconsin Light, 10th Battery, Capt. Yates V. Beebe

Second Brigade
Capt. Arnold Sutermeister

Indiana Light, 4th Battery, Lieut. Henry J. Willits
Indiana Light, 8th Battery, Lieut. George Estep
Indiana Light, 11th Battery, Capt. Arnold Sutermeister
Indiana Light, 21st Battery, Lieut. William E. Chess
1st Wisconsin Heavy, Company C, Capt. John R. Davies

CAVALRY[b]

SECOND BRIGADE (SECOND DIVISION)
Col. Eli Long
98th Illinois (mounted infantry), Lieut. Col. Edward Kitchell

[a]Temporarily attached to Third Division, Fourth Army Corps.
[b]Corps headquarters and the First and Second Brigades and 18th Indiana Battery, of the First Division, at and about Alexandria, Tenn.; the Third Brigade at Caperton's Ferry, Tennessee River. The First and Third Brigades, and the Chicago Board of Trade Battery, of the Second Division, at Maysville, Ala.

17th Indiana (mounted infantry), Lieut. Col. Henry Jordan
2d Kentucky, Col. Thomas P. Nicholas
4th Michigan, Maj. Horace Gray
1st Ohio, Maj. Thomas J. Patten
3d Ohio, Lieut. Col. Charles B. Seidel
4th Ohio (battalion), Maj. George W. Dobb
10th Ohio, Col. Charles C. Smith

POST OF CHATTANOOGA

COL. JOHN G. PARKHURST
44th Indiana, Lieut. Col. Simeon C. Aldrich
15th Kentucky, Maj. William G. Halpin
9th Michigan, Lieut. Col. William Wilkinson

ARMY OF THE TENNESSEE

MAJ. GEN. WILLIAM T. SHERMAN[a]

FIFTEENTH ARMY CORPS[b]

MAJ. GEN. FRANK P. BLAIR, JR.
First Division
Brig. Gen. Peter J. Osterhaus

---

[a]General Sherman had under his immediate command the Eleventh Corps and the Second Division, Fourteenth Corps, of the Army of the Cumberland; the Second and Fourth Divisions, Fifteenth Corps, and the Second Division, Seventeenth Corps.

[b]The Third Division, Brig. Gen. James M. Tuttle commanding, at Memphis, La-Grange, and Pocahontas, Tenn.

First Brigade
Brig. Gen. Charles R. Woods

13th Illinois: Lieut. Col. Frederick W. Partridge
Capt. George P. Brown
3d Missouri, Lieut. Col. Theodore Meumann
12th Missouri: Col. Hugo Wangelin
Lieut. Col. Jacob Kaercher
17th Missouri, Col. John F. Cramer
27th Missouri, Col. Thomas Curley
29th Missouri: Col. James Peckham
Maj. Philip H. Murphy
31st Missouri, Lieut. Col. Samuel P. Simpson
32d Missouri, Lieut. Col. Henry C. Warmoth
76th Ohio, Maj. Willard Warner

Second Brigade
Col. James A. Williamson

4th Iowa, Lieut. Col. George Burton
9th Iowa, Col. David Carskaddon
25th Iowa, Col. George A. Stone
26th Iowa, Col. Milo Smith
30th Iowa, Lieut. Col. Aurelius Roberts
31st Iowa, Lieut. Col. Jeremiah W. Jenkins

Artillery
Capt. Henry H. Griffiths

Iowa Light, 1st Battery, Lieut. James M. Williams
2d Missouri Light, Battery F, Capt. Clemens Landgraeber
Ohio Light, 4th Battery, Capt. George Froehlich

SECOND DIVISION
Brig. Gen. Morgan L. Smith

First Brigade
Brig. Gen. Giles A. Smith
Col. Nathan W. Tupper

55th Illinois, Col. Oscar Malmborg
116th Illinois: Col. Nathan W. Tupper
Lieut. Col. James P. Boyd
127th Illinois, Lieut. Col. Frank S. Curtiss
6th Missouri, Lieut. Col. Ira Boutell
8th Missouri, Lieut. Col. David C. Coleman
57th Ohio, Lieut. Col. Samuel R. Mott
13th United States, 1st Battalion, Capt. Charles C. Smith

Second Brigade
Brig. Gen. Joseph A.J. Lightburn

83d Indiana, Col. Benjamin J. Spooner
30th Ohio, Col. Theodore Jones
37th Ohio, Lieut. Col. Louis von Blessingh
47th Ohio, Col. Augustus C. Parry
54th Ohio, Maj. Robert Williams, Jr.
4th West Virginia, Col. James H. Dayton

Artillery

1st Illinois Light, Battery A, Capt. Peter P. Wood
1st Illinois Light, Battery B, Capt. Israel P. Rumsey
1st Illinois Light, Battery H, Lieut. Francis De Gress

FOURTH DIVISION
Brig. Gen. Hugh Ewing

First Brigade
Col. John M. Loomis

26th Illinois, Lieut. Col. Robert A. Gillmore
90th Illinois: Col. Timothy O'Meara
Lieut. Col. Owen Stuart
12th Indiana, Col. Reuben Williams
100th Indiana, Lieut. Col. Albert Heath

Second Brigade
Brig. Gen. John M. Corse
Col. Charles C. Walcutt

40th Illinois, Maj. Hiram W. Hall
103d Illinois, Col. William A. Dickerman
6th Iowa, Lieut. Col. Alexander J. Miller
15th Michigan,[a] Lieut. Col. Austin E. Jaquith
46th Ohio: Col. Charles C. Walcutt
Capt. Isaac N. Alexander

Third Brigade
Col. Joseph R. Cockerill

48th Illinois, Lieut. Col. Lucien Greathouse
97th Indiana, Col. Robert F. Catterson
99th Indiana, Col. Alexander Fowler
53d Ohio, Col. Wells S. Jones
70th Ohio, Maj. William B. Brown

Artillery
Capt. Henry Richardson

1st Illinois Light, Battery F, Capt. John T. Cheney
1st Illinois Light, Battery I, Lieut. Josiah H. Burton
1st Missouri Light, Battery D, Lieut. Byron M. Callender

SEVENTEENTH ARMY CORPS

SECOND DIVISION
Brig. Gen. John E. Smith

First Brigade
Col. Jesse I. Alexander

63d Illinois, Col. Joseph B. McCown
48th Indiana, Lieut. Col. Edward J. Wood
59th Indiana, Capt. Wilford H. Welman
4th Minnesota, Lieut. Col. John E. Tourtellotte
18th Wisconsin, Col. Gabriel Bouck

Second Brigade
Col. Green B. Raum

---

[a]Detached at Scottsborough, Ala.

Col. Francis C. Deimling
Col. Clark R. Wever

57th Illinois, Maj. Pinckney J. Welsh
17th Iowa: Col. Clark R. Wever
Maj. John F. Walden
10th Missouri: Col. Francis C. Deimling
Lieut. Col. Christian Happel
24th Missouri, Company E, Capt. William W. McCammon
80th Ohio, Lieut. Col. Pren Metham

Third Brigade

Brig. Gen. Charles L. Matthies
Col. Benjamin D. Dean
Col. Jabez Banbury

93d Illinois: Col. Holden Putnam
Lieut. Col. Nicholas C. Buswell
5th Iowa: Col. Jabez Banbury
Lieut. Col. Ezekiel S. Sampson
10th Iowa, Lieut. Col. Paris P. Henderson
26th Missouri, Col. Benjamin D. Dean

Artillery
Capt. Henry Dillon

Cogswell's (Illinois) Battery, Capt. William Cogswell
Wisconsin Light, 6th Battery, Lieut. Samuel F. Clark
Wisconsin Light, 12th Battery, Capt. William Zickerick

ORGANIZATION OF THE

CONFEDERATE ARMY

In the Chattanooga Campaign

REPRINTED FROM *War of the Rebellion: A Compilation of the Official Records of the Union and Confederate Armies*

Organization of the Army of Tennessee, General Braxton Bragg, C.S. Army, commanding, November 20, 1863[a]

GENERAL HEADQUARTERS
1st Louisiana (regular), [Col. James Strawbridge]
1st Louisiana Cavalry, [Maj. J.M. Taylor]

LONGSTREET'S ARMY CORPS[b]

M'LAWS' DIVISION

Kershaw's Brigade

2d South Carolina, Col. John D. Kennedy
3d South Carolina, Col. James D. Nance
7th South Carolina, Col. D. Wyatt Aiken
8th South Carolina, Col. John W. Hengagan
15th South Carolina, Col. Joseph F. Gist
3d South Carolina Battalion, Lieut. Col. William G. Rice

---

[a]The artillery assignments indicated were made in circular of this date from General Bragg's headquarters. Return of strength for this date not found.
[b]Detached November 4, for operations in East Tennessee.

Humphreys' Brigade

13th Mississippi, Col. Kennon McElroy
17th Mississippi, Col. William D. Holder
18th Mississippi, Col. Thomas M. Griffin
21st Mississippi, Col. William L. Brandon

Wofford's Brigade

16th Georgia, Col. Henry P. Thomas
18th Georgia, Col. S.Z. Ruff
24th Georgia, Col. Robert McMillan
Cobb's Legion, Lieut. Col. Luther J. Glenn
Phillips' Legion, Lieut. Col. E.S. Barclay
3d Georgia Battalion Sharpshooters, Lieut. Col. N.L. Hutchins, Jr.

Bryan's Brigade

10th Georgia, Col. John B. Weems
50th Georgia, Col. Peter McGlashan
51st Georgia, Col. Edward Ball
53d Georgia, Col. James P. Simms

Artillery Battalion
Maj. Austin Leyden

Georgia Battery, Capt. Tyler M. Peeples
Georgia Battery, Capt. Andrew M. Wolihin
Georgia Battery, Capt. Billington W. York

Hood's Division
Jenkins Brigade

1st South Carolina, Col. Franklin W. Kilpatrick
2d South Carolina Rifles, Col. Thomas Thomson
5th South Carolina, Col. A. Coward
6th South Carolina, Col. John Batton
Hampton (South Carolina) Legion, Col. Martin W. Gary
Palmetto (South Carolina) Sharpshooters, Col. Joseph Walker

Robertson's Brigade

3d Arkansas, Col. Van H. Manning

1st Texas, Col. A.T. Rainey
4th Texas, Col. J.C.G. Key
5th Texas, Col. R.M. Powell

Law's Brigade

4th Alabama, Col. Pinckney D. Bowles
15th Alabama, Col. William C. Oates
44th Alabama, Col. William F. Perry
47th Alabama, Col. Michael J. Bulger
48th Alabama, Col. James L. Sheffield

Anderson's Brigade

7th Georgia, Col. W.W. White
8th Georgia, Col. John R. Towers
9th Georgia, Col. Benjamin Beck
11th Georgia, Col. F.H. Little
59th Georgia, Col. Jack Brown

Benning's Brigade

2d Georgia, Col. Edgar M. Butt
15th Georgia, Col. Dudley M. DuBose
17th Georgia, Wesley C. Hodges
20th Georgia, Col. J.D. Waddell

Artillery Battalion
Col. E. Porter Alexander

South Carolina Battery, Capt. William W. Fickling
Virginia Battery, Capt. Tyler C. Jordan
Louisiana Battery, Capt. George V. Moody
Virginia Battery, Capt. William W. Parker
Virginia Battery, Capt. Osmond B. Taylor
Virginia Battery, Capt. Pichegru Woolfolk, Jr.

HARDEE'S CORPS

CHEATHAM'S DIVISION

Jackson's Brigade
1st Georgia (Confederate), Maj. James C. Gordon
5th Georgia, Col. Charles P. Daniel
47th Georgia[a], Capt. J.J. Harper
65th Georgia[a], Lieut. Col. Jacob W. Pearcy
2d Georgia Battalion Sharpshooters, Lieut. Col. Richard H. Whiteley
5th Mississippi, Maj. John B. Herring
8th Mississippi, Maj. John F. Smith

Moore's Brigade
37th Alabama, Col. James F. Dowdell
40th Alabama, Col. John H. Higley
42d Alabama, Lieut. Col. Thomas C. Lanier

Walthall's Brigade
24th and 27th Mississippi, Col. William F. Dowd
29th and 30th Mississippi, Capt. W.G. Reynolds
34th Mississippi, Col. Samuel Benton

Wright's Brigade
8th Tennessee, Col. John H. Anderson
16th Tennessee, Col. D.M. Donnell
28th Tennessee, Col. Sidney S. Stanton
38th Tennessee, Lieut. Col. Andrew D. Gwynne
51st and 52d Tennessee, Lieut. Col. John G. Hall
Murray's (Tennessee) Battalion, Lieut. Col. Andrew D. Gwynne

Artillery Battalion
Maj. Melancthon Smith

Alabama Battery, Capt. William H. Fowler
Florida Battery, Capt. Robert P. McCants
Georgia Battery, Capt. John Scogin
Mississippi Battery (Smith's), Lieut. William B. Turner

HINDMAN'S DIVISION

Anderson's Brigade

[a]Assigned November 12, 1863.

7th Mississippi, Col. William H. Bishop
9th Mississippi, Maj. Thomas H. Lynam
10th Mississippi, Capt. Robert A. Bell
41st Mississippi, Col. W.F. Tucker
44th Mississippi, Lieut. Col. R.G. Kelsey
9th Mississippi Battalion Sharpshooters, Capt. W.W. Tucker

Manigault's Brigade

24th Alabama, Col. N.N. Davis
28th Alabama, Maj. W.L. Butler
34th Alabama, Maj. John N. Slaughter
10th and 19th South Carolina, Maj. James L. White

Deas' Brigade

19th Alabama, Col. Samuel K. McSpadden
22d Alabama, Capt. Harry T. Toulmin
25th Alabama, Col. George D. Johnston
39th Alabama, Col. Whitfield Clark
50th Alabama, Col. J.G. Coltart
17th Alabama Battalion Sharpshooters, Capt. James F. Nabers

Vaughan's Brigade

11th Tennessee, Col. George W. Gordon
12th and 47th Tennessee, Col. William M. Watkins
13th and 154th Tennessee, Lieut. Col. R.W. Pitman
20th Tennessee, Col. Horace Rice

Artillery Battalion
Maj. Alfred R. Courtney

Alabama Battery, Capt. S.H. Dent
Alabama Battery, Capt. James Garrity
Tennessee Battery (Scott's), Lieut. John Doscher
Alabama Battery (Waters'), Lieut. William B. Hamilton

BUCKNER'S DIVISION[a]

---

[a]Detached November 22 for operations againt Burnside in East Tennessee. Reynold's brigade and the artillery were recalled.

Johnson's Brigade

17th and 23d Tennessee, Lieut. Col. Watt W. Floyd
25th and 44th Tennessee, Lieut. Col. John L. McEwen, Jr.
63d Tennessee, Maj. John A. Aiken

Gracie's Brigade

41st Alabama, Lieut. Col. Theodore G. Trimmier
43d Alabama, Col. Young M. Moody
1st Battalion, Alabama (Hilliard's) Legion, Maj. Daniel S. Troy
2d Battalion, Alabama (Hilliard's) Legion, Capt. John H. Dillard
3d Battalion, Alabama (Hilliard's) Legion, Lieut. Col. John W.A. San-
ford
4th Battalion, Alabama (Hilliard's) Legion, Maj. John D. McLennan

Reynolds' Brigade

58th North Carolina, Col. John B. Palmer
60th North Carolina, Capt. James T. Weaver
54th Virginia, Lieut. Col. John J. Wade
63d Virginia, Maj. James M. French

Artillery Battalion
Maj. Samuel C. Williams

Mississippi Battery (Darden's), Lieut. H.W. Bullen
Virginia Battery, Capt. William C. Jeffress
Alabama Battery, Capt. R.F. Kolb

WALKER'S DIVISION[a]

Maney's Brigade[b]

1st and 27th Tennessee, Col. Hume R. Feild
4th Tennessee (Provisional Army), Capt. Joseph Bostick
6th and 9th Tennessee, Lieut. Col. J.W. Buford

---

[a]Transferred from Longstreet's corps November 12, 1863, and regiments of Gregg's
brigade distributed to Bate's, Maney's, and Smith's brigades.
[b]Transferred from Cheatham's division November 12, 1863.

41st Tennessee,[c] Col. Robert Farquharson
50th Tennessee,[c] Col. Cyrus A. Sugg
24th Tennessee Battalion Sharpshooters, Maj. Frank Maney

Gist's Brigade

46th Georgia, Lieut. Col. William A. Daniel
8th Georgia Battalion, Lieut. Col. Leroy Napier
16th South Carolina, Col. James McCullough
24th South Carolina, Col. Clement H. Stevens

Wilson's Brigade

25th Georgia, Col. Claudius C. Wilson
29th Georgia, Col. William J. Young
30th Georgia, Col. Thomas W. Mangham
26th Georgia Battalion, Maj. John W. Nisbet
1st Georgia Battalion Sharpshooters[a], Maj. Arthur Shaaff.

Artillery Battalion
Maj. Robert Martin

Missouri Battery, Capt. Hiram M. Bledsoe
South Carolina Battery, Capt. T.B. Ferguson
Georgia Battery, Capt. Evan P. Howell

BRECKINRIDGE'S ARMY CORPS

CLEBURNE'S DIVISION

Liddell's Brigade

2d and 15th Arkansas, Maj. E. Warfield
5th and 13th Arkansas, Col. John E. Murray
6th and 7th Arkansas, Lieut. Col. Peter Snyder
8th Arkansas, Maj. Anderson Watkins

[c]From Gregg's brigade.
[a]Assigned November 12, 1863.

19th and 24th Arkansas,[b] Lieut. Col. A.S. Hutchinson

Polk's Brigade

1st Arkansas, Col. John W. Colquitt
3d and 5th Confederate, Lieut. Col. J.C. Cole
2d Tennessee, Col. William D. Robinson
35th and 48th Tennessee, Col. Benjamin J. Hill

Smith's Brigade

6th and 10th Texas Infantry and 15th Texas (dismounted) Cavalry,
Col. Roger Q. Mills
7th Texas,[c] Col. Hiram B. Granbury
17th, 18th, 24th, and 25th Texas Cavalry (dismounted) Maj. William
A. Taylor

Lowrey's Brigade

16th Alabama, Maj. Frederick A. Ashford
33d Alabama, Col. Samuel Adams
45th Alabama, Lieut. Col. H.D. Lampley
32d and 45th Mississippi, Lieut. Col. R. Charlton
15th Mississippi Battalion Sharpshooters, Capt. Daniel Coleman

Artillery Battalion
Maj. T.R. Hotchkiss

Arkansas Battery (Calvert's), Lieut. Thomas J. Key
Texas Battery, Capt. James P. Douglas
Alabama Battery (Semple's), Lieut. Richard W. Goldthwaite
Mississippi Battery (Swett's), Lieut. H. Shannon

STEWART'S DIVISION[a]

Adams' Brigade

13th and 20th Louisiana, Col. Leon von Zinken

---

[b]Transferred from Smith's brigade November 12, 1863.
[c]Transferred from Gregg's brigade November 12, 1863.
[a]See organization of this division October 31, 1863.

16th and 25th Louisiana, Col. Daniel Gober
19th Louisiana, Col. W.P Winans
4th Louisiana Battalion, Lieut. Col. John McEnery
14th Louisiana Battalion Sharpshooters, Maj. J.E. Austin

Strahl's Brigade

4th and 5th Tennessee, Col. Jonathan J. Lamb
19th Tennessee, Col. Francis M. Walker
24th Tennessee, Col. John A. Wilson
31st Tennessee, Col. Egbert E. Tansil
33rd Tennessee, Lieut.Col. Henry C. McNeill

Clayton's Brigade

18th Alabama, Maj. Shep. Ruffin
32d Alabama, Capt. John W. Bell
36th Alabama, Col. Lewis T. Woodruff
38th Alabama, Col. Charles T. Ketchum
58th Alabama, Lieut. Col. John W. Inzer

Stovall's Brigade

40th Georgia, [Col. Abda Johnson]
41st Georgia [Col. William E. Curtiss]
42d Georgia, [Col. R.J. Henderson]
43d Georgia, [Col. Hiram P. Bell]
52d Georgia, [Maj. John J. Moore]

Artillery Battalion
Capt. Henry C. Semple

Georgia Battery (Dawson's), Lieut. R.W. Anderson
Arkansas Battery (Humphreys'), Lieut. John W. Rivers
Alabama Battery, Capt. McDonald Oliver
Mississippi Battery, Capt. Thomas J. Stanford

BRECKINRIDGE'S DIVISION
Lewis' Brigade
2d Kentucky, Lieut. Col. James W. Moss
4th Kentucky, Maj. Thomas W. Thompson
5th Kentucky, Col. H. Hawkins

6th Kentucky, Lieut. Col. W.L. Clarke
9th Kentucky, Lieut. Col. John C. Wickliffe
John H. Morgan's dismounted men.

Bate's Brigade[a]

37th Georgia, Col. A.F. Rudler
4th Georgia Battalion Sharpshooters, Lieut. Joel Towers
10th Tennessee,[b] Col. William Grace
15th and 37th Tennessee, Lieut. Col. R. Dudley Frayser
20th Tennessee, Maj. W.M. Shy
30th Tennessee,[b] Lieut. Col. James J. Turner
1st Tennessee Battalion,[b] Maj. Stephen H. Colms.

Florida Brigade[c]

1st and 3d Florida, Capt. W.T. Saxon
4th Florida, Lieut. Col. E. Badger
6th Florida, Col. Jesse J. Finley
7th Florida, Lieut. Col. Tillman Ingram
1st Florida Cavalry (dismounted), Col. G. Troup Maxwell

Artillery Battalion
Capt. C.H. Slocomb

Kentucky Battery (Cobb's), Lieut. Frank P. Gracey
Tennssee Battery, Capt. John W. Mebane
Louisiana Battery (Slocomb's), Lieut. W.C.D. Vaught

STEVENSON'S DIVISION

Brown's Brigade[a]

3d Tennessee[d], Col. Calvin H. Walker
18th and 26th Tennessee, Lieut. Col. William R. Butler
32d Tennessee, Capt. Thomas D. Deavenport
45th Tennessee and 23d Tennessee Battalion, Col. Anderson Searcy

---

[a]Transferred from Stewart's division November 12, 1863.
[b]Transferred from Gregg's brigade November 12, 1863.
[c]Organized November 12, 1863.
[d]In Gregg's brigade October 31, 1863.

Cumming's Brigade[e]

34th Georgia, Col. J.A.W. Johnson
36th Georgia, Lieut. Col. Alexander M. Wallace
39th Georgia, Col. J.T. McConnell
56th Georgia, Lieut. Col. J.T. Slaughter

Pettus's Brigade[a]

20th Alabama, Capt. John W. Davis
23d Alabama, Lieut. Col. J.B. Bibb
30th Alabama, Col. Charles M. Shelley
31st Alabama, Col. D.R. Hundley
46th Alabama, Capt. George E. Brewer

Vaughn's Brigade[b]

3d Tennessee (Provisional Army)
39th Tennessee
43d Tennessee
59th Tennessee

Artillery Battalion[c]
Capt. Robert Cobb

Tennessee Battery, Capt. Edmund D. Baxter
Tennessee Battery, Capt. William W. Carnes
Georgia Battery, Capt. Max Van Den Corput
Georgia Battery, Capt. John B. Rowan

WHEELER'S CAVALRY CORPS[d]

[e]Regimental commanders, not reported in original, are supplied from Stevenson's roster.
[a]Reassigned to division November 12, 1863.
[b]Note on original: "Exchanged prisoners; but few reported."
[c]According to Stevenson's return, his artillery battalion consisted at this date of Carnes', Corput's, and Rowan's batteries, and the 20th Alabama Battalion, viz: Company A, Capt. Winslow D. Emery, Company B, Capt. Richard H. Ballamy, and Company C, Capt. T.J. Key.
[d]The First Brigade of Wharton's division, Martin's division, Armstrong's division (the 5th Tennessee excepted), and all the artillery (except Huwald's battery) detached under Wheeler's command.

MAJ. GEN. JOSEPH WHEELER
Wharton's Division
Maj. Gen. John A. Wharton

First Brigade
Col. Thomas Harrison

3d Arkansas, Lieut. Col. M.J. Henderson
65th North Carolina (6th Cavalry), Col. George N. Folk
8th Texas, Lieut. Col. Gustave Cook
11th Texas, Lieut. Col. J.M. Bounds

Second Brigade
Brig. Gen. Henry B. Davidson

1st Tennessee, Col. James E. Carter
2d Tennessee, Col. Henry M. Asby
4th Tennessee, Col. William S. McLemore
6th Tennese, Col. James T. Wheeler
11th Tennessee, Col. Daniel W. Holman

MARTIN'S DIVISION
Maj. Gen. William T. Martin

First Brigade
Brig. Gen. John T. Morgan

1st Alabama, Lieut. Col. D.T. Blakey
3d Alabama, Lieut. Col. T.H. Mauldin
4th Alabama [Russell's], Lieut. Col. J.M. Hambrick
Malone's (Alabama) Regiment, Lieut. Col. James C. Malone, Jr.
51st Alabama, Capt. M.L. Kirkpatrick

Second Brigade
Col. J.J. Morrison

1st Georgia, Lieut. Col. S.W. Davitte
2d Georgia, Lieut. Col. F.M. Ison
3d Georgia, Lieut. Col. R. Thompson
4th Georgia, Col. Isaac W. Avery
6th Georgia, Col. John R. Hart

ARMSTRONG'S DIVISION
Brig. Gen. Frank C. Armstrong

First Brigade
Brig. Gen. William Y.C. Humes

4th Tennessee [Baxter Smith's], Lieut. Col. Paul F. Anderson
5th Tennessee, Col. George W. McKenzie
8th Tennessee [Dibrell's],
9th Tennessee, Col. Jacob Biffle
10th Tennessee, Col. Nicholas N. Cox

Second Brigade
Col. C.H. Tyler

Clay's (Kentucky) Battalion, Lieut. Col. Ezekiel F. Clay
Edmundson's (Virginia) Battalion, Maj. S.P. McConnell
Jessee's (Kentucky) Battalion, Maj. A.L. McAfee
Johnson's (Kentucky) Battalion, Maj. O.S. Tenney

KELLY'S DIVISION

First Brigade
Col. William B. Wade

1st Confederate, Capt. C.H. Conner
3d Confederate, Col. W.N. Estes
8th Confederate, Lieut. Col. John S. Prather
10th Confederate, Col. Charles T. Goode

Second Brigade
Col. J. Warren Grigsby

2d Kentucky, Col. Thomas G. Woodward
3d Kentucky, Col. J.R. Butler
9th Kentucky, Col. W.C.P. Breckinridge
Allison's (Tennessee) Squadron, Capt. R.D. Allison
Hamilton's (Tennessee) Battalion, Lieut. Col. O.P. Hamilton
Rucker's Legion, Col. E.W. Rucker

Artillery

Tennessee Battery, Capt. A.L. Huggins
Tennessee Battery, Capt. Gustave A. Huwald
Tennessee Battery, Capt. B.F. White, Jr.
Arkansas Battery, Capt. J.H. Wiggins

RESERVE ARTILLERY[a]

Maj. Felix H. Robertson

Missouri Battery, Capt. Overton W. Barret
Georgia Battery (Havis'), Lieut. James R. Duncan
Alabama Battery (Lumsden's), Lieut. Harvey H. Cribbs
Georgia Battery, Capt. Thomas L. Massenburg

DETACHED

Roddey's Cavalry Brigade

4th Alabama, Col. William A. Johnson
5th Alabama, Col. Josiah Patterson
53d Alabama, Col. M.W. Hannon
Moreland's (Alabama) Battalion, Lieut. Col. M.D. Moreland
Georgia Battery, Capt. C.B. Ferrell
KINLOCH FALCONER
Assistant Adjutant-General

[a]Sengstak's (Alabama) battery, assigned November 19, not accounted for.

Bibliography

Primary Materials

Records

War of the Rebellion: A Compilation of the Official Records of the Union and Confederate Armies. 129 vols. Washington, D.C., 1880–1901.

Collected Works, Memoirs, Diaries, Reminiscences, Papers

Alexander, E.P. *Military Memoirs of A Confederate: A Critical Narrative.* New York, 1907.

Angle, Paul M., ed. *Three Years in the Army of the Cumberland: The Letters and Diary of Major James A. Connolly.* Indianapolis, 1959.

Athearn, Robert G., ed. *Soldier in the West: The Civil War Letters of Alfred Lacey Hough.* Philadelphia, 1957.

Basler, Roy P., ed. *The Collected Works of Abraham Lincoln.* 8 vols. New Brunswick, N.J., 1953.

Bauer, Jack, ed. *Soldiering: The Civil War Diary of Rice C. Bull, 123rd New York Volunteer Infantry.* San Rafael, Calif., 1977.

Beatty, John. *Memoirs of a Volunteer, 1861–1863.* New York, 1946.

Brown, Norman D., ed. *One of Cleburne's Command: The Civil War Reminiscences and Diary of Captain Samuel T. Foster, Granbury's Texas Brigade, CSA.* Austin, Tex., 1980.

Buell, Clarence C., and Robert U. Johnson, eds. *Battles and Leaders of the Civil War.* 4 vols. New York, 1887–88.

Commager, Henry Steele, ed. *The Blue and the Gray: The Story of the Civil War as Told by Participants.* 2 vols. Indianapolis, 1950.

Confederate Veteran. 40 vols. Nashville, 1893–1932.

Eisenschiml, Otto, and Ralph Newman, eds. *The Civil War: The American Iliad as Told by Those Who Lived It.* New York, 1956.

Grant, Ulysses S. *Personal Memoirs of U.S. Grant.* 2 vols. New York, 1885.

Jones, J.B. *A Rebel War Clerk's Diary.* 2 vols. Philadelphia, 1866.

Longstreet, James. *From Manassas to Appomattox.* Philadelphia, 1896.

Lyle, W.W. *Lights and Shadows of Army Life.* Cincinnati, 1865.

MacArthur, Douglas. *Reminiscences.* New York, 1964.

Parsons, E.B. "Missionary Ridge," *Military Order of the Loyal Legion of the United States, Wisconsin Commandery.* Milwaukee, 1891.

———. "Sheridan," *Military Order of the Loyal Legion of the United States, Wisconsin Commandery,* Milwaukee, 1891.

Porter, Horace. *Campaigning With Grant.* New York, 1897.

Roman, Alfred T. *The Military Operations of General Beauregard.* 2 vols. New York, 1884.

Rusling, James M. *Men and Things I Saw in Civil War Days.* New York, 1899.

Scribner, B.F. *How Soldiers Were Made; or the War As I Saw It Under Buell, Rosecrans, Grant, and Sherman.* New Albany, Ind., 1887.

Sherman, William T. *Memoirs of General William T. Sherman.* 2 vols. New York, 1875.

Simon, John Y., ed. *The Papers of Ulysses S. Grant.* 10 vols. Carbondale, Ill., 1973–82.

Sorrel, G. Moxley. *Recollections of a Confederate Staff Officer.* Edited by Bell I. Wiley. Jackson, Tenn., 1958.

Tapp, Hambleton, and James C. Klotter. eds. *The Union, The Civil War, and John W. Tuttle: A Kentucky Captain's Account.* Frankfort, Ky., 1980.

Thomas, Benjamin P., ed. *Three Years With Grant As Recalled by War Correspondent Sylvanus Cadwallader.* New York, 1955.

Toney, Marcus B. *The Privations of a Private.* Nashville, 1905.

Tower, R. Lockwood, ed. *A Carolinian Goes to War: The Civil War Narrative of Arthur Middleton Manigault, Brigadier General, C.S.A.* Columbia, S.C., 1983.

Vandiver, Frank E., ed. *The Civil War Diary of General Josiah Gorgas.* University, Ala., 1947.

Walton, Clyde C., ed. *Private Smith's Journal: Recollections of the Late War.* Chicago, 1963.

Warner, J.H. *Personal Glimpses of the Civil War: Nineteenth Tennessee.* Chattanooga, 1914.

Wiley, Bell Irvin, *Four Years on the Firing Line*, by James C. Nisbet. Jackson, Tenn., 1963.

Wilson, James H. *Under the Old Flag.* 2 vols. New York, 1912.

Wyeth, John A. *With Sabre and Scalpel.* New York, 1917.

Young, J. Russell. *Around the World with General Grant.* 2 vols. New York, 1879.

Unit Histories

Barnes, James A., et al. *The Eighty-Sixth Regiment Indiana Volunteer Infantry.* Crawfordsville, Ind., 1895.

Boyle, John Richards. *Soldiers True: The Story of the One Hundred and Eleventh Pennsylvania.* New York, 1903.

Briant, C.C. *History of the Sixth Regiment Indiana Volunteer Infantry.* Indianapolis, 1891.

Canfield, S.S. *History of the Twenty-First Regiment Ohio Volunteer Infantry.* Toledo, 1893.

Clark, Charles T. *Opdycke Tigers: One Hundred and Twenty-Fifth Ohio Volunteer Infantry.* Columbus, Ohio, 1895.

Collins, George K. *Memoirs of the One Hundred and Forty-Ninth Regiment New York Volunteer Infantry.* Syracuse, N.Y., 1891.

Cope, Alexis. *The Fifteenth Ohio Volunteers and Its Campaigns in the War of 1861–1865.* Columbus, Ohio, 1916.

Duke, John K. *History of the Fifty-Third Regiment Ohio Volunteer Infantry during the War of the Rebellion, 1861–1865.* Portsmouth, Ohio, 1900.

Eddy, Richard. *History of the Sixtieth Regiment New York State Volunteers.* Philadelphia, 1864.

Ford, Thomas J. *With the Rank and File.* Milwaukee, 1898.

Hannaford, E. *The Story of a Regiment: A History of the Camps and Associations in the Field of the Sixth Regiment of Ohio Volunteer Infantry.* Cincinnati, 1868.

Haynie, J.H. *The Nineteenth Illinois.* Chicago, 1912.

History of Battery M, First Illinois, Light Artillery, by members of the Battery. Princeton, Ill., 1892.

History of the Services of the Third Battery Wisconsin Light Artillery in the Civil War of the United States, compiled principally from members themselves. Berlin, n.d.

Horrall, S.F. *History of the Forty-Second Indiana Volunteer Infantry.* Chicago, 1892.

Leeper, Wesley Thurman. *Rebels Valiant: Second Arkansas Mounted Rifles (Dismounted)*. Little Rock, 1964.

McMurray, W.J. *History of the Twentieth Tennessee Regiment Volunteer Infantry, C.S.A.* Nashville, 1904.

Oates, William C. *The War Between the Union and the Confederacy, and Its Lost Opportunities, With a History of the Fifteenth Alabama Regiment and the Forty-eight Battles in Which It Was Engaged.* New York, 1905.

Obreiter, John. *History of the Seventy-Seventh Pennsylvania Volunteers.* Harrisburg, Pa., 1905.

Payne, Edwin W. *History of the Thirty-Fourth Illinois Infantry.* Clinton, Iowa, n.d.

Perry, Henry F. *History of the Thirty-Eighth Regiment Indiana Volunteer Infantry.* Palo Alto, Calif., 1906.

Royse, Isaac Henry Clay. *History of the One Hundred and Fifteenth Regiment Illinois Volunteer Infantry.* Terre Haute, Ind., 1900.

Sykes, E.T. *Walthall's Brigade.* Columbus, Miss., 1905.

Watkins, Samuel R. *"Co. Aytch," Maury Grays, First Tennessee Regiment.* Jackson, Tenn., 1952.

Worsham, W.J. *The Old Nineteenth Tennessee Regiment, C.S.A.* Knoxville, 1902.

Wright, Henry H. *A History of the Sixth Iowa Infantry.* Iowa City, Iowa, 1923.

Manuscripts

J. Patton Anderson Papers. William P. Palmer Collection, Western Reserve Historical Society, Cleveland, Ohio.

J. Patton Anderson Papers. P.K. Yonge Library of Florida History, Univ. of Florida, Gainesville.

P.G.T. Beauregard Papers. Record Division—Rebel Archives—War Department, National Archives, Washington, D.C.

Braxton Bragg Papers. William P. Palmer Collection, Western Reserve Historical Society, Cleveland.

E.S. Bruford Papers. Record Division—Rebel Archives—War Department, National Archives, Washington, D.C.

Simon B. Buckner Papers. Henry E. Huntington Library, San Marino, Calif.

Chickamauga-Chattanooga National Military Park Library
E.E. Betts letters
Henry Campbell diary

Carrol H. Clark diary
John Ely diary
John Geary letters
W.W. Gifford recollections
Jacob Goodson letter
G.E. Goudelock letters
Henry W. Howard and James A. Howard letters
R.D. Jamison letters and recollections
Abram E. Kipp letters
John Lewis letter
Benjamin B. Mabry letters
W.R. Montgomery letters
Axel H. Reed diary
Robert J.B. Thigpen letter
Robert Watson diary
Frank Wolfe letter

Jefferson Davis Papers. Louisiana Historical Association Collection, Howard-Tilton Memorial Library, Tulane University, New Orleans.

William J. Hardee Papers. Alabama State Department of Archives and History, Montgomery.

Stoddard Johnson Journal. William P. Palmer Collection of Braxton Bragg Papers, Western Reserve Historical Society, Cleveland.

St. John Liddell Journal. Daniel C. Govan Papers, Southern Historical Collection, Univ. of North Carolina, Chapel Hill.

James Rawlins Papers. Chicago Historical Society.

Tennessee State Library and Archives, Nashville

Confederate Collection
John E. Gold reminiscences
Joel T. Haley letters
John W. Harris letters
Minerva McKamy recollections
W.M. Pollard diary
W.E. Yeatman memoirs

Civil War Veterans Questionnaire
Joseph P.J. Hoover
Joseph K. Marshall
M.L. Morrison
Joseph E. Riley

Elihu Washburn Papers. Illinois State Historical Library, Springfield.

Newspapers

Aberdeen Examiner, Aberdeen, Mississippi
Atlanta Confederacy

Secondary Materials

Books

Boatner, Mark M., III. *The Civil War Dictionary*. New York, 1959.

Bridges, Hal. *Lee's Maverick General: Daniel Harvey Hill*. New York, 1961.

Bryan, Charles W., Jr. "The Civil War in East Tennessee." Ph.D. diss., Univ. of Tennessee, 1978.

Buck, Irving A. *Cleburne and His Command*. Jackson, Tenn., 1959

Catton, Bruce. *Grant Takes Command*. Boston, 1968.

———. *This Hallowed Ground*. New York, 1956.

Cist, Henry M. *The Army of the Cumberland*. New York, 1882.

Connelly, Thomas L. *Autumn of Glory: The Army of Tennessee, 1862–1865*. Baton Rouge, 1971.

Connelly, Thomas L., and Archer Jones. *The Politics of Command: Factions and Ideas in Confederate Strategy*. Baton Rouge, 1973.

Davis, William C. *Breckinridge: Statesman, Soldier, Symbol*. Baton Rouge, 1974.

Dodson, W.C., ed. *Campaigns of Wheeler and His Cavalry, 1862–1865*. Atlanta, 1899.

Downey, Fairfax. *Storming of the Gateway: Chattanooga, 1863*. New York, 1960.

Dyer, John P. *From Shiloh to San Juan: The Life of "Fightin' Joe" Wheeler*. Baton Rouge, 1961.

Flint, Roy K. "The Battle of Missionary Ridge." M.A. thesis, Univ. of Alabama, 1960.

Foote, Shelby. *The Civil War: A Narrative*. 3 vols. New York, 1958–75.

Fuller, J.F.C. *The Generalship of Ulysses S. Grant*. New York, 1929.

———. *Decisive Battles of the U.S.A.* New York, 1942.

288   Chattanooga—A Death Grip on the Confederacy

Geary, Mary de Forest. *A Giant in Those Days.* Brunswick, Ga., 1980.

Govan, Gilbert E., and James W. Livingood. *The Chattanooga Country, 1540–1962: From Tomahawk to TVA.* New York, 1952.

Hebert, Walter H. *Fighting Joe Hooker.* New York, 1944.

Henry, Robert S. *"First With the Most" Forrest.* Indianapolis, 1944.

———. *The Story of the Confederacy.* Indianapolis, 1931.

Horn, Stanley F. *The Army of Tennessee: A Military History.* New York, 1941.

Horn, Stanley F., ed. *Tennessee's War, 1861–1865, Described by Participants.* Nashville, 1965.

Hughes, Nathaniel Cheairs. *General William J. Hardee: Old Reliable.* Baton Rouge, 1965.

Lamers, William M. *The Edge of Glory: A Biography of General William S. Rosecrans, U.S.A.* New York, 1961.

Lewis, Lloyd. *Sherman: Fighting Prophet.* New York, 1932.

Liddell-Hart, Basil H. *Sherman, Soldier, Realist, American.* New York, 1929.

Livermore, Thomas L. *Numbers and Losses in the Civil War in America, 1861–1865.* New York, 1969.

Livingood, James W. *Hamilton County.* Memphis, 1981.

McDonough, James Lee. *Stones River—Bloody Winter in Tennessee.* Knoxville, 1980.

McFeely, William S. *Grant: A Biography.* New York, 1981.

McKinney, Francis F. *Education in Violence: The Life of George H. Thomas.* Detroit, 1961.

McWhiney, Grady. *Braxton Bragg and Confederate Defeat: Field Command.* New York, 1969.

Manchester, William. *American Caesar: Douglas MacArthur, 1880–1964.* Boston, 1978.

Mitchell, Joseph B. *Decisive Battles of the Civil War.* New York, 1955.

Nevins, Allan. *The War for the Union.* 4 vols. New York, 1960.

O'Connor, Richard. *Sheridan the Inevitable.* Indianapolis, 1953.

Patten, Cartter. *Signal Mountain and Walden's Ridge.* Signal Mountain, Tenn., 1962.

Polk, William M. *Leonidas Polk: Bishop and General.* 2 vols. New York, 1915.

Potter, David M. *Division and the Stresses of Reunion: 1845–1876.* Glenview, Ill., 1973.

Purdue, Howell and Elizabeth. *Pat Cleburne, Confederate General: A Definitive Biography.* Hillsboro, Tex., 1973.

Sartain, James A. *History of Walker County, Georgia.* Dalton, Ga., 1932.

Seitz, Don C. *Braxton Bragg: General of the Confederacy.* Columbia, S.C., 1924.

Thomas, Emory M. *The American War and Peace: 1860–1877.* Englewood Cliffs, N.J., 1973.

———. *The Confederate Nation: 1861–1865.* New York, 1979.

Thomas, Wilbur. *General George H. Thomas: The Indomitable Warrior.* New York, 1964.

———. *General James "Pete" Longstreet, Lee's "Old War Horse": Scapegoat for Gettysburg.* Parsons, W. Va., 1979.

Tucker, Glenn. *Chickamauga: Bloody Battle in the West.* Rpt. Dayton, Ohio, 1972.

Turchin, John B. *Chickamauga.* Chicago, 1888.

Van Horn, Thomas B. *The Life of Major General George H. Thomas.* New York, 1882.

———. *History of the Army of the Cumberland.* Cincinnati, 1873.

Wiley, Bell I. *The Life of Billy Yank: The Common Soldier of the Union.* New York, 1971.

Articles and Booklets

Buck, Irving A. "Cleburne and His Division at Missionary Ridge and Ringgold Gap," *Southern Historical Society Papers,* 49 vols. 1876.

Burt, Jesse C. "Fighting With 'Little Joe' Wheeler," *Civil War Times Illustrated,* May 1960.

Hay, Thomas R. "The Battle of Chattanooga." *Georgia Historical Quarterly,* June 1924.

Jewett, Leonidas M. "The Boys in Blue at Missionary Ridge," *Military Order of the Loyal Legion of the United States, Ohio Commandery VI.* Cincinnati, 1908.

Livingood, James W. "Chattanooga's Crutchfields and the Famous Crutchfield House." *Civil War Times Illustrated,* Nov. 1981.

Longacre, Edward G. "A Perfect Ishmaelite: General 'Baldy' Smith." *Civil War Times Illustrated,* Dec. 1976.

McWhiney, Grady. "Braxton Bragg." *Civil War Times Illustrated,* April 1972.

Stephenson, P.D. "Reminiscences of the Last Campaign of the Army of Tennessee, from May, 1864, to January, 1865," *Southern Historical Society Papers*, XII (1884), 38–39.

Sullivan, James R. *Chickamauga and Chattanooga Battlefields*. National Park Service Historical Handbook. Series No. 25. Washington, D.C., 1956.

Tucker, Glenn. "The Battle of Chickamauga." *Civil War Times Illustrated*, Aug. 1971.

———. "The Battle of Chickamauga." *Civil War Times Illustrated*, May 1969.

Index

291